To
WEE BARFE,
SOUTHERN COMFORT.
ROCK 'N' ROLL !!
SHAUN X

Attention-Seeking Missile

ATTENTION-SEEKING MISSILE

THE MAKING OF A MENTALIST

Mereo Books

2nd Floor, 6-8 Dyer Street, Cirencester, Gloucestershire, GL7 2PF
An imprint of Memoirs Books. www.mereobooks.com
and www.memoirsbooks.co.uk

Attention-Seeking Missile
ISBN: 978-1-86151-147-8

First published in Great Britain in 2025
by Mereo Books, an imprint of Memoirs Books.

The address for Memoirs Books can be
found at www.mereobooks.com

Mereo Books Ltd. Reg. No. 12157152

Typeset in 11/17pt Garamond
by Wiltshire Associates.
Printed and bound in Great Britain

This book is dedicated to the other two points of our iron triangle:
Michaela and Tank.

CONTENTS

The sea is aquamarine,
We thought to bring back your dreams from the ocean.
A figurehead figurine –
We led you on to the dreams time had woken.

Rod Legge (1947 – 2009)

foreword

There was great music on the radio in the late 1970s and early 80s – particularly on John Peel's late-night show. Poly Styrene turned the world Dayglo, whilst her band X-Ray Spex pounded out the rhythms – saxophone hammering over guitars and drums. Patrik Fitzgerald sang his caustic ballads and as I write this, the words of All Sewn Up come back to me, making the passage of nearly fifty years seem like yesterday. Always there were The Ramones – blistering two-minute songs of genius about the adventures of Sheena, Judy and Ramona. They were innovative and eclectic times. Enthusiasts with no experience in the music business produced wonderful singles – The Flys, Clive Pig and the Hopeful Chinaman, The Only Ones and all the rest – classics of pop. That fine record shop Henry's at 116, St. Mary's Street, Southampton, stocked them all.

There was little live original music in Lymington. A group called Cuba played at the Literary Institute in New Street and it was good to hear the records played at full volume on the loudspeakers rather than the tinny transistor radio at home. But there was nothing else. Long gone was the Stone Cellar on Lymington Quay where Jimmy Crackcorn brushed away the blue-tailed fly and the place rocked to skiffle in the late 1950s.

Rod Legge, the town's great songwriter, who taught the guitar to Robert Cook of The Cropdusters, had become too shy and withdrawn to play in public. But there were unexpected surprises. His home-produced cassette Setley Pond and the Stars of Aesculapius featured a reflective monologue on the pond – its numinous magic and the people that loved it. The narrative was framed by two beautiful instrumental pieces – more resonant and evocative with every passing year – and a collection of songs. The quotation at the top of the page is from Rod's Song of the Dolphin.

By good fortune, I heard about The Peeping Toms and attended their debut at the Railway Inn, in Station Street. It was an ideal venue – compact and atmospheric. The music soared – Johnny Ramone barre chords growling behind lyrics that were powerful, original and witty. It was the first of many such nights and lunchtimes in the town –particularly at Ye Olde English Gentleman in Queen Street.

The music was in the same spirit as those other artists I have mentioned – the verve and élan that separates the memorable from the mundane, the great from the ordinary. It was a tradition in the town continued by Adamski and Birdy. All of Shaun's groups shared those qualities and this fine book recalls them all – the times, the people and the music – bringing back so many memories.

Colin Insole

CHAPTER 1

THE DEVIL WITHIN

My full name is Shaun David Morris. I was born on the 23rd of January 1963 at Hythe Hospital in Hampshire, England, slap bang in the middle of one of the worst winters on record. Low temperatures and snowfalls brought Britain to a standstill, and it was called the Big Freeze. I am part of the baby boomer generation; my star sign is Aquarius, and my Chinese zodiac sign is the Tiger. Queen Elizabeth II was on the throne, and the Conservative government was in power, with Harold Macmillan, Prime Minister. The British instrumental group The Shadows were at number one in the UK singles chart with their hit *Dance On!* and the same band topped the album chart with *Out of the Shadows*.

My father, David, was a chemical engineer from South Wales who worked at the Esso oil refinery in Fawley, just down the road from Hythe, and my mother, Carole, was a hairdresser from London, who served her apprenticeship at Selfridges department store in the heart of the city. Mum and her older sister Anne were child evacuees during the Second World War and spent the duration of those turbulent times living with a family in their farmhouse in Ledbury, in rural Herefordshire. Tragically, their mother died when they were young ladies, and unfortunately, I never got to meet her.

I have two younger siblings: a sister, Gail, born in February 1965, and a brother, Richard, born in April 1971. Dad was a clever man. As an only child from a poor background, growing up in a small Welsh village, his teachers recognised his academic potential from an early age, and encouraged him to go on to grammar school. Dad's father was a bus driver and conductor, and his mother was a dinner lady at the local school. They didn't have a lot of money, but they managed to save up enough to make this happen.

At the time, my family were living in a bungalow in Copsewood Road, Hythe; in the house directly behind us lived my parents' good friends Bill and June Wagland and their daughter Nicola, who was the same age as me. Nicola was the first friend I ever had, and we were always playing together as youngsters. Two boys, Gareth and Kelly, came along later. The Waglands moved to another home in Hythe soon afterwards, and eventually to a house in the village of Boxford, Suffolk. Both families never let distance become an obstacle though and regularly kept in touch.

It's no exaggeration to say I entered this world with the fire burning fiercely under my feet. On a family holiday in Italy, when I was barely two years old, Mum and Dad went out for a meal together one evening, leaving me in the care of a babysitter. I somehow managed to smash up my wooden cot and they had to call in the local *falegname* (carpenter) to repair it. *A dimple on the chin, the devil within.* The carpenter nicknamed me *Testardo*, which translates into hothead in Italian.

Whilst we were spending quality time together down at the beach on this groovy little holiday, my parents had to physically remove my sandals to prevent me from running straight across the burning hot sand into the sea. For much of my formative years, my mother kept me on reins, for reasons only known to her and my father. I'd like to think I wasn't so out of control as an ankle-biter that I needed to be restrained like that. I can only guess it had a lot to do with being one of the terrible twos at the time, children of that age being notoriously erratic. Toddler's Law.

Growing up in Hythe as a kiddie, I'd play with wooden building blocks, plasticine and something called Fuzzy Felt. At lunchtimes during the week, I'd be glued to *Watch with Mother*, which was a BBC television programme aimed specifically at tiny-tots and pre-school children. Some of my favourite *Watch with Mother* shows were *Andy Pandy, Flower Pot*

Men, Bizzy Lizzy and *The Woodentops.* There was *Camberwick Green, Trumpton* and *Chigley,* as well as *The Herbs, Pogle's Wood, Joe,* and *Mary, Mungo and Midge.* Apart from *Watch with Mother,* TV programmes catered for the very young at the time included *Hector's House, The Clangers, Ivor the Engine* and *Noddy and Friends.* These shows would only keep the average 1960s toddler amused for short periods of time, before we'd inevitably grow restless and bored out of our tiny little minds. Before the programmes had even ended, I'd often wander off on my own, seeking other, more stimulating entertainment.

Who can ever forget that fictional pirate on the TV, Captain Pugwash, who sailed the high seas in his ship, The Black Pig, assisted by the delightfully named Seaman Stains, Master Bates and Roger the Cabin Boy; the latter was the title of a Bamboo Vipers song I wrote many years later. *Captain Pugwash, 'The Bravest Buccaneer,'* pompous, but likeable, was always trying to outwit his scheming mortal enemy, the fearsome pirate Cut-Throat Jake, captain of *The Flying Dustman,* who spoke with a stereotypical West Country accent and was easily recognisable by his eye patch and enormous black beard.

Later, there was *Jackanory, Tarzan, Magpie, Vision On, The Double Deckers, Crackerjack!* and *the Pink Panther Show* to keep us amused. *Dr Who* used to be on the TV on Saturday afternoons, and the programme would terrify me when I was a child. The slightest glimpse of one of *Dr Who's* many enemies, such as The Daleks, the Cybermen, Sea Devils and Abominable Snowmen would send me scurrying for cover behind the sofa in the lounge. Asleep in my bed at night, I'd have recurring nightmares about these frightening television villains.

Then there was the children's TV programme *Animal Magic,* presented by an enigmatic man called Johnny Morris, who used to mimic the various animals at Bristol Zoo, we'd watch on intently, as he talked in an implied special language to chimpanzees, giraffes, toucans and other residents of the zoo, much like a modern-day Dr Doolittle, if you like. Many years later, because I shared the same surname as him, I managed to convince an awful lot of people that Johnny Morris was in fact my uncle, on my father's side of the family. The first person I told this to, a woman I'd known for years, believed me wholeheartedly, exclaiming, 'Wow Shaun, that's amazing! I never realised you were related to the great Johnny Morris! You kept that one quiet!' Subsequently, I managed to keep up the pretence, and in effect, the whole thing snowballed.

When Johnny died in 1999, I received several emails and condolence cards from folk expressing their deepest heartfelt sympathy. It was then that I realised I couldn't keep up this charade for any while longer. It was time for me to come clean, once and for all, in total respect for the man. I can categorically state here and now, that as far as I'm aware, I am in no way whatsoever related to Johnny Morris. I've certainly talked to more than a few animals in my life, but they're of the human variety, not your average elephant, panda, flamingo or sea turtle.

It's a miracle that any of us survived childhood in the 1960s. Parents exposed kids to second-hand smoke and let them run wild in the streets. Sugar was in everything, and hazards lurked everywhere. Little children would sit in the passenger seat of a car without a seatbelt. Mum or Dad would just fling an arm in front of you if they had to brake quickly. Infants sometimes rode in unattached baby seats. In the 60's, cribs had few of the safety measures in place today. Dangerous drop rails, slats so wide an infant's head could get stuck, places where tiny fingers could get caught, and choking hazards were just a few of the problems.

We'd bounce on trampolines without nets, and the risks were many. There were sprains, breaks and falling on your head when one of the neighbourhood kids jumped hard enough to send you flying. Play parks were potential death traps. Poorly maintained roundabouts, swings and slides were the norm. Mothers would let little ones play with pots and pans while they cooked, and didn't worry too much about them getting hold of the chemicals under the kitchen sink.

There were no such thing as childproof medicine caps. Electrical outlets were there for stabbing with a fork, and small choking hazards abounded. Young children would walk to and from school alone and ride bikes without helmets. They'd hitch lifts from complete strangers and play outside unsupervised all day. Kids wandered around in packs, looking for stuff to do. Adults often had no idea of their children's whereabouts for long stretches of time.

When I was about three years old, I climbed up the loft ladder in our house to hand Dad a pencil he'd asked for. The rubber at the top of the pencil was missing, leaving a small, exposed jagged piece of metal. I slipped on the ladder, and falling, nearly took my eye out with it. Blood flowed everywhere, and I was rushed to Hythe hospital, where they stitched me up.

During hot weather, children would spend hours outside without suntan lotion. Street entertainment consisted of playing with marbles and aiming them into the small holes in manhole covers. There were hopscotch boards written with chalk on the tarmac. Everyone moved out of the way when cars came, and when the cars drove off, the games resumed.

There was hide 'n' seek and kiss chase. Kids would drink from garden hoses and public water fountains to keep hydrated, ingesting unsafe levels of lead. Some of the toys children played with in those days could kill you. Kids would swing from the highest branches of tall trees unfazed and climb up onto asbestos roofs to play.

Indoor games included Spin the Plate; if you were fortunate enough to lose, you might find yourself stood there in front of the older girl from next door, in your bedroom with no clothes on. On car journeys, it was common for children to kneel on the back seat and pull faces and stick their tongues out at the driver in the car behind. Back then, parents were allowed to spank and hit their kids when they angered them. My parents' weapon of choice was the wooden spoon. If I'd been especially naughty, Dad would give me the option of the rounded side of the spoon, or the flat side with nails in it.

We could hear Mr Whippy coming from miles away. When the ice cream van pulled into our road, chimes blaring, we'd all run out with the pennies our mums had given us. There were Red Devils, Zooms, Funny Faces, Choc Ices, Fabs and Wonder Woppas. In the sweetshop, we'd spend our pocket money on Black Jacks and Fruit Salads, Gobstoppers, Sherbert

Dips and Anglo bubble gum. Sometimes, when we could afford it, we'd buy ourselves a tube of Spangles, or if we were feeling flush, an Aztec Bar.

Throughout my early childhood, Dad would drive the family down to the village of Cadoxton in the Vale of Glamorgan, South Wales, to stay with my grandparents at their home in Underwood Road. I absolutely loved it there and got to know all the boys in the immediate area. I remember Andrew Ovard, Christopher Morris, Philip Jones, Peter Hughes, Christopher Elias and Gary and Alan Philips. We got up to plenty of the usual mischief and I have great memories from that time.

A couple of doors down from my grandparents' house was a convenience store. It was run by a lovely young couple, Malcolm and Wendy Mayers. Wendy was a buxom blonde woman, and Malcolm fitted the stereotype of your classic Welshman. He had a swarthy complexion and sported a thick moustache and wore glasses. Many years later, when my brother Richard was studying at Edinburgh University, he decided to travel down to Cadoxton and pay a surprise flying visit to the Mayers' home. He knocked on the front door and Malcolm slowly opened it. Rich smiled at him and excitedly said 'Hi Malcolm, do you remember me? I'm Richard Morris, David's son. How are you? I haven't seen you in ages!' Malcolm just stood there in the doorway staring at him with complete indifference, and replied, 'When are you gonna lose that university accent?' Priceless.

My dad's father was Maurice Thomas Morris, who we called 'Dadcu', which is Welsh for Grandad. He was married to a woman we referred to as Nanny Nee, and was a kind man who loved children and would do anything he could to help them. Dadcu also loved a pint of beer and would often go for a drink in The Green Dragon and The Crown & Sceptre pubs in Cadoxton. Sometimes, he'd venture further afield in search of good company and liquid refreshment. He'd take the short bus ride from Cadoxton to Neath, and head for the Castle Hotel in the town centre.

When staying at Dadcu and Nanny Nee's house in the late 60's and early 70s, I was given Welsh cakes to eat and drank cups of tea that tasted like heaven; completely different to what I was used to at home in England. I think it had something to with the Welsh water at the time. Dadcu had this endearing habit of tapping his teaspoon sharply twice on the side of his teacup every time he sat down at the kitchen table.

There's an iconic black and white photograph of Dadcu standing on one of the golden beaches at the scenic and historic Gower Peninsula in Southwest Wales, the UK's first designated Area of Outstanding Natural Beauty. He's wearing a string vest and a pair of trousers with the braces dangling and has a fag hanging out of his mouth. I think he looks really cool in that photo.

During WW2, Dadcu was stationed with the Royal Air Force in India. I remember the various small souvenir metal animals he'd brought home to Wales with him after the war; one of them a malevolent looking Indian cobra, *Naja naja*. There were concrete bomb shelters in everyone's back gardens in Cadoxton, as there were all over the country in those dark days. Dad once told me a story about how he was playing outside with his friends one day, standing on top of one of these bomb shelters, when a German Heinkel bomber flew overhead. It had just unloaded its payload of bombs over the city of Swansea, only eight miles away.

My mother's father was called Montague Joseph Plass and was lovingly known to all our family as Grandad. He worked most of his life as a travelling salesman, and after moving down from Twickenham in Middlesex, he lived in a flat in Bournemouth with his second wife Roma, up until he died in 1993. His own father was a German ex-pat, who was living and working in England when World War One broke out. Throughout the duration of the war, he was interned in Alexandria Palace in London. The British Government couldn't take the risk of allowing potential enemy saboteurs and spies to operate undercover in the country. Ultimately, it's these people who win wars. Grandad once told me that his father, although under suspicion, was never mistreated by the British authorities.

Years later, during WW2, Grandad himself was posted first to Cairo in Egypt, in the northeastern corner of Africa, then to Nigeria in West Africa, where he rose to the rank of Major. He remained in Nigeria until the end of the war. Because his father was German, he was originally in the

Pioneer Corps, also known as the 'Not to Be Totally Trusted Regiment.' Later he was transferred to the Royal West Africa Frontier Force (WAFF). I do know he spent a considerable amount of his wartime service in the desert.

After the war ended, Grandad travelled extensively throughout West Africa, absorbing the culture of some of the exotic countries in the region. When I was a young boy, he used to regale me with tales of his experiences out there and showed me some of the many wonderful souvenirs he'd brought back home with him.

In 1980, Grandad suffered a serious heart attack while on holiday in Cuba with his wife Roma and had to be medevacked by helicopter to a hospital in the capital, Havana. The medical staff there were bang on it and they thankfully managed to save his life. On another occasion, closer to home, he was electrocuted while mowing his front lawn at his flat in Bournemouth. He'd unwittingly cut through the power cable of his Flymo and a neighbour found him lying down, sprawled out and sizzling on the grass. Luckily, he survived his encounter with a lawnmower, unlike me, on that fateful day back in 1979.

Grandad had a younger sister called Vera; Great Aunt Vera, who resided in a house in Totteridge, North London, not that far from where the famous Irish comedian Spike Milligan lived. She worked in an office in the city and was a strong, independent woman who said it like it was. My mother often drove Gail, Richard and I up to London to stay with her, especially during half-term. We used to have some great times there. One Saturday afternoon, it must have been around 1970, I recall a smiling Cliff Richard, the very man, wearing a pair of sunglasses, coming out of a pet shop in Totteridge before jumping into his car and driving away.

Apart from Great Aunt Vera, Grandad had a younger brother, Gusty, who was a hairdresser at the acclaimed Steiner's salon in London's Mayfair. Uncle Gusty lived in Loughton, Essex with his wife Eunice and two daughters, Susan and Hilary. Susan eventually moved to a town on the coast near Cairns in Queensland, Australia, where she married a decorated Vietnam veteran helicopter pilot who'd seen more than his fair share of action in the war.

Once, after travelling out to Australia to stay with his daughter, Gusty became hopelessly lost in the outback. He'd been on a day trip with some other people and had somehow managed to become separated from the rest of the group. He was missing for around twenty-four hours and the local police had to send out a search party to look for him. There were even distress calls put out over radio stations in the area, appealing for any information regarding his last known whereabouts. In the event, Gusty was eventually found alive and kicking in a ditch after spending a whole night under the beautiful stars of the Australian bush; understandably shaken, but certainly not stirred.

My dad was fanatical about the Welsh Rugby Union team, and on one occasion in the late 1960s I recall him picking up my little sister and playfully throwing her onto the sofa, running around the living room, arms aloft and screaming with joy, ecstatic that Wales had just scored a try. The names Gareth Edwards, JPR Williams, Barry John, Dai Morris, Brian Price, Phil Bennett and Mervyn Davies are forever etched in my mind.

During the 1950s, my father was a student at the University of Birmingham, and it was there that he met my mother. He was a tidy soccer player, a tenacious midfielder, and at one point captained the combined British Universities football team. Dad even played on the same side as the great Billy Wright, who was an English centre-back who spent his whole career with Wolverhampton Wanderers and was the first footballer in the world to earn one hundred international caps.

I loved playing football from a very early age and would spend hours on my own having a kickabout in my back garden at home in Hythe. I guess I inherited that passion from my dad. He took me to my first professional match in 1970, or possibly 1971. I recall it was Southampton v Manchester City at The Dell. In all honesty, although I thought I was at the time, I wasn't really that good at football, compared to some of the other boys I knew. I think I was quite a skilful player, adept at the intricacies of the game, but due to my stature, and more to the point, my basic attitude, I lacked the physicality and determination needed to succeed on the main stage.

One Saturday afternoon, I think it was sometime around 1973, the father of my friend Simon Molineaux, who was called Dave, drove the pair of us to The Dell to watch a Football Combination game between Southampton and Oxford United. Because it was the reserves playing, there was hardly anybody there in in the ground. We were standing on the terraces behind one of the goalposts and kept harassing the Oxford goalkeeper for his autograph. Eventually, the goalie turned his head back towards us, and grabbing a pen from somewhere, jogged over and quickly scrawled down his signature on each of our match programmes. Whilst he was doing this, Southampton happened to go on the counterattack and scored, smashing in a goal into the empty net, right in front of us. That poor goalkeeper's face was a picture, a mixture of anger and frustration, and Simon and I couldn't contain ourselves from laughing.

Later, in the early 80s, playing for the Old English pub soccer team in a match one Sunday morning on Pilley recreation ground, I was more interested in the magic mushrooms that were growing on the pitch than the game. I certainly didn't hold a candle to my father's talent as a footballer, that's for sure. I recall future Cropdusters driver Dave Bindon played on our side in that match and banged something up his nose just before kick-off. I don't know what it was, but it clearly did the job, as he ended up scoring a hat trick.

I supported City for a short while after that game, even to the point of wearing one of their sky-blue home shirts, until a local boy, Islington-born Charlie George, scored the winner in extra time for Arsenal in the 1971 FA Cup Final at Wembley, securing the league and cup double for the club. At the top of Copsewood Road, where I lived, was a small, featureless sloping grassy area on a hill known to the locals as The Green. It was a place my sister and I used to go to for sledging on a rickety, hastily put-together homemade wooden contraption in the winter, after it had been snowing heavily, and was covered top to bottom in ice.

Immediately after watching the match live on colour television, which was a novelty at the time, I headed off there for a game of football with some boys who were friends of mine. Everybody there that sunny spring

Saturday afternoon in May '71 was convinced they were Charlie George, repeatedly mimicking his iconic goal celebration, sinking to the turf and lying on their backs, their arms outstretched. It was an amazing day and something I'm sure I'll never forget.

My grandfather on my mother's side, the man we knew as Grandad, who was in the fabled Not to Be Totally Trusted Regiment during World War Two, was a real Arsenal fan and used to watch the Gunners regularly at Highbury as far back as the 1930s. From an early age, he was persistent, if nothing else, in drumming it into me that 'The Arsenal' were the team to support; the only one that mattered. From the moment Charlie's screamer hit the back of the net there was only one club for me.

In 1968, aged five, I started my formal education at Hythe Infants' School. I can remember getting into serious trouble early on after I got caught swinging on the chains in the boys' toilets, pretending to be Tarzan King of the Jungle. The old headmaster, Mr Brinton, cornered me in the corridor after assembly one morning. He gave me a proper dressing down in front of the other school kids and started whacking me across my backside with a hymn book. I remember the book coming apart at the seams and the tattered yellowing pages flying everywhere. I was immediately sent to an empty classroom in disgrace, on isolated detention.

One of my abiding memories of those far-off days was the small bottles of milk we were given daily, which were well past their sell-by date, and the child milk monitors who distributed them. I recall being forced by the teachers to eat a piece of raw carrot in the playground every lunchtime. One such teacher was a sour, cranky old woman called Miss Clough, who could be an absolute tyrant. She used to patrol the dining hall religiously, making sure we ate every scrap of food that was on our plates. I can still remember the words she uttered at us every single day at school: 'No waste. I won't tolerate waste!'

My best friends at school back then were two boys called Simon Molyneaux, who I mentioned earlier, and David Hammond. Simon lived in one of the houses behind us and my father used to call him Simon de Montfort, after the 13th century nobleman. Dad put in a gate in the fence that divided the Molyneaux's back garden from ours. This meant young 'Mr de Montfort' and I had easy access whenever we wanted to play together.

In the cold, dark winter mornings, Mum would serve my sister and me a bowl of Ready Brek cereal for breakfast and give us each a Vitamin C tablet to take. We used to wear a bright orange reflective sash across our winter coats so we could be seen by the traffic in the darkness. We flickered like the flames of a fire, and they called it the 'Ready Brek glow'. It really makes me laugh, when schools nowadays shut down completely at the merest hint of a falling snowflake. In our day, not going to school because of inclement weather wasn't an option; we just had to get on with it.

I remember, when I was five years old, walking to school on horrendous, freezing cold winter mornings in blizzard-like conditions. I could hardly see two feet in front of me through the snowstorms and struggled to keep my balance on the dangerous, icy pavements. I was at constant risk of slipping on the ice and falling onto the road. The perils of sliding under the wheels of oncoming vehicles were all too real, and I recall being nearly run over by cars on a couple of occasions.

Closing schools because of adverse weather conditions is a prime example of how times have changed since I was a kid. Nowadays, things couldn't be more different. Whereas we'd be expected to attend school even in the event of incendiary bombs raining down on top of us, today's generation of schoolchildren have been encouraged to come up with any excuse not to go. During periods of cold weather, the boilers always seem to break down, and the teachers won't risk driving short distances to work in case they have an accident on the roads.

These days, kids complain, 'Oh my god, a snowflake just landed on my head! It really hurt! What am I going to do? I don't think I'll be able to go to school today because I won't be able to concentrate properly.' Or: 'I saw this weird snowman yesterday. It had an evil face, and it freaked me out! I think I might need counselling. Mummy, is it okay if I stay at home today?' Or: 'I don't see why I should be outside in the cold. I'm not an Eskimo, for god's sake! There might be polar bears out there that could eat me alive. Is it okay if I have the day off school?' In this context, 'Snowflake' is the operative word.

When I was in the comfort of my own home, I'd play with plastic toy soldiers, Matchbox cars and Meccano. There was Hot Wheels, Supercars, Spirograph, Jack Straws, Tiddly Winks, Subbuteo and Twister. Board games in the 60's, included Snakes and Ladders, Mousetrap, Operation, Ludo, Headache, Home You Go! Ker Plunk and Frustration. If it wasn't pissing down with rain outside, I'd sometimes put on my treasured Cowboys and Indians fancy dress costumes, and run around the back garden, whooping and howling away like a combination of a mental modern-day Milky Bar Kid and Sitting Bull on Ritalin; a boy possessed. Another memory I have from around this time was Grandad buying me an authentic German lederhosen outfit, complete with obligatory feather cap. There's an old colour photograph of me wearing it at a children's birthday party in Hythe in the late 60s.

My mother once told me a story about a lady who was an acquaintance of hers. I was around three or four years old at the time, and Mum had taken me out with her to the local shops in Hythe in my pushchair. She bumped into her friend outside one of the shops, and the lady, turning her attention to me, bent down on her knees, smiled, and asked, 'And what do you want to be when you grow up, Shaun?' Staring back at her for a moment, I triumphantly replied 'A gorilla!' I'd like to think I meant 'guerilla,' but there it is.

I can remember joining the local Tufty Club, where children were taught about road safety by a cute little red squirrel called Tufty Fluffytail and his faithful furry friends Willie Weasel, Bobby Brown Rabbit and Harry Hare. I was unceremoniously thrown out of the Tufty Club after only a couple of weeks but can't recall the reason why. Probably because I was being a little shit. I was also in the Hythe division of the Boy's Brigade for a short while and recall a coach trip up to London one day to watch the Royal Tournament at Earl's Court Exhibition Centre. The Royal Tournament was the world's largest military tattoo and pageant, held by the British Armed Forces.

Another memory that sticks in my mind is something that happened at Balmer Lawn in Brockenhurst around this time. Mum and her friend June Wagland had taken us and her three kids there so we could enjoy a picnic together by the river. I was showing off in front of Nicola and jumped headfirst into the water. A pothole opened beneath me, and I remember sinking further and further down into the mire. It was petrifying. If it hadn't been for a vigilant man who happened to be standing a few yards away on the riverbank and was keeping an eye on us, I surely would have drowned. Without hesitation, leaping into the water, he pulled me out of the murky depths just in the nick of time and saved my life. Shaking with terror, I burst into tears and ran towards my mother to tell her what had happened. That was my first brush with death when it came to messing about on the river. It certainly wasn't my last, as you'll find out later.

In November 1971 my family moved into a new four-bedroom house in Broad Lane, in the town of Lymington, not that far away from Hythe. It was at Lymington Junior School in Emsworth Road, that I met some children who would become my best friends, many of whom I'm still in touch with today. Vivid memories from that time include having to eat our school lunch in the local parish hall, and playing soccer in Physical Education lessons, where we'd practise heading techniques with an old-style football that was so heavy it felt more like a medicine ball when you made contact with it.

I'd discovered a love of music from a very early age. My parents used to play their records all the time on the stereo in the living room, and Dad owned an 8-track cassette player. I remember listening to the songs of the 60's on the radio. Dad was into the American country singer/songwriter and guitarist Glen Campbell in a big way, so hit singles like *By the Time I Get to Phoenix*, *Wichita Lineman* and *Galveston* were played in our house constantly.

My parents also owned a large assortment of music catered specifically for children, mostly in the form of vinyl LPs; a number of which were multi-coloured. On Saturday mornings I'd sometimes listen to the BBC radio children's programme *Junior Choice,* hosted by Ed 'Stewpot'

Stewart. One song I remember being played frequently on *Junior Choice* was *A Windmill in Old Amsterdam* by Ronnie Hilton. Another one was *My Brother* by Terry Scott.

When I was growing up in Hythe, as a youngster I listened to records by the likes of Ken Dodd and the Diddymen and Pinky and Perky. I remember numbers such as *Puff the Magic Dragon* and traditional English nursery rhymes like *Little Boy Blue*. When I moved to Lymington, in 1971, I graduated on to songs in the music charts; *Apeman* by The Kinks, *Won't Get Fooled Again* by The Who, *Get it on* by T-Rex, The Move's *Blackberry Way* and the innuendo-laden novelty song, *Ernie (The Fastest Milkman in the West)* by Benny Hill. Later, while living in France in '72 and '73, I remember *Little Willy* by The Sweet, Mott the Hoople's *All the Young Dudes* and *Son of My Father* by Chicory Tip. The following year, there was Slade's *Cum on Feel the Noise*, *Can the Can* by Suzi Quatro, *Dynamite* by Mud, *See My Baby Jive* by Wizard and Alvin Stardust's *My Coo-Ca-Choo*. In 1974, the American band Sparks released their single *This Town Ain't Big Enough for Both of Us*. I loved Sparks, and I guess you could say they were the first band I really got into.

In a visual sense, kids back in those days were exposed to that supremely ridiculous BBC children's TV programme, *Blue Peter*, which was aired on Monday and Thursday afternoons each week. For me, *Blue Peter* is synonymous with milk bottle tops, sticky back plastic, cereal boxes, squeezy bottles, feats of derring-do, and the omnipresent *Blue Peter* badge. Valerie Singleton, the show's female presenter at the time, would create such random things as Daleks out of Swiss rolls and sandwiches, and 'Here's one I made earlier' became a common catchphrase. Looking back, it was all completely innocent, of course, and to its credit, *Blue Peter* raised an awful lot of money through its regular charitable appeals.

Later, during the early 80s, there was the perpetually vandalised Percy Thrower Garden at BBC TV Centre, named after the famous pipe smoking gardener, horticulturist, broadcaster and writer. Incidentally, I always believed the senseless damaging of the garden was an inside job; the culprit more than likely being Percy Thrower himself. 'Why would Percy vandalise his own garden? I hear you ask. That's a question I'm afraid I can't answer. All I can say is that we grew up in a strange era, where logic, reason and proportion went out the window. Is it any wonder we turned out the way we did? I don't think so.

The children of my generation were force fed such interminable amounts of this kind of nonsensical bullshit, at such an early age, you simply wouldn't believe it. Many of us didn't want to watch boring television programmes like *Blue Peter;* what we desperately needed was a hefty dose of pure, thrilling escapism. Supermarionation TV series such as *Thunderbirds, Joe 90, Stingray* and *Captain Scarlet* were the answer to our prayers and were far more appealing to us youngsters. It wasn't simply the corporate media's erroneous attempt at specifically targeting us kids in those days, for their own ends and to ensure the money kept rolling in. It also entailed craftily doctoring the viewing figures to keep everyone in the business onside.

One of the *Blue Peter* presenters, John Noakes, used to have a boat moored in a shipyard in Lymington. Noakes would come down here with his excitable Border Collie, Shep. 'Get down, Shep!' became a John Noakes *Blue Peter* catchphrase in the 70s. Whether it's true or not, I heard he could be an ill-tempered so and so, often shouting his mouth off at random people for no apparent reason whatsoever. 'Get down Shep! Good boy! Well done, you've earned yourself a Blue Peter badge.'

It was at the original Lymington Junior School, in 1971, that I first encountered my great mate David Dutton, who introduced himself by throwing an orange at me from across the playground. I was also acquainted for the first time with Roger Figgures and Mark Tinley, both of whom I ended up making music with years later. Other characters worth a mention from those long-ago days at Lymington Juniors include Kevin Upton, Andrew Plumbly, Dean Lancaster, Peter Clapham, Mark Lavis, Peter Golden and Graham Flood.

I remember spending an awful lot of time round Roger Figgures' house. I'd regularly go round there for tea on Thursday afternoons after school. Roger had an uncle called Dick, who was always immaculately dressed in a suit, and he would turn up with several comic magazines for him; *The Beano* and its sister comic, *The Dandy,* were the two I remember the most. *The Beano* featured well-known comic strip characters such as Dennis the Menace, Minnie the Minx, The Bash Street Kids, Billy Whizz, Lord Snooty and his Pals, and of course, Roger the Dodger. The Dandy had Desperate Dan as its mascot, along with other characters like Beryl the Peril and Korky the Cat.

In February 1972 I had to say goodbye to my newfound friends, as my father took on a new assignment at the Exxon oil refinery in Port-Jérôme-sur-Seine, near the commune of Nôtre-Dame-de-Gravenchon in Normandy, France. Initially, my family lived in a spacious first-floor flat above a convenience store in Nôtre-Dame-de-Gravenchon. Later, we moved to a three-bedroom house in a street not far away.

At my new all-boys junior school, I struggled with the French language at first, but after a lot of practice, I became fluent in around three months. We used to have the day off every Wednesday and attended sports sessions at the town hall on Saturday mornings. At school lunchtimes during the week, I ate at home and always had a large glass of the ubiquitous Normandy cider with my meal. After finishing lunch, I returned to school for afternoon lessons.

Talking of family meals, for many years afterwards, my father would often complain about how much gravy my mother was putting on his dinner. I'll never forget his words at the time: 'Christ, Carole, what are you doing? It's swimming in the stuff! Are you trying to drown me, or something?!' When Dad was convinced he'd been served too much food on his plate, he'd say, 'Bloody hell, Carole, I can't eat all that! There's enough there to feed an army!'

My abiding memories of living in France back then include a dictator of a school headmaster, who ripped into me on my very first day at school for bringing in several small plastic toy tanks and armoured personnel carriers to play with. My first impression of him was that he was an over the top, authoritarian Frenchman who'd probably realised, belatedly, that he'd made the wrong career choice. He was all Gallic shrugs, bad breath and pointy beard; the latter seemed to thrust itself forward independently, as if its owner had no control over its actions, daggerlike into your face, whenever he was talking to you.

I also recall pupils having to wear these dodgy-looking multi-coloured nylon tunics in class. I ended up befriending most of the outsider kids who'd moved to France from different European countries, some of them refugees. Several of them would often come over to our house to play whatever games happened to be popular at the time. Spin the Plate was out of the question, as we were all boys in it together. Towards the end of my fourteen months living in Nôtre-Dame-de-Gravenchon, I introduced some of my schoolmates to the distinctly English game of cricket.

In the basement of our house, I set up a table football game and I would spend hours at a time down there. One hilarious incident I recall was when I stayed the night round the house of an American friend of mine called Fred Zumwalt, in the middle of the week. I'd only packed a pair of pyjamas, not my school uniform, and because the authorities wouldn't let you wear ordinary clothes on the premises, such as a T-shirt and jeans, I spent the whole day at school in my PJs. My classmates were pissing themselves at the sight of me, I can tell you, and I laughed along with them. I might well have been the object of ridicule, but I really couldn't have cared less at the time. I didn't give a flying fuck what anyone thought.

In April 1973, Dad's assignment in France came to an end and we moved back to the UK, and our house in Lymington. Whilst I was living abroad, a new junior school had been built in Avenue Road, complete with swimming pool. It was here that I was reunited with my old schoolmates. One of them, Dean Lancaster, freaked out when he saw me again in the school canteen. Dean dropped his dinner tray on the floor, blobs of shepherd's pie, mushy peas and tomato ketchup going everywhere, and excitedly gave me a welcome hug. For some reason, Dean was convinced I was French for a long while afterwards.

I really enjoyed it at that school and performed well in class because I had the right motivation behind me, not least because of two certain unforgettable people. We had a husband and wife teaching separate classes in the fourth year of juniors, Mr and Mrs Howell. Mr Howell wrote children's books in his spare time and his wife provided the vivid illustrations for them. On Friday afternoons, after a lesson in lino cutting, he would regale us with fantastical tales about marsh sprites, ice pixies, wood gnomes and the like.

The Howells lived in the nearby village of Sway and had a swimming pool in their back garden. From time to time, they'd invite pupils from their classes over to their house, where we'd drink glasses of ice-cold fizzy lemonade, and frolic in the pool. Mr Howell taught me to dive properly by placing a leaf between my ankles and making sure it was still there after I'd hit the water.

There was a boy in my class at Lymington Junior School whose name was Christopher Jones. He'd moved down here with his family from somewhere in the Midlands in the early 70s, and his parents managed the Solent Mead old people's home in Church Lane, right opposite the house where the Tinleys lived. Because Chris was a chubby boy, at our end of term Christmas nativity play, in 1973, Mrs Howell cast him as 'Fairy Tankerbell' in a festive storyline she'd written herself, especially for the occasion.

Chris was required to wear a tight-fitting pink tutu and pretty ballerina slippers to match. He sported little cardboard wings and carried a silver wand, and everyone found the whole thing hilarious. I'm not sure what Tinley's exact role was in the nativity play, but I do recall him dressed as Father Christmas and sitting in a box that was covered in tin foil. For the grand finale, he shot up out of the box, arms and legs flailing all over the place, much to the amusement of the people watching in the audience.

Chris Jones was a good nipper, and we used to spend quite a bit of time together in those days. One Saturday afternoon, while we were out riding our bikes around the leafy lanes of Pennington, he suddenly lost control of his bicycle, went straight over the handlebars and fell headfirst into a ditch full of stinging nettles. Chris was understandably freaking out, and in a lot of pain. I grabbed hold of his arm and hauled him out of the ditch, and we rode back to his place as fast as we could. When we arrived, his concerned mother grabbed a pot of Calamine lotion from somewhere and smeared it all over the nettle rash on Chris's body. It provided instant relief for him, thank goodness.

It was at the new Lymington Junior School that I initially met my good friend Kevin Joyce; another one I would become musically involved with in the years to come. I was also introduced for the first time to two other boys there; the vivacious Laurence Sunderland, nicknamed 'Midge', and his good mate Steven Strobel, who was as mad as a March hare.

Laurence was always good for a laugh. During the school summer holidays one year, he travelled down to Wales with me, to stay at my grandparents' home in Cadoxton for a week. He got on famously with all the local lads while we were there, and they christened him 'Spiderman' after he uninhibitedly shimmied up a drainpipe at the school at the end of Underwood Road and climbed onto the roof, where he proceeded to whoop with delight and attempted to dance like John Travolta, spinning all over the place until he fell over. I must admit, it was certainly funny.

One standout memory I have concerning Steven Strobel, is something he did during the late 70s. The pair of us were larking around at the sports ground in Lymington one evening, when Steve picked up a discarded old metal floodlight casing off the grass and placed it on his head. Shrieking like a distracted banshee, he began tear-assing across the playing field, zigzagging here, there and everywhere. He resembled a cross between the Tin Man character in the movie *The Wizard of Oz* and a 1950s vintage wind-up toy robot. It was a side-splitting spectacle to behold.

I remember a couple of crazy episodes while attending that school. During wet playtime one day, my friend Mark Tinley plugged something dangerous into a live socket in the classroom which nearly electrocuted a poor girl sat nearby. Around this time, Tinley went down the local dump and tossed a lighted match into a discarded petrol can. The resulting explosion sent pieces of metal flying into his forehead, and they're still embedded in his skull to this day.

Break times at Lymington Juniors would mainly consist of playing games of soccer with tennis balls and marbles with gigantic ball bearings or marching round the playground mimicking the sound of a machine gun, pretending you were in the army. Boys and girls played Tag, Dizzies, Simon Says, British Bulldog, Leapfrog, Elastics, Oranges and Lemons, Clackers, Skipping, Rock Paper Scissors, Headers and Volleys, Yo-yoing, Cat's Cradle, Stuck in the Mud, Conkers, Piggy in the Middle and Kick the Can.

Playground songs included Ibble Obble Black Bobble, One Potato Two Potato, Ingle Angle Silver Bangle, What's the Time? Half Past Nine, A Sailor Went to Sea Sea Sea, Apples Peaches Pears and Plums and the Clapping Song. Then there were the obligatory football chants. For example: 'Two four six eight, who do we appreciate?' And 'We hate Nottingham Forest; we hate Everton too.' 'Come and have a go if you think you're hard enough.' Songs the boys might sing on the playground were *My Old Man's a Dustman* and *My Friend Billy's Got a 10-foot Willy*, *Yum Yum, Bubble Gum, Jesus Christ Superstar* and *Mary Had a Little lamb*.

One afternoon on the sports field, all the boys in our year divided into two separate groups: 'Skinheads' and 'Grebos'. I remember somebody yelling 'Charge!' and the two groups clashing together in one almighty sprawling mass of bodies, wrestling each other to the ground and excitedly and repeatedly asking each other, 'Are you a Skinhead or a Grebo?' It all seems so ridiculous now, but it was a wonderful release at the time. Then there was kiss chase, and I recall everyone was in love with the Chamberlain twins at the time, Wendy and Jackie, who were in the year below me.

Some of the things schoolboys came out with in my era were utterly ridiculous. For instance, they'd say, 'My mate said you wanted a fight with me?' 'No, I didn't.' 'Are you calling my mate a liar?' I mean, how do you get out of that one? 'Shut your mouth!' 'Make me!' 'I don't make shit, shit comes natural!' This one doesn't make any sense at all. 'What are you looking at? Do you want a photo or something?'

Then there was the school snitch, always trying to drop other kids in the shit. 'Miss, he's got chewing gum in his mouth, and you said we're not allowed to eat sweets in the classroom. Na na na na na, you're in trouble.' 'Sir, he just pinched me on the arm. And he swore at me. I didn't do anything, honest.' On a more serious note, boys sometimes reached the point where they would throw stones at one another, usually over something totally trivial. I still bear a few physical scars from these meaningless, spiteful juvenile playground altercations.

Later, when I was at comprehensive school, one of the boys in my year, David Norris, used to go into Forbuoys newsagents in Pennington each morning and systematically buy tons of different sweets from the jars of confectionary lined up on the shelf: Sherbet lemons, bon bons, cough candy, pear drops, sherbet pips, mint imperials, rhubarb and custards, aniseed balls, cola cubes, snowies, dolly mixtures, jelly beans, Murray mints, pineapple chunks, sweet peanuts, chocolate limes, fruit jellies, Pontefract cakes, extra strong mints, humbugs. Norris would buy insane amounts of these sweets, and devour the lion's share himself, on a daily basis. Where he got the money from is no one's business. At breaktimes, the boy would stand on the playing field and shout 'Scramble!' at the top of his voice. He'd then casually throw paper bags full of the sweets up in the air. Every boy within hearing range would immediately stop what they were doing and converge on the playing field as if their lives depended on it. Norris would be standing there lording it over them and dishing out the goodies while boys were scrambling around him on the grass in desperation, tearing each other apart over a sherbet pip.

I suppose those were the only times Norris had any measure of control over anything in his life. It was his way of attracting the attention he so obviously craved. David Norris, *King of* Confectionary. King Con. I'm sure he imagined himself as some modern-day male equivalent of Mother Teresa of Calcutta. It was all completely innocent, of course, but what a weird thing to do; it really was.

I used to spend a lot of time round my mate David Dutton's house. Glam Rock was taking hold of the nation, and we'd spend endless hours listening to the latest records by Slade, T-Rex, The Sweet, Suzi Quatro, Mud and the now disgraced Gary Glitter. I remember on Thursday evenings we'd watch *Top of the Pops* on his parents' TV. Dave was as funny as fuck, eating stone cold baked beans straight from the can and dancing round the kitchen with an inane grin on his face, displaying a set of perfectly formed gleaming white teeth. Dave's dad Barry was a great, independently minded guy who was a big part of my childhood. He was a larger-than-life personality, just like his son, and he owned a hi-fi shop in Early Court, just off Lymington High Street. Barry always seemed to me, even as a young kid, to exude that positive, alternative outlook on life. Dave's mum was called Jackie, and she would unfailingly make me feel welcome whenever I visited their home.

I used to love Saturday mornings. We'd watch programmes like *The Banana Splits, Skippy* and *the Partridge Family* on TV, then some of us would ride around on Chopper pushbikes, if we were lucky enough to own one. We'd buy Panini football stickers to put in our albums. If you had more than one sticker featuring the same player, you'd take them into school the following Monday morning to swap with your mates on the playground. 'Got, got, haven't got, haven't got, got, got' etc.

At the time, Roger Figgures' uncle owned a toy shop on the High Street, and one Sunday afternoon we snuck in there while he was was taking a nap upstairs. The new football season had hardly got underway, and seeing a box full of shiny packets of stickers, we swiped the lot. For good measure, Roger helped himself to a couple of boxes of Subbuteo accessories on our way out. Before most boys had even set eyes on a new football sticker, we had virtually the entire collection in our albums.

Occasionally, we'd head on down to Doey's Dump on a scavenging mission, seeing what bits and bobs we might find there. Several years later, many of the boys would spend long periods of their spare time standing on the steps of Sperrings, a newsagent on the Hight Street, that also sold vinyl records. It's now a Costa Coffee. There, dressed in parka coats, pinstriped flares and penguin shoes, they'd while away the hours chewing gum, bogging people out and generally watching the world go by. It was almost like a rite of passage. Woe betides anyone from neighbouring New Milton who dared crossing the cattle grid and come over into Lymington. The lads were fiercely territorial and wouldn't tolerate invaders in their own backyard. The words 'Fight, fight, fight' could sometimes be heard, accompanied by insults and crude hand gestures. Then the obligatory chasing out of town began. Looking back, a lot of it circled around the boys protecting the girls. They felt threatened and feared outsiders turning up on their doorstep and making off with their love interests. I suppose it was all part of the great growing up process.

When we weren't at school, you could usually find me and my mates kicking a ball about in Grove Gardens or Woodside Park. Eventually, we decided to form our own football team, which we named The Hornets, and the first game we played was against Elmer's Court School. It wasn't so much a school, more a place of refuge for disadvantaged boys from London who suffered from various chest problems and other afflictions. They were sent down here for a better quality of life, and the sea air helped with their breathing problems. The match ended in disaster as they beat us 6-2 in a humiliating rout. We were thrashed by a team of asthmatics, and that was hard to take.

We played a few more matches over the course of the following months, with varying degrees of success. Just about everyone I knew turned out for The Hornets at least once, regardless of whether they were any good at football or not. Some of the lads who played for us were completely useless, but it didn't matter because at the end of the day, they were enthusiastic participants and embraced the spirit of it all. It was a whole world of fun, and no one really cared if we won, drew or lost.

Over the course of the next few years, several of the Hornets played for local, more distinguished football clubs such as Pennington Lads, Lymington Sprites, Lawrence Boys and Dibden Dolomites. Some of us even outlandishly claimed to have represented imaginary teams like Sowley Sedge Warblers, Norley Wood Numbats, Tiptoe Tsetse Flies and Keyhaven Komodo Dragons. Behave. What on earth were we talking about? The Dibden Dolomites were real though and actually existed. I remember, many years later, a mate of mine having a scrap with their manager one night in Ye Olde English Gentleman pub in Lymington.

Notable people from the Hornets Hall of Shame include Mike Case and his brother Reg, Roger Figgures, Gary Webb, Glen Limburn, Jamie Dunford, Tony Jones, David Powell, Ali Blandford-Newson, John Wild,

Nick Smith, Richard and Paul Cooper, the McCarthy brothers, and of course, Dave Dutton. I remember we had a meeting one day, and decided The Hornets needed a proper football strip to make us look more professional. The lads finally agreed on orange and black striped shirts with numbers on the back, black shorts and orange and black socks. Everyone was excited about the whole thing, but the problem was, how were we going to pay for the kit? Unsurprisingly, the boys' parents weren't interested at all in helping the team out financially, so we had to think of another way of raising the money.

In the end we opted for the idea of an organised sponsored walk, from Lymington to East Boldre, six miles away, and back again. Feeling confident we'd raise enough funds, I went to Smith's sports shop at the top of town and placed an order with Mike Smith, the owner, for twelve brand new football kits. This turned into another disaster, as hardly anyone was prepared to sponsor us for some strange reason. Anyway, we went ahead with the walk regardless; that is, the few of us who could be bothered. So it was, one dismal Saturday afternoon in October, that we crossed the toll bridge and trudged off on our ill-conceived adventure into the nether regions of the New Forest.

The weather that day was atrocious. Lashed by the rain and shivering in the cold, we made for a pitiful sight as we slowly made our way along the winding country lanes, trying to avoid the water-filled ditches. It seemed like an eternity before we finally reached East Boldre. Tired and bewildered, soaked to the skin, we muttered among ourselves about the hopelessness of the situation we had found ourselves in.

We headed back on the return journey at a snail's pace, and with a sense of foreboding. By now it was completely dark, and morale was at an all-time low. The weather showed no sign of letting up. In fact, it was getting worse. It was late into the night when our small band of weary, despondent souls crawled back into Lymington and our beds.

The outcome of this whole fiasco became glaringly apparent when the football kits were delivered to the sports shop. After the ill-fated sponsored walk, a furious Mike Smith tried repeatedly and unsuccessfully to contact me, demanding payment. I don't know if he ever managed to return the kits to the manufacturer without having to pay anything, or if he found a way of shifting them on to someone else. Anyway, I didn't really care, to be honest. I quickly forgot about the whole matter and moved on with my life.

There was a lad called Tony Hayter who lived at the top of the road across from our house, right next to a good mate of mine called Glen Limburn. Glen's sister, Tina, was in the same year as me at school. I vividly recall our well-respected schoolteacher, Mrs Howell, gathering several of us together in her classroom in July 1974. Her last words to us before we left Lymington Juniors for good were 'Please listen to my advice pupils. Whatever you do in the future, stay well away from Tony Hayter. He's a very bad boy and trouble with a capital T. He's been to Borstal and it's wise not to associate with him in any way.' Tony was a few years older than us, and we were all terrified of him, and for good reason.

One day, I and a group of boys, the McCarthy brothers, who lived nearby, came up with a hare-brained scheme to shoot Tony with bows and arrows. We marched up to his house at the top of Ambleside Road thinking we were clever, armed to the teeth and ready to finish him off once and for all. He suddenly appeared out of nowhere, snarling, sporting a feather cut, Oxford bags, platform shoes and a real bad attitude. We panicked and ended up firing our arrows into the air and dropping the bows, then legged it down the road as fast as we could. After that little incident, I just knew Tony wouldn't rest until he'd beaten the absolute crap out of all of us.

One morning during half term, Tony was walking down his road with a mate of his called Paul Cleal. He caught a sudden glimpse of me in my parents' driveway and the pair of them stormed into our garden seeking retribution. Luckily, I'd managed to hide myself in amongst the cabbages on our vegetable patch, at the back of the house, blending in as best I could, and they never found me.

Ironically, Tony and I became firm friends a few years later after I helped him home when he was in a bad way, after being jumped by a couple of local neanderthals. Regarding archery, I remember me, Roger Figgures and the McCarthy brothers standing in a field firing aluminium-tipped arrows vertically into the sky, then just stupidly waiting to see if they came down and nailed us through the head. When you look back on it, I suppose the whole thing was completely nuts, but boys will be boys.

Not long after, a group of us formed the Black Eagle Gang (Schwartze Adler). Our mission in life was to intercept foreign spies, enemies of the state and perceived internal subversive elements. Our headquarters was in a treehouse in Roger Figgures' back garden, and we flew the flag with pride. The members of the Black Eagle Gang were as follows: Roger (Command and Control), me (Forward Scout), Kevin Upton (Long Range Reconnaissance), Clinton McCarthy (Military Advisor), Spencer McCarthy (Interpreter) and Scott McCarthy (Perimeter Sentry).

One night, after we'd set out the Claymores (directional anti-personnel mines), someone happened to stroll into our position undetected and set them off. Scott was assigned perimeter defence that night but failed miserably in stopping the infiltrator. He was summarily executed by firing squad at dawn the following morning for falling asleep on guard duty. Actually, we tied him to an elderly neighbour's gate, then rang her doorbell and ran off. She hurriedly came out of her house to find Scott swinging back and forth like a pendulum on a clock.

Throughout the mid to late 70s, I hung out with the McCarthy brothers a lot. I called them the Three Musketeers. It was at their house, just down the road from me, that I first met my future wife, Michaela Dennett. She was three years below me at school. She had a feather haircut and was nicknamed Suzi by a boy called Graham Mustey, who was in the same year as me at school, after Suzi Quatro. She famously wore Suzi's hairstyle and still does. Michaela was a bit of tomboy and a force to be reckoned with, I'd say.

Another time involving the McCarthy's, I was invited to stay at their dad John's house for the weekend. It was 1974. There were a few other boys there on the Saturday afternoon, and Spencer and I thought it would be a great idea to piss in one of their *Coke* cans. Anyway, to cut a long story short, Scott grassed us up and I was promptly driven home in disgrace in his dad's De Tomaso Mangusta car. Fortunately, John just dropped me off without saying a word and didn't come into our house. If he had, I would have been in serious trouble for that one.

On another occasion, I was hanging out with the brothers, bored and with nothing to do, when we stumbled upon a derelict house, tucked away down a track just off our road. We entered the property illegally, as you do, and discovered an old 17th century musket underneath a bed. After a split second of deliberating, we decided we were going to keep the musket and gave it to Scott to take care of. A few days later, the shit hit the fan when the owner of the musket traced the theft back to us. Clinton, Spencer and I denied all knowledge of the incident, planting the blame squarely on poor Scott's shoulders.

Our next-door neighbour at the time was a miserable elderly woman called Mrs Holt, who wouldn't even acknowledge you. She was a right old bag for sure. For instance, if a football was kicked over the fence into her garden, it would end up on the bonfire. She was a spinster with a chip on her shoulder, and we never once saw her smile. My parents bought my brother Richard a beautiful, beige-coloured pedigree kitten, Berlioz, as a present for his 2nd birthday. Although we've never been able to prove it, we're convinced that woman killed him by deliberately laying down weedkiller in her flowerbed.

One day, an old family friend from Hythe, David Fisher, came over to stay for the weekend. We decided to exact our revenge. Finding a dead frog in the road, we speared it on a stick and planted it on Mrs Holt's front lawn, in full view of her living room window. I recall us carrying out an impromptu voodoo ceremony around the frog and hoping Mrs Holt would just disappear. Forever. My wish came true a year or so later when I was told by someone who knew her that she had been attacked and partially eaten by a leopard whilst on safari in Zimbabwe. Whether this was true or just another urban myth, it really didn't matter, as we never saw the woman again.

CHAPTER 2

MIXING WITH THE BIG BOYS

In September 1974, I started at Priestlands Comprehensive School in Pennington. On first impression, the teachers seemed to me as if they were from some kind of alien, long-lost world. There was a distinct lack of connection between them and the pupils. Our headmaster, the rarely seen and perpetually elusive Mr Platt, was a weak, waspish, god-fearing sliver of a man. When he was addressing the school assembly, his head would shoot back and forth like a demented turkey. He came across as distant, stuffy and unapproachable. For me, even at such a tender young age, Platt appeared as a pious and dutiful figure of fun who commanded little respect. I could never take him seriously.

Platt's deputy, Mr Haynes, or 'Bopper' as he was known, could be a nasty piece of work. A stickler for discipline, he would stalk the school corridors, instilling fear and terror in the pupils. When it came to corporal punishment, it was Haynes who dished it out. He kept a cane in his office and seemed to get a thrill out of inflicting pain onto schoolboys' backsides, as a few of us can readily testify. He really was a sadistic bastard, that man. Throughout my five years at Priestlands, Bopper appeared to be everywhere and nowhere, all at the same time.

The one member of staff I was most wary of was Mr Dollery, Desmond Dollery, the Technical Drawing teacher. He was an ex-Royal Navy deep-sea diver who had seen active service during World War Two, or so rumour had it. He was ultra strict and wouldn't tolerate even the slightest bit of misbehaviour in his classroom. In every single TD lesson I attended at Priestlands school, the mere sight of the hard-line, uncompromising expression on Dollery's unsmiling weatherbeaten face would keep me on a razor's edge. It was that bad. No matter how hard I tried, I just couldn't get a grasp of the subject.

I was hopeless at Technical Drawing, something Dollery knew only too well, and in his cynical, ex-military eyes, I was someone who was beyond redemption. In an important TD exam I sat in the second year, I scored the grand total of five percent, and I only got that for writing my name down correctly on the examination paper.

The French teacher, Vivian Wilmshurst, was an irritating man. When he was asking you a question, he had this habit of saying 'Mmm? Mmm?' at the end of the sentence. For example, 'Have you done your homework yet? Mmm? Mmm?' I remember Wilmshurst berating my friend Kev Joyce one day, for wearing badges on his school blazer. 'And what are these? Mmm? Mmm? Take that paraphernalia off at once! Who do you think you are? Come on, chop chop. Mmm? Mmm?'

Educator in the French language by day, local scoutmaster by night, the man would delve deep into your psyche when you were ill and shouldn't have been at school in the first place. He'd take advantage of you when you were at your most vulnerable, and when you least expected it. He was weird, without a doubt, odd squad with a capital O, in my opinion. There was something about the man that gave me the creeps.

The very first song I ever wrote was titled '*I Hate Viv Wilmshurst.*' The whole idea was conceived in Roger's bedroom at *Sandpipers*; the house he lived at with his mother Jo, and three sisters, Jill, Anne and Jane, in Normandy Lane, Lymington. He'd recently bought himself a cheap electric guitar from Woolworths on the High Street, and added a basic twelve-bar blues tune to accompany my schoolboy punk lyrics. Was '*I Hate Viv Wilmshurst*' a vindictive song? Probably. Was it ever gonna make us a load of money? Probably not.

I remember a teacher called Mrs Evans. She was a right old battleaxe and more than a few of the pupils despised her with a passion. I've never heard a woman holler so much, and so loudly, in my life. I'm sure her overall intention was to engender fear and discipline into us all, but to me, she simply came across as some neurotic, cartoonish basket case. In hindsight, I'm sure many of these teachers were reasonably all right if you met them outside of the rigid, stifling school environment, but I didn't want them anywhere near me, so there you go.

At Priestlands school, I immediately struck up friendships with some of the other boys. One of them was a boy called Simon English, nicknamed Urk, after the Urko character in the television series, *The Planet of the Apes*. There was also Stephen Elliott, nicknamed Stump. He resided at a place called Culverley House in Brockenhurst, and he could be as funny as hell. He possessed the driest sense of humour and would often have us all in stitches. Before Stump moved down to these parts, he had lived with his family in Berlin, where his father was stationed with the British Army.

Another resident of Culverley House was John Caslake, nicknamed Jibber. He didn't arrive at Priestlands until the second year, after moving to the area from Brunei in Southeast Asia, where his father had been employed as a teacher. Much later, in the early 1980s, my band Peeping Toms knocked up a red backdrop featuring a black marker pen drawing of Jibber, complete with oversized erect penis. We even used to play a cover of *Babylon's Burning* by The Ruts, changing the song title to *Jibber's Bike's Burning*, after his motorbike caught fire one day, while riding back to Lymington from New Milton.

There was a family called the Moreys who lived in the tiny village of Pilley, two miles away from Lymington. One of the sons was in our school year, albeit fleetingly. On intake day he did a runner, hopping over the fence and evaporating into the ether forever. He never returned, preferring instead to spend the next five years fishing for minnows in a stream in Boldre, known as The Shallows.

Pilley boasted the largest population of Moreys on earth at that time. There were literally hundreds of them concentrated together under the same roof. They had to put a doorway in between two adjoining council houses so they could accommodate them all. Morey spotters from all over the country would descend upon Pilley in their droves. They brought with them a kind of twitcher's list, eagerly ticking off the various species, once they'd been sighted. There was the relatively common field Morey, the crested sand Morey, the ant-eating puffy-cheeked wood Morey, the flying fan-tailed swamp Morey, the false effervescent night Morey, Fotheringay's speckled reticulated ice Morey and, would you believe it, a Morey-impersonating Morey. There was even a *Collins Observer Book of Moreys* on sale in the local bookshops at the time. Joking aside, they were simply a harmless family going about their business like everyone else. I know some of them personally, and they're good people.

Years later, one of the Moreys, I'll call him Snuffy, travelled up to London in the van with us for a Cropdusters gig at The Powerhaus in Islington, North London. I remember him freaking out at Fleet service station on the way up there, because he'd never seen automatic doors before. They completely blew his mind. 'Ere you, what are these fucking things for, eh?' he asked a couple of us, confusedly. I also recall him punching some bloke's lights out in the mosh pit while the band were onstage that night, because he'd accidentally trodden on his toe. To make matters worse, Snuffy shat himself in the van on the journey home.

Apparently, the next day, in the Morey family's front garden, several other members of the clan hoisted the guy up in the air and proudly carried him shoulder high through the main street in Pilley, parading him for all to see. They were as pleased as punch, and chanting triumphantly, 'Ere look! Snuffy's been to London, you. Snuffy's been to London! Good old Snuffy! Aaaaaaaaarrrrrhhhh!'

My favourite teacher at Priestlands was a man called Mr Visick, although I can't for the life of me remember what subject he taught. He was a former WW2 aircraft pilot and mad as a box of frogs – absolutely barking. He'd come out with crazy stuff like 'I was talking to a pair of brass mosquitoes yesterday evening' and 'Have you seen a zinc caterpillar around here recently?' 'You'd better watch out for those titanium grasshoppers, they're very untrustworthy, you know.'

The guy was completely nuts, but in a good way. His classroom was the school library, and he allowed us to express ourselves and let us play records on his stereo during lessons. I'd like to think Mr Visick was a massive influence on all of us and a great inspiration. He was a charismatic, laidback, clever and very funny man. 'Why, only the other day, I happened upon three magnesium fireflies who appeared down on their luck. I told them things surely couldn't be that bad and they immediately perked up. You see, you never really know, do you?' As a teacher, Mr Visick was unique.

Several of the Physical Education teachers at Priestlands didn't appear to be that much older than us. One of them, Mr Clumsty, was an arrogant, bullying rugby-type person. One morning, when we were still in the first year, all the boys were congregated in the sports hall for a PE lesson, wearing only our dark blue shorts. Clumsty gestured for us to gather round him, then instructed everybody to express themselves while moving in one direction around the hall, in organised fashion. Most of us simply jogged slowly round the circuit, but a few others attempted forward rolls and handstands or performed cartwheels. Mark Tinley decided to run in the opposite direction to everyone else, pretending he was riding a motorbike, revving sounds emanating loudly from his mouth, going against the grain. Clumsty went berserk, dragging Tinley across the hall and throwing him onto a gym mat. He made the rest of us sit down and watch while he admonished him for rebelling against the collective. The bastard threatened him before kicking him about on the floor. I'll never forget the look of fear on Tinley's face. He was only eleven years old, for fuck's sake.

Another PE teacher, Mr Lavender, would often be waiting for us in the boys' changing room after a sports session. When he was satisfied each boy had taken all his kit off, he'd direct us to the showers, where he'd steal furtive glances at our naked young bodies. Licking his lips and shuffling about uncomfortably, he'd momentarily fix his gaze upon our pre-pubescent genitals. Lavender seemed to take an unhealthy interest in our physical development, if you know what I mean. We nicknamed him 'the willy watcher'.

Around the second year, I began to distrust the powers that be who were running this place of learning. I was losing my desire and determination to knuckle down and work hard to make something out of myself. I lacked the ambition to succeed academically and quickly grew bored out of my mind with all the lessons, timetables and rigid bullshit rules and regulations. I didn't care much about the future; I was only interested in the here and now. I couldn't concentrate properly in class and hated having to do homework. Art and English were the only subjects I found vaguely stimulating in any sort of way. Even French lessons rapidly became a chore. Being able to speak the language helped immensely at first, but I gradually became uninterested, and before long I couldn't remember certain words and phrases I'd learned from my time in France.

In retrospect, the only meaningful thing I got out of going to school was seeing my mates and mucking about, listening to music, playing stupid pranks, the jolly japes and the banter. I just wanted to have fun and not be suffocated by all the crap that most of the teachers were spouting at us at the time. In my mind, attending Priestlands every day was a social event. It couldn't be anything else.

Every year the fair would come to Pennington Common, and all the kids would become excited at the prospect of going on the amusement rides; the rollercoaster, Ferris wheel, ghost train and bumper cars, or dodgems as they were known. There's an ancient ballad called *Scarborough Fair*, reworked by the American folk rock duo Simon and Garfunkel, which was the lead track on their 1966 album *Parsley, Sage, Rosemary and Thyme*. Simon Vincent adapted the lyrics to the song, and in a thick, overblown Hampshire accent, sang them to a few of us in the school playground one morning. 'Are you going up the fair tonight? I'll meet you by the coconut shy. Remember me? I knocked six down last time. And I'll be trying for seven tonight.'

I remember a brief period when schoolboys in our year would go up to each other and ask, 'Going up fair tonight?' The correct reply to the question was supposed to be 'Nah, going down club.' One afternoon in the school corridor, Mike Case approached Graham Flood and asked, 'Going up fair tonight?' Graham stared at him for a moment, before punching him in the stomach. I think Graham was sick to death of boys constantly walking up to him and stupidly asking, 'Going up fair tonight?' and he'd simply reached the end of his tether and just snapped.

At lunchtimes in the main school hall, Mrs Marsh, the dinner lady, would tell us off for acting about while we were in the queue, waiting for her to serve us our food. 'Behave yourselves, or you won't get none!' she'd bawl at us. When I look back to those days in the 70s, I can't believe the stuff they were feeding us schoolchildren. Liver and bacon with a dollop of dry mashed potato and peas as hard as bullets, and stodgy sponge pudding with pink banana custard, were just two of the school meals that tormented my very soul. 'Behave yourselves, or you won't get none!'

Our art teacher in the second year, Mr Hart, played in a rock band from Dorset called Rusty Blade. He was a hippie type from Darlington, in the north-east of the country, with frizzy afro hair and a goatee beard. My immediate impression of him was that he was an out there kind of guy and he was all right. However, it didn't take long for me to get on his wrong side. One afternoon, while he was stood up addressing the class, Dave Dutton leant across the table and whispered in my ear, 'Do something stupid nipper!' I promptly leapt up like a maniacal jack-in-the-box, shouting 'Ali Bongo!' at the top of my voice.

Mr Hart was hell bent on making an example out of me, and in front of everyone, he started cruelly twisting my ear and threatening me. I must admit it hurt like fuck. He was a great, dedicated cross-country runner, and when he realised I wasn't that bad at long-distance running myself, he began to change his opinion of me, even to the extent of encouraging me to take part in several organised running events across Hampshire and Dorset.

I remember the Environmental Science lessons at Priestlands School, and they were indeed mental. The teacher, Mrs Jarvis, was a lovely woman, but I could never understand what the fuck she was talking about. She'd stand there, in front of the class, saying things like, 'Photosynthesis enables levels of oxygen and carbon monoxide in the atmosphere to balance. Without it, we'd quickly run out of oxygen. Now class, if this were to occur, there'd be no more Sally Seed, no more Lucy Leaf, no more

Bobby Bluebottle, no more Seamus Squirrel, no more Edgar Elephant and no more children learning about Environmental Science at school. 'Put it this way. If Wayne had a shipment of bananas, and Sammy the Cloud suddenly appeared in the sky above him, what do you think would happen next? Kevan?'

Kevan Lane was a small, timid, harmless boy, who rarely said anything at all. He'd turn a deep crimson red, look down at the floor, and shuffle his feet awkwardly whenever a teacher asked him a question. For some reason, he'd always glance across the classroom at me and mumble 'Shut up Shaun! Shut up Shaun!' Why it was my fault the teacher had asked him a question, I've got no idea.

I'll never forget the day Kevan was asked to read out a passage from an Environmental Science book in front of the rest of the class. He spoke so quietly that even the boy sitting right next to him couldn't hear him properly. Mrs Jarvis intervened on his behalf. 'Speak up Kevan, you're doing fine. What's the next sentence in the book? Come on, you can do it!'

At this point, Kevan was blushing uncontrollably, his face the colour of beetroot. He was really embarrassed and was struggling terribly to pronounce the words 'root nodules.' Mrs Jarvis intervened once more, prompting him. 'Come on Kevan, you're almost there.' After an agonising few seconds, he finally managed to splutter out 'Rrrrrrrrrrrrrrooooooot nodules! Shut up Shaun! Shut up Shaun!'

Mrs Jarvis then said 'Bravo Kevan. Didn't he do well, everybody? I think he deserves a round of applause and a Jelly Baby for being such a brave little soldier. Don't the rest of you agree? What's your favourite colour Jelly Baby, Kevan? I've got a packet of them here in the drawer.' Talk about patronising. I seem to recall Kevan anxiously whispering back to her, 'Red please, Mrs Jarvis.'

Another time, Kevan was nervously reading an extract out of a book, while the rest of the pupils listened on intently. When he came to the word 'rhododendrons' he began having a meltdown. Try as he might, he simply couldn't pronounce it. The pressure was on. The whole classroom was engulfed in a deathly silence, eagerly anticipating what Kevan was going to say next. After what felt like an eternity, he stammered 'Rrrrrrrodidumdums! Shut up Shaun! Shut up Shaun!'

Looking back, Kevan was probably on the verge of a nervous breakdown at the time. I often wonder what became of him. Someone recently told me they'd heard he'd moved up to Darwen in Lancashire decades ago, where he'd settled down, got married and somewhere along the line, found God. I don't know whether the information carries any credence or not, but whatever he's doing, it's his life and good luck to him. Amen.

I recall sitting in a classroom one day, and our tutor attempting to explain something mathematical to the pupils. As an example, she focused on a boy called Barry Holloway and asked him how many brothers and sisters he had. Bemused, Barry thought about the question for a moment, then rolled his eyes around and mumbled, 'Now let me see. There's Ollie, Molly, Dolly, Lollie, Polly, Holly. Umm, who else is there?' Scratching his head in mild puzzlement, he continued, 'Ah, yes, then there's Wally, and we've got a dog called Tolly. He's a collie. Golly!'

Barry then went silent and began staring vacantly up at the ceiling of the classroom, as if he was trying to remember whether he'd missed out the names of any of his brothers and sisters. He started muttering quietly to himself, 'There's Ollie, Molly, Dolly, Lollie, Polly, Holly...' At this point, the tutor sharply interrupted him. 'All right Barry, that's enough for now. I think we get the gist of what you're saying.' Barry began rolling his eyes once more and gazed up at the ceiling again, an inane look spreading across his face. It was extraordinary, to say the least.

After I'd returned from France, I joined the local Cub Scout group in Lymington. I had a good time while I was in the cubs because some of my best friends from school were enrolled there. We were all in it together and we had a lot of fun. The Cub Scout leaders were called Akela and Bagheera, after the animal characters in Rudyard Kipling's famous story *The Jungle Book*, and I remember them loudly addressing us with the words 'Pack, pack pack!' and 'Cubs do your best!' to which we'd all enthusiastically reply in unison, 'We will do our best!'

When I look back on those long-ago halcyon days, they are full of memories of such things as Bob-a-Job Week, a visit to a local donkey sanctuary, tug of war, obstacle courses, ill-fitting short trousers, woggles and colourful merit patches. Fortunately, the flamboyant dandy peer Lord Montagu kept a healthy distance, and thankfully didn't bother us in any way.

Joking aside, back in the summer of 1952, Monty, who resided at Beaulieu Palace House, not far away from Lymington, was arrested and charged with the serious crime of molesting a 14-year-old Boy Scout. He'd invited the lad to join him for a swim in the River Solent, near the grounds of his estate. The boy accused Monty of sexually attacking him in his beach hut; something he always vehemently denied, although he later admitted to being bisexual. In the event, Lord Montagu appeared at Lymington Magistrates Court, where he was booed and jeered by a mob of around 250 people. After an agonising three-week wait, he was cleared of the charges. Then the real nightmare began.

In January 1954, Monty and two other men, his cousin, Dorset landowner Michael Pitt-Rivers and the then diplomatic correspondent for the Daily Mail, Peter Wildeblood, were arrested and charged with consensual homosexuality with two young RAF airmen, Eddie McNally and John Reynolds. Their arrests were part of a crackdown on homosexuals by Churchill's government, amidst a backdrop of Cold War paranoia following the defection of gay spies Guy Burgess and Donald Maclean to the Soviet Union. McNally and Reynolds turned Queen's Evidence and testified for the prosecution against the three defendants in court. The exact charge was conspiracy to incite certain male persons to commit serious offences with male persons. The subsequent trial at Winchester Assizes in Hampshire caused a national, if not, international scandal, and Monty nearly suffered a mental collapse over the whole affair.

The Montagu case shook the Establishment to its very core and changed the course of British legal history. The three men were found guilty, with Lord Montagu handed a 12-month prison sentence. The other two men received eighteen months each. Many people at the time were outraged, believing the three men were victims of a witch hunt by the anti-gay press.

As it transpired, the two airmen were threatened with expulsion from the RAF if they didn't testify against them.

The Montagu case ultimately led to the decriminalisation of homosexuality in the United Kingdom. Personally, I believe Lord Montagu, Michael Pitt-Rivers and Peter Wildeblood were made scapegoats by certain members of the establishment, mainly the then Home Secretary, Sir David Maxwell Fyfe. These people aimed to expunge homosexuality from society and went after high profile people before the law changed.

There's a pub in Beaulieu named after the man, the Montagu Arms, where they serve RBS IPA (Receptive Boy Scout Indian Pale Ale) on draught. I've never tried it myself, but apparently, it's an extremely popular drink with the customers. Another well-loved tipple on offer in the pub is their flagship real ale, called Monty's Revenge, which has the reputation of being exceedingly rich and smooth in flavour. They've even got a signature cocktail in honour of him, Monty on the Beach. The cocktail's ingredients are a closely guarded secret, known only to a very few select people.

Me and my mates have always flippantly known the pub as the Scout's Bottom. After Lord Montagu's conviction all those years ago, road signs in the New Forest were defaced with lewd graffiti such as 'Caution Bender to the Left', 'Bend to the Right Not Likely' and 'Don't Bend Over in Beaulieu'.

The next stage of the journey meant enrolling in the 9th Lymington Sea Scouts. I was the only one out of my mates who was forced to join, and I was gutted. I absolutely hated every minute of being a Sea Scout. I resented having to attend the meetings every Friday evening after a week at school, and it tainted the weekend for me. I remember my ridiculous initiation ceremony where I was perched on a wooden swing seat and hoisted up by rope through a hatch on the first floor of the scout hut, to the shrill sound of pipe whistles echoing above me. Led by the indefatigable Scoutmaster Tibby Turner, it was an experience I'd rather forget.

Tibby the Scoutmaster was something of an enigma. He was a plump chap, with a moon-shaped face and keen blue eyes, approaching his mid-sixties. He had a balding head and wore glasses. He spoke with a thick

Hampshire accent and could be quite grumpy at times. However, he was passionate about what he was doing and a true believer. A bachelor by choice, he lived in a small cottage at the bottom of our road. Occasionally, he helped in the organisation of regional scouting events that we were all expected to attend.

One such jamboree took place over the course of a summer weekend in Brockenhurst. Scout groups from all over the area converged on a large field at New Park for two days of camping, hiking, orienteering, bushcraft and night manoeuvres I remember outdoor activities included obstacle courses and a football tournament. In the evening, we'd all gather round the campfire to toast marshmallows, and join in hearty renditions of such timeless scouting classics as *Ging Gang Goolie, Kumbaya (Come Be with Me), The Grand Old Duke of York, Campfire's Burning, Five in the Bed, One Finger One Thumb* and *Oh Dear! What Can the Matter Be?*

There were organised competitions between rival scout groups that weekend. The 1st Pennington Scouts were there, and I was at school with a couple of them at the time, Tony Burns and Colin Whitlock, who remain good friends of mine that I'm still in touch with today. One of the competitions was called Housekeeping, and some of my fellow sea scouts from the 9th Lymington, and I, set out to sabotage it. Good housekeeping meant ensuring the area around the scouts' sleeping tents were clean and tidy, properly maintained, and with no visible litter strewn about.

The Pennington scouts went over and above the call of duty. They put up a sign, so everybody knew who they were, a washing line and even a flagpole. After foraging about earnestly in the forest for hours, they returned to the campsite with pieces of wood, assorted bits of foliage and a smug look on their faces. They constructed a wire perimeter fence outside their tent, and sprinkled pebbles around it for effect. The only thing missing was a vegetable plot.

I can't for the life of me remember whose idea it was, but we ended up making a 'woomerang'. This was a crude type of home-made slingshot (catapult) arrow, with a wooden shaft, sharp-edged point, and cardboard fins. In the early hours of Sunday morning, under the light of a silvery moon, we crept silently out of our tent on a mission and raised hell.

Launching the woomerang at the Pennington scouts' tent, it flew straight through the canvas. There was an almighty ripping sound, and panicked cries could be heard coming from the tent's inhabitants, who'd been fast asleep at the time. I remember instantly thinking that this was probably not my finest move, but they'd been taking all this far too seriously, and I hadn't wanted to be there in the first place. Anyway, we scurried back inside our tent in fits of laughter, waiting for the repercussions that would surely follow later that morning. Amazingly, we got away with it. Nothing was ever mentioned about the incident.

Around lunchtime, the district commissioner arrived on site to inspect the scouts, and hand out prizes to the competition winners. Because of the obvious tear in the 1st Pennington's tent, they didn't win the housekeeping prize. Someone else did. They stood there incredulous, as the district commissioner congratulated my bunch of unlikely lads and awarded us the prize for winning the organised football tournament. As our team leader gleefully accepted the trophy on our behalf, we were roundly applauded by everybody, except of course, the Pennington Scouts.

One Sunday afternoon in late autumn, not long after the New Park shenanigans, several of us were driven deep into the forest on an orienteering exercise. Before long, we were hopelessly lost and detached from the rest of the scout group. Trudging aimlessly through thickets and fields, we became totally disorientated. Not one of us could read a compass, and it seemed as if we were walking around in circles.

Eventually, we forded a brook, climbed a fence, and found ourselves in a muddy field full of cows. I'd made the foolish decision earlier to wear a pair of brand-new Puma trainers my parents had bought me. One of the cows suddenly charged at us, and in a desperate bid to escape the rampaging beast, I became stuck in the mud. Fearing the worst, I frantically tried to free myself. I succeeded, but at the cost of one of my trainers, which I had to leave behind in that godforsaken place.

Unbeknown to our group of unwilling participants, they'd sent out a search party looking for us. Somehow, they finally managed to locate us in a forest clearing, in the middle of nowhere. As we hopped into the back seat of the car, a weaselly, thin, bespectacled man, who was sitting in the passenger seat, turned his head around, admonishing us for inconveniencing him on his precious Sunday afternoon. I never knew who he was, or how he was connected to the sea scouts, but the bloke was a bit of a tool. When I arrived back home, I walked through the front door wearing only one trainer. My parents were livid.

Once, while in the 9th Lymington Sea Scouts, we were all bussed down to Portsmouth for a grand tour of HMS *Victory*, the iconic 18th century flagship, forever associated with the heroic exploits of the inspirational Admiral Horatio Nelson at the Battle of Trafalgar in 1805. Nelson is regarded as one of the greatest naval commanders in history. After an informative history lesson about the *Victory*, we were required to stand in formation on the dockside while a Rear Admiral from the Royal Navy walked down the line, inspecting us from head to toe. What the fuck for, I'll never understand. It wasn't like we were about to be packed off to war or anything.

Anyway, the Rear Admiral, with quiet authority, started slowly pacing up and down in front of us, his arms behind his back. Walking past, his eyes met mine, and then he asked the burning question, 'Have you ever been on a modern ship?' Because a good friend of my dad's, Peter Scott, was the captain of a small warship called a minesweeper at the time, and my family had recently been guests of his on there, I replied to him that I had indeed spent time aboard a modern ship. 'And what type of ship was it?' he asked. Shuffling uncomfortably for a moment, I told him it was a minesweeper. Fellow sea scout and friend from school, Simon Vincent, who was stood in line right next to me, couldn't contain himself and was doubled up, crying with laughter. He thought a minesweeper was a kind of metal detector, used in such unusual pursuits as hobby-level gold prospecting and the unearthing of valuable buried treasure. Simon associated minesweepers with nerdy old men pottering around in fields and meadows in the British countryside, with their camouflage trousers and knee pads, and didn't get it at all.

The Rear Admiral just looked at me impassively, then moved on down the line towards his next target; a short, anaemic spotty boy with a bamboozled expression clearly visible on his face. I could just about make out what the Rear Admiral was saying to him. 'Come on, stand up straight lad. And how long have you been in the Sea Scouts?' The boy muttered back, 'Uh, I don't know sir.'

The Rear Admiral, sounding confused, replied, 'Surely you must know how long you've been in the Sea Scouts. A year? Six months? Have you ever been on a modern ship?' The boy just stood there, rigid, without saying anything, and the Rear Admiral, staring at him intensely for a split second, continued further on down the line. Tibby Turner, you promised me the world, but you delivered a dockyard in Portsmouth.

Tibby was undoubtedly a respectable kind of guy and hats off to him for sacrificing his spare time for ungrateful little shits like us. I'm sure he meant well, but it was the way in which he came across. Obsessed with the outdated Baden-Powell ethos of scouting, he lived and breathed the whole sorry thing. It was firmly embedded in his DNA, and he'd never give you a moment's peace.

One lousy Sunday afternoon, after a few of us had been summoned to the scout hut, he decided, in his infinite wisdom, that it would be a good idea to pair us up and send us out to sea in dinghies. Looking back, I'm convinced he was deliberately trying to kill us. Tentatively donning my life jacket, a sudden realisation hit me. There were only five dinghies, but there were nine of us present. One of us would be on our own, the odd one out. As it transpired, that unfortunate person was me. Anyway, we set out to sea, and that's when the ordeal began. Within minutes, I started losing control of the oars. I found myself spinning helplessly towards the wash of an oncoming Isle of Wight passenger ferry. It was terrifying. I remember abandoning all hope, certain I was going to perish in the Solent. Mike Case and Chris Shepherd, in a separate dinghy nearby, were pissing themselves with laughter at my predicament.

Then, just as I was about to be sucked down into the ferry's propellors, a speedboat appeared suddenly out of the blue and rescued me from the brink of death. The crew hauled me aboard their boat, attached a rope to the dinghy, and we made our way back to dry land. Staggering ashore, and understandably traumatised by the experience, I thanked the speedboat crew for saving my life. Tearing off my life jacket, I slumped down on the ground in annoyance. I looked up and noticed Tibby standing in the doorway of the scout hut, hands on hips, shaking his head in exasperation. He appeared genuinely disappointed that I was still alive.

By now, I'd had it up to here with Tibby Turner and his goddamned Sea Scouts. From that moment on, I was determined to never set foot in that blessed scout hut again. On Friday evenings, I'd change into my uniform, as normal, but instead of heading off to the meeting, I'd go round my schoolfriend Mark Pallant's place. Mark lived in a flat above a bookshop on Lymington High Street.

The pair of us would spend the time drinking cups of hot, milky coffee and playing Striker. Striker was a simple 70s five a side table-top football game, when compared to its cousin, the more illustrious Subbuteo. The objective of Striker was scoring as many goals as possible against your opponent by pressing the plastic football players' heads to make their legs kick the ball. Later, there was an upgrade of the game called Super Striker, which came packaged in an enormous box, complete with diving, twisting goalkeepers.

Anyway, I kept up this pretence for a while, before my parents received a letter from Tibby demanding to know where I'd been for the past few weeks. I told Mum I was adamant I didn't want to go there anymore, and that I wasn't into wasting my Friday evenings doing something I hated. I just wanted to go out and play with my friends. She finally agreed I could leave the Sea Scouts, and I breathed a huge sigh of relief. Free from the spectre of Tibby Turner and his nautical nightmare at last, I felt a whole lot happier.

Looking back on the mid 1970s, it seemed such a drab time to be alive. Everything was brown and dull. Glam rock was on its last legs, and the likes of David Essex, Peters and Lee, Kenny, Wings and Donny & Marie Osmond never did anything for me. As I mentioned earlier, I was into Sparks though and bought their first three albums from the splendidly named Klitz Records on the High Street. They had a booth at the back of the shop where you could listen to the latest records on headphones before deciding whether you wanted to buy them.

As a child, I suffered from asthma and quite severe bouts of bronchitis. I can remember being off school and lying flat out on the carpet in the lounge at home in the daytime, wheezing, coughing up phlegm and feeling worse than terrible. On the television would be stuff like Rainbow, Fingerbobs, Pipkins, or Crown Court. The opening theme tune to Crown Court still haunts me to this day. There was also the incredibly boring Programmes for Schools and Colleges.

Much of this period in my life remains a blur. I do remember a few notable incidents though. One evening, after David Dutton's parents had gone out for a meal at a local restaurant, he nicked his dad's car and took it for a spin. He was thirteen years old. After being chased along roads for miles at high speed by the police, he ended up crashing the car into a ditch. The following Friday, Dave's exploits were splashed all over the front page of the local newspaper, the *Lymington Times*.

I was a paperboy in those days, and wary of dogs after an Alsatian bit me when I was younger, while playing in the road outside our house in Hythe. I remember early one morning being bitten on the leg by an out-of-control Border Collie. It happened on the pavement in the street as I was delivering newspapers. The dog ran up to me and sank its teeth into my thigh before running off. Its owner, a dour, balding, chubby middle-aged bloke who seemed to have a chip on his shoulder, witnessed the whole incident, then unbelievably, had the nerve to blame me for antagonising the animal in the first place. He became aggressive and started shouting at me. I just laughed at him and gave him the finger and carried on up the road with my sack of newspapers.

Another disturbing episode I can recall was when a good friend of my mother's came over to our house to babysit Gail, Richard and me, while my parents went out somewhere for the evening. Chuckling to myself in my bedroom, I quickly removed all my clothes and tiptoed quietly down the stairs. I calmly opened the door to the living room, where the babysitter was sat quietly watching television, and walked over and stood directly in front of her, stark bollock naked, without saying a word.

Recoiling in horror, she looked me up and down for a moment, then spluttered out the immortal words 'For God's sake Shaun, put some clothes on! You're twelve years old now! What on earth would your mother and father say?' I guess I was testing her to see what her reaction would be. She was a lovely lady, and I encountered her on many occasions in the ensuing years. Nothing was ever mentioned about the incident again. It was our special secret, or so I wanted to believe, anyway.

Meanwhile, at Priestlands, things were going from bad to worse. My school reports were appallingly bad. So bad in fact, that I'd throw them in the bin before my parents had the chance to read them. The same criticisms were being levelled at me repeatedly: 'Has the ability but won't apply himself.' 'In class, Shaun often comes across as if he's totally away with the fairies. He needs to apply himself and concentrate a lot more if he wants to go on and achieve anything meaningful in life.' 'There's a distinct lack of effort on Shaun's part. He needs to show more determination.' 'Appears to have his head in the clouds most of the time. Must try harder.'

There was a boy in the year above us at school called David Gregory. He had longish straight greasy hair and was covered in acne and wore glasses. David played the bass guitar, and the music he listened to was a million miles away from what floated my boat at the time. He was into Pink Floyd, Genesis, Yes, Rush and progressive rock bands in general, and the only words you could ever get out of him were 'Yeah man.'

'All right David? There's a small ball of fluff on your shirt collar.' 'Yeah man.' 'Hi David, did you watch the news last night? Russia's declared war on the rest of the world and we're all heading for oblivion. We're fucked mate.' 'Yeah man.' 'David, I hate to tell you, but I was walking past your house this morning and couldn't help but notice your mother getting gang-banged in your front garden by a load of builders working on the property next door. I hasten to add, she looked like she was thoroughly enjoying every minute of it.' 'Yeah man.'

David Gregory had one of those faces that's extremely hard to forget. He reminded me of Shaggy from the Hanna-Barbera TV production Scooby-Do. My mate Geoff Neal couldn't get his head around Gregory. He would scrawl pictures of his face on every classroom desk at any given opportunity. Gregorys, they were known as, and they were everywhere. 'David, do you know you're famous? There are drawings of you all over the school desks.' 'Yeah man.' Yeah man, yeah man. I recall one evening in the late 70s, Geoff and I turning up unannounced at Gregory's house and peering through his bedroom window. He was practising his bass guitar and stopped playing the instrument momentarily to pick his nose. Yeah man.

The summer of 1976 was an absolute scorcher, by anyone's estimation. Britain basked in an unprecedented heatwave which seemed to go on forever. There were wildfires raging through forests and across woodland, crops failed, and reservoirs dried up. Railway lines buckled, tarmac melted, and hosepipe bans were put in place due to water rationing. During late June and early July, the mercury went completely off the scale. Large swathes of coastal southern England were invaded by massive swarms of greenfly, closely followed by their natural predator, the starving and aggressive seven-spotted ladybird. Billions of them. It was a seemingly apocalyptic event, a plague of biblical proportions.

Against this backdrop of relentless, sweltering sunshine and inexhaustible multitudes of bothersome insects, I'd spend the school summer holiday of '76 down by the outdoor seawater baths in Lymington and playing never-ending games of badminton, would you believe, with Roger Figgures in his back garden. There was a BBC television sitcom running at the time, about a Royal Artillery concert party sweating away in the tropical heat of Burma during the final months of the Second World War, called *It Ain't Half Hot Mum*. In a strange way, the show echoed what we were experiencing in the UK that summer.

The lyrics to *It Ain't Half Hot Mum's* theme tune went like this:

Meet the gang because the boys are here, the boys to entertain you.
With music and laughter to help you on your way.
To raising the rafters with a hey, hey, hey!

*With songs and sketches and jokes old and new, we mess about,
you won't feel blue.*

So, meet the gang because the boys are here, the boys to entertain you.

We are here to make you feel gay, so give us a cheer with a hey, hey, hey!

*Just gather around and put down your gun, we mess about,
there's plenty of fun.*

So, meet the gang because the boys are here, the boys to entertain you.

B-O, B-O-Y-S, Boys to entertain you.

I used to love getting up to no good when I was younger, but not in a bad way. I just possessed a mischievous spirit, that was all. One day during spring half term – I think we were in our third year of school at the time – me and my mates decided to re-enact a stunt I'd initially learned about, and taken part in, with the boys I was friends of in Wales during the early 70s. It was called the Grand National. What this entailed, was a bunch of us gathering near the back garden of the first in a row of houses, in a road chosen at random.

The ultimate objective was to tear through each individual back garden together, one after another, as fast as our legs would carry us. We had to overcome any obstacle that was put in front of us before clearing the final hurdle. The plan then was to regroup in the road outside the end house in the row, after we'd completed our mission.

The most exciting aspect of the Grand National was you'd never know who or what was waiting for you on the other side of someone's garden fence or hedge. There might be a friendly old man there watering his tomatoes, a lady hanging out her washing, a treacherous fishpond, or a snarling Doberman Pinscher patrolling its territory. It was the fear of the unknown. That was the buzz, and that's the reason why we did it.

Anyway, one bright sunny morning, a group of around a dozen of us were huddled together in the road, ready for the challenge that lay ahead. We'd already targeted a row of around ten houses beforehand. These were situated in Waterford Lane, Lymington, which was adjacent to Broad Lane, where I lived. We couldn't wait for our very own attempt at the Grand National to get underway. It was such a long time ago; I can't quite remember the names of everyone who took part in this exercise in mischief. I do recall Brent Jones being there. Possibly, Mike Case, Laurence Sunderland and Angus McDonald as well.

Upon the sound of a bugle, which was our prearranged signal to charge forward into the breach, we surged towards the first garden fence. In trepidation, and with adrenaline pumping, we scaled it as one. We were a tight knit unit that day, on a path to glory. The fence buckled under the combined weight of us all, sending many of us sprawling onto the manicured garden lawn.

I glanced to my left, and immediately locked eyes with an elderly woman sitting in the conservatory, a cup and saucer in her hand. Some of us were in hysterics. I remember looking back at the conservatory. On closer inspection, I realised that we'd rudely interrupted someone's coffee morning. There were a dozen or so ladies present, and they were all speechless. They simply couldn't believe what was unfolding in front of them.

Waving at them, we wished them well and soldiered on to the next objective, a daunting eight-foot-high hedge. Throwing ourselves at the greenery with gusto, one on top of another, we managed to navigate the obstacle successfully. Falling headfirst into the garden, we discovered we'd landed among a collection of terracotta gnomes. A few of the gnomes got smashed to pieces amid all the confusion. The next barrier standing in our way was another hedge, identical to the previous one. We cleared it without too much trouble and found ourselves on someone's patio. That's when it all went wrong.

A furious voice shouted out from somewhere, 'Who the hell are you? What do you think you're doing trespassing in my garden? You've got a bloody nerve! Get out of here now, before I box your ears! I mean it! Go on then, what are you waiting for? Get the hell out of here, now!' A clearly irate, middle-aged man started coming towards us, menacing and red-faced with rage, his fists tightly clenched. We scattered as fast as possible and made a mad dash for the garden gate. Pouring through, we managed to escape the clutches of Mr Infuriated and get the hell out of Dodge. Apart from a few minor cuts and bruises, we emerged relatively unscathed. From then on, there would be no more messing around, uninvited, in other peoples' gardens. No more Grand Nationals.

My friends and I used to get up to some crazy stuff. We'd long since moved on from childish pranks, like tying someone's door handle to a flowerpot in their front garden, then ringing the doorbell. We'd hang around just long enough to watch the person open the door, making the pot swing against the wall of the house with a crash, before scarpering.

Among other stupid stunts we pulled when we were very young was one which involved giving a couple of older boys a load of lip, hoping we'd wound them up enough, so they'd charge after us. It was the thrill of the chase. Pure excitement. I can't recall who was with me on this occasion, but I seem to remember there were three of us present.

The incident happened one evening, after we'd foolishly mouthed off at two gangly youths who were complete strangers to us. They were loitering down a country lane, fifty yards or so away, and decided to teach us a lesson in manners. They started to run towards us, gesturing with their fists and shouting angrily. We hotfooted it down the lane and bolted over a turnstile into some large wide-open fields, our pursuers hard on our heels. Running as fast as our legs could carry us, we kept on going, determined to put as much distance as possible between us and the lads chasing us.

After a long while navigating our way through the fields, we realised we were making good ground, and it looked as if we were shaking them off. Sure enough, an hour or so into the manhunt, they reluctantly gave up the pursuit. Flicking V signs at us, they turned around and slowly walked away in the opposite direction, disappearing into a clump of trees. Who know what those two youths would have done had they caught up with us. In hindsight, it was a foolish move on our part to goad and insult them like we did, and we were just asking for trouble.

During summer holidays in the late 1970s, the Girl Guides Association would organise weeklong camping trips down to our neck of the woods, staying in a field in Walhampton, just across the river from Lymington. Guides from far and wide would travel here for seven days of map and compass, first aid, knots, tracking and stalking and fire lighting. Other activities the girls might take part in included sailing, canoeing and weather lore. A few supervisors would always accompany them on their camping holiday, helping to pitch up the six-berth tents the guides would be sleeping in and oversee the preparation and cooking of simple meals on the campfire.

I can't for the life of me remember whose bright idea it was originally, but plans were put in place to form a nighttime raiding party. This entailed groups of us boys camping out in tents ourselves, in some of our parents' back gardens. The ultimate purpose of the exercise was to head out undetected to the field in Walhampton, where the guides had set up camp. Once there, we'd approach in total silence, then pull the guy ropes out, so the tent collapsed onto its sleeping occupants, creating havoc. Then we'd beat a hasty retreat in the direction we'd come in from.

Only a very few of us took part in the first raid, codenamed *Operation Mary*. I remember Kevin Joyce was there, along with Brent Jones, Laurence Sunderland, Mike Case, John Wild, Roger Figgures, Angus McDonald, Chris Shepherd and myself. Together, we comprised a small team. It was much better having limited numbers of boys sneaking around quietly, than a large group of lumbering oafs clanking about loudly at night, advertising their presence.

After it had been established that the guides had arrived and secured their camp, we set the operation in motion. At zero hour, under the cover of darkness, we crept out of our tents without making a sound and headed off to a prearranged assembly point. There, we psyched ourselves up for the top-secret mission that lay ahead. Leaving the assembly point, we crossed the toll bridge and turned left onto a footpath that ran parallel to the Lymington River and Undershore Road. Bulrushes swaying in the breeze, we walked single file, adrenaline pumping, and eventually arrived at a large wooden gate. Hopping over it, we stealthily made our way towards the target. We were now in the field adjacent to the one the guides were camping in.

Within minutes, we had reached the fence that divided the two fields and climbed over it. Heading directly towards our final objective, in total silence, we came to the first in a row of half a dozen tents. Yanking on the guy ropes, it immediately began to fall in on itself. Hysterical cries could be heard coming from inside the tent as we quickly moved on to the next one. Repeating the process, and getting a similar reaction, we were soon tugging at the guy ropes of the third tent.

By now, there was so much commotion going on that the adult supervisors had woken up and were now emerging from their tents. A couple of men screamed at us to stop what we were doing at once and leave the guides alone. One of them raced across the field in his pyjamas and jumped into the seat of a Ford Cortina car parked nearby. Turning on the ignition and putting the headlights on full beam, he sped towards us. Panicking, our cover blown, we made the decision to separate. Racing away from the scene in different directions, to a cacophony of shrieks filling the night air, it was every man for himself. The Cortina didn't know which one of us to focus on and go after. Our small band of merry mayhem makers split apart, but the core of us ended up reuniting on the footpath we'd travelled in on.

We eventually reached the road, but right at that moment the Cortina appeared out of nowhere and we ended up having to leap over the walls of various peoples' homes to get away from it. The driver was apoplectic with rage, on a search and destroy mission, intent on getting hold of at least one of us and bringing us to justice. Luckily, he never got to get his hands on us. We were too well hidden in the shrubbery, blending in with the surroundings. Around ten minutes later, the man drove off back to the campsite. When the dust settled, we emerged from the shadows and made our way home.

I took part in two more Girl Guide tent raids after that one. The first, codenamed Operation Mungo, was a venture into the familiar territory of the field at Walhampton, with mostly the same people. This time we terrorised a different group camped there. Yet again, we managed to evade capture. My third and final raid, codenamed Operation Midge, was a meticulously planned mechanized one, on a camp in a water meadow at a place called Sowley. Leading the offensive on their Puch Maxis were Kevin Joyce, Angus McDonald and Chris Shepherd. They formed the three-pronged trident heading the raid. Behind them followed the infantry. That is, the rest of us. Struggling to keep up, we floundered about in the long, wet grass in pitch darkness. The terrain proved extremely difficult that night, but eventually, we got our shit together and reconnected with Kev, Angus and Chris.

The key to the success of this mission was the element of surprise. Four hundred metres from the campsite, the guys turned off the engines on their mopeds and removed their crash helmets. Pulling on balaclavas, we spent the next few minutes monitoring the situation and accessing our options. We then moved into position, preparing to strike. Creeping silently towards the silhouettes of the tents in front of us, we hit the first one, pulling frantically on the guy ropes. The tent slowly started to come down and we could hear the predictable sounds of distress coming from under the canvas.

Before we had the chance to home in on tent number two, the alarm was raised, and we had to abandon the mission. We could hear shouting in the distance and car engines starting up. The whole campsite was suddenly illuminated in bright light. Kev and the two other riders dashed to their mopeds and led a forced retreat across the meadow. The foot soldiers followed behind, trying to keep up and laughing uncontrollably. No one bothered to chase after us and we made it back without encountering any problems.

Unfortunately, word soon spread across town about our nocturnal escapades. People would approach us in the street, begging to be included on the next raid. That's when I stopped going altogether. I knew it would be foolhardy to undertake a mission with too many people on board. I thought it was suicidal, and so it proved.

Not long afterwards, a whole bunch of teenage boys and girls, perhaps twenty of them, attempted to achieve what he had done before them. They succeeded in letting down a tent at Walhampton and evaded the supervisors, but by now the authorities had got wise to what was happening. As they made their way home that night, the police were waiting for them on the toll bridge. Some tried desperately running away but most were eventually caught and apprehended. Others just stood there rooted to the spot, like rabbits in the headlights, resigned to their fate.

The cops made several arrests that night, and the ringleaders were taken to Lymington police station and banged up in the cells. I don't think anyone was ever charged with an offence, but they were issued with a verbal warning and told never to do anything so stupid again. Also, some of the parents were notified about their child's misbehaviour. As far as I'm aware there were no more raids conducted in our area of operations. The all too brief, but exhilarating, golden era of tent raiding was over, closing the page on another chapter in my life.

I remember one day during the summer of 1978; my parents ordered a new set of garden furniture. It arrived shortly after, fully wrapped in gigantic separate cardboard boxes. When the tables and chairs had been removed, I went over to look at the empty boxes. The one that contained the table was so large you could stand upright inside it, without your head touching the top. This gave me an idea. I thought what a laugh it would be to get a couple of my mates to repackage the box with me still in it, then carry it up the road and deliver it to some unsuspecting person's house not too far away. The scheme entailed finding a house whose owners were probably away on holiday at the time. As it was the height of summer, this surely wouldn't be hard to do.

As soon as we'd pinpointed a suitable property, we'd try and establish whether the owners' neighbours would likely be at home. The plan then was for Geoff Neale, if he was up for it, and one other guy to carry me up the neighbours' path to the front door and ring the bell. When the person opened the door, Geoff would introduce himself as a delivery driver from a company we'd invented the name of, called Cuthbert's Garden Furniture Specialists. Explaining that he'd intended to drop the delivery off at the address next door but couldn't get a response when he rang the doorbell, he'd ask the person if it was ok to leave the box with them until the owners returned.

All going well, the person would agree to it and allow Geoff and the other guy to carry the box through the door and into the hallway. They'd thank the person, say their goodbyes, then walk back down the garden path and away. I envisaged standing there silently in that cardboard box, in a stranger's home, for around ten minutes, before bursting out through the top of it like a maniacal jack-in-the-box. I'd then escape through the front door and run home to safety.

I spoke to Geoff about my plan, and he thought the whole thing was fucking hilarious. We'd need three of us to pull off this stunt, and we quickly found a willing volunteer, although I can't remember exactly who the guy was. Anyway, we hatched a plan of attack whereby the two 'delivery men' would come over to my place the following evening and lift me into the garden table box. They'd then close the top of the box and seal it with masking tape, making the job look as professional as possible. When they'd done this, the pair of them would change into official looking, white delivery driver's overalls they'd managed to obtain, the real deal. Then, they'd carry me off up the road to my destiny.

It was now D Day, and time to put our plan into action. Geoff and the other guy picked up the box and carried it carefully out of our garden. We headed up Church Lane and into Daniel's Walk, where our target was located. Arriving at the house, Geoff rang the bell. The person inside, a woman, opened the door and gestured for them to come in and drop the box off in the hallway, as arranged.

The problem was the box wouldn't fit through the doorway. It was far too big. As Geoff and the other guy struggled in vain to push the box over the threshold, I remember thinking this wasn't going to work, and they'd never be able to get me in there. Twisting and turning, the guys gave it their all, but however much they tried, it simply wasn't going to happen.

Just then, I heard Tinley's unmistakeable voice coming from somewhere nearby. He happened to be riding past the house on his pushbike at the time, and seeing what was going on, shouted, 'Don't believe them, it's a practical joke!' Thinking it was now or never, I shot up vertically, launching myself through the masking tape at the opening to the box, howling like a man possessed. Waving my arms about wildly, I banged my head on the top of the doorframe. I immediately locked eyes with a middle-aged woman; a look of utter disbelief etched across her face. Gasping, she went into panic mode, and screamed out 'In God's name, go!' then kicked the empty box away from the house, slamming the door shut on us, before bolting it. Thinking she'd probably call the police, we got out of there as fast as we could. Although our plan had ultimately failed, we'd had a mighty fine time trying to make it work. What a fucking laugh that was. I'll never forget it.

In the meantime, life carried on as normal. A welcome respite from the tedious French and the excruciating Technical Drawing and Mathematics lessons came in the form of infrequent Friday night discotheques, which were held at the school youth club, located on the premises. The DJ on these occasions was usually a short, unassuming guy named John Robinson, or 'Blue' as he was affectionately known. DJ Blue was an affable chap, with his scraggly long blonde hair and classic 70s regular beard, and every time you saw him, he'd be dripping in denim. Denim hat, denim overcoat, denim jacket, denim shirt, denim vest, denim jeans, denim long johns, denim belt, denim headband, denim wristband, denim socks, denim shoes, denim underwear, denim watch strap, denim turntables; you name it, Blue had it. Denim, denim, denim.

I still can't get my head around why it took me so long to fathom out the reason everyone called the man Blue. How could I have missed something so blatantly obvious? It was the colour of his clothes, of course. But never mind, eh? Years later, long after I'd left school, I bumped into Blue, and the only thing blue about him was his eyes. You know, I could have sworn they were brown the last time I saw him.

DJ Blue would spin the latest hits from the music charts, playing records by the likes of Leo Sayer, Tina Charles, The Drifters and David Cassidy, as the lights flashed and we bumbled about in an ungainly manner on the dance floor. The boys tended to wear large-collared patterned shirts, Oxford bag trousers with unfathomable pockets and Dr Marten boots. The girls favoured brightly coloured tight-fitting tops or jumpsuits, and sneakers, although many were fully caught up in the Bay City Rollers teen idol phenomenon at the time. The Bay City Rollers were a Scottish boy band who achieved incredible worldwide success in the mid-1970s, and their young, besotted fans would display their obsession with their heroes by wearing calf-length tartan trousers and wrapping tartan scarves around their wrists. At the end of the night, Blue would put on decelerating smoochers by The Commodores, Barry White, Carly Simon, 10cc, John Denver and David Soul.

These school discos could be entirely unpredictable. If you were lucky, a girl might ask you to dance with her. Most boys were usually unlucky and just hunkered down in chairs on the periphery of the dancefloor, looking embarrassed and not knowing what to do with themselves. Several sipped Coca-Cola or lemonade from plastic cups, appearing jumpy and easily startled. Some of the girls simply whiled away the time pointing their fingers in various directions at random fellow pupils and giggling nervously.

On Saturday evenings, there were sometimes organised events happening at Lymington Community Centre in Cannon Street. The youth club there put on discos and my Canadian schoolfriend Scott Brynen was the resident DJ for a while. In those days, there was a hall you could go to in New Street called the Literary Institute, or the Lit, as it was known to us. It was permanent home to the renowned Tony's School of Dancing, and boy, could Tony dance some. We enjoyed many good nights in there. The Lit had a proper stage and creaking wooden floorboards. It hosted private functions, with live bands playing from time to time.

Another place to go to if you fancied putting on your dancing shoes and socialising with your friends was a room upstairs at the back of the old Angel Hotel in the High Street, known as the Angel Ballroom. I remember a few hot and sweaty nights in there. Then of course, you might receive an invitation to a friend's birthday party at their home, or maybe in a hall or other type of venue they'd hired out for the occasion.

It's amazing when you think places like the Literary Institute and that room at the Angel Hotel aren't used for musical events anymore. As is the case everywhere, these seminal local buildings now either get knocked down by greedy developers, or just sit there, neglected by their owners and allowed to rot. What a waste.

The months passed and nothing much changed. Then, in September 1977, I bought my first punk rock record, the single *Holidays in the Sun* by the Sex Pistols. I'd already got my hands on the *In the City* single by The Jam a few months previously, but I considered them to be more of a mod band. They weren't punk enough in my opinion, although many people would disagree. That same year, I bought the debut album by The Stranglers, *Rattus Norvegicus*, on vinyl. I used to play the record loudly on my parents' stereo in the mornings to fire me up, before heading off to school. It's a brilliant album; an absolute belter.

A few of my mates and me bought into the whole punk rock phenomena, spiking up our hair and dying it in various colours. We'd wear tattered old suit jackets covered in safety pins, and Pistols, Clash and Damned badges. We wore ripped up T-shirts and bondage trousers. I remember getting Mum to take in the legs of my school trousers and turn them into drainpipes.

In my year at Priestlands, there were only a handful of punks. Apart from myself, there was Urk, Stump, Roger Figgures, Gary Webb and two girls: Andre Whitren and Claire Doughty. Clair's other half, Dougie, was a couple of years above us, and was one the first punks around these parts. In the year below me, there was a girl called Cathy McColl, and she was bang into punk rock as well.

Cathy got banned from school for wearing Dr Martens boots. She was told they were for boys only, for fuck's sake. One of the teachers, Mrs Roberts, burst into tears when Cathy walked into class with green spiky hair, after watching the Sex Pistols on Top of the Pops. She pierced her nose with a safety pin and got sent straight to Bopper Haynes.

I'll never forget the day we went on an organised coach trip up to London. It was just before we broke up for the school summer holidays. It was a gorgeous sunny morning as we boarded the coach, in high spirits, looking forward to the day ahead. I was sat in one of a row of five seats at the rear of the coach with Dave Dutton, Wayne Baker, Charlie Haselden, who was the local vicar's son, and Steven 'Numbo' Nixon, who got his nickname because he smoked Players No 6 cigarettes.

We arrived in London late in the morning and disembarked from the coach with our packed lunches and pocket money. As I recall, the teachers allowed us to go off and do our own thing for the day, if we promised to return for the pickup, at the designated time and place, for the coach journey home. Forming separate groups, people moved off in different directions, eagerly looking forward to their day out in the big city.

Some of the pupils headed towards the city's major attractions, such as the Natural History Museum, Science Museum or the Tower of London. Others paid a visit to Madam Tussaud's or London Zoo or hung around the water fountains on Trafalgar Square. Our group, the five of us who had occupied the seats at the rear of the coach, made our way excitedly to the King's Road in Kensington.

I remember spending the day wandering up and down the King's Road, taking in all the sights and sounds. We saw groups of punks hanging out in Sloane Square and we visited independent record stores. American Christian bible bashers would stand on the pavement outside their headquarters, trying to get your attention by waving religious pamphlets at you, hoping you'd come inside to sign your life away and join the faith.

After we'd eaten our packed lunches of sandwiches, crisps and an apple, and finished our fizzy drinks, we carried on up and down the road for the next couple of hours, before slowly walking back to the pickup point. We arrived there in good time and reboarded the coach with the other kids, for the return journey home. The trip back was uneventful, although someone apparently flicked a piece of chewing gum at a couple of people sitting in seats in front of us. The sticky gum ended up entangled in their hair and they couldn't get it off.

The following morning, we headed off to school as normal, and after registration, attended a full school assembly in the main hall. Mr Armitage was our Head of Year and was taking assembly that day. We called him 'Beaky' on account of his enormous, prominent nose. When the assembly was over, he said 'Right, everyone can go now, apart from those from the fourth year who went on the school trip to London yesterday.' As all the other pupils filed out of the hall, I remember thinking what the hell was going on.

When the hall was clear, Armitage rose from his chair, an infuriated expression on his face. He told us Excelsior Coaches had just rung the school and complained about finding chewing gum stuck to some of their coach seats. They said it would cost a lot of money to have them properly cleaned. Armitage was becoming increasingly enraged, pacing about the hall, his nose turning a deep purple. Failing to compose himself, he launched into an angry tirade, demanding to know who'd thrown the chewing gum.

As we sat there in silence, Beaky decided to turn detective. Making us all stand up, he rearranged the seats in identical fashion to the layout of those on the coach. He was morphing into Colombo before our very eyes. He then made each of us sit down in the corresponding seat to the one we'd sat on yesterday. Armitage was not a happy man, that's for sure. Determined to find the culprit, or culprits, he began ranting on about angles and trajectories, trying to find out exactly from where the gum had been thrown. He finally whittled it down to the five of us who'd been sitting on the rear seats. He dismissed everyone else, and they shuffled out of the hall to their morning lessons.

Armitage told Dave, Charlie, Numbo, Wayne and me to remain seated. He came over to us with piercing, accusatory eyes, waiting for one of us to crack. When nobody uttered a word, he ordered us out of the hall and made us walk over the playground to another building. We climbed the stairs, and Armitage asked if anyone had anything to say, waiting for one of us to own up. Getting no response, he made the five of us stand up against the wall, noses pressed firmly against it. Then he walked into his office and closed the door.

It was mid-afternoon on a Friday, and we were standing against the wall for what seemed like hours. Armitage eventually emerged from his office, and then the interrogations began. I recall Numbo Nixon was the first one to get called in for a grilling. We could hear Armitage shouting at him and banging his fists on the table. Fifteen minutes later, Numbo reappeared, looking flustered. One after another, we were hauled into the office for questioning. Everyone pleaded innocence and then the bell rang, signalling the end of the school day, and time to go home. Armitage, his big, protruding nose throbbing, and turning the colour of dark purple, and frustrated that he couldn't extract a confession out of any of us, advised us all to use the weekend to think long and hard about the consequences, should we choose to remain silent.

The following Monday morning we were each summoned again by Armitage for another gruelling torture session. Up against the wall we stood once more. The whole thing was becoming unbelievable, turning into a dystopian nightmare, to be honest. I genuinely didn't know who'd thrown the chewing gum. Again, Numbo was the first one of us to get interrogated. Failing to get him to confess, Armitage decided to try a different method of approach.

He called the rest of us into his office individually and informed each of us that Numbo had finally cracked under pressure and admitted to being the culprit. He was hoping we'd say we knew he was the guilty party all along, and implicate him, but that we'd kept silent to protect him. It was a deceitful ruse, and ultimately, it didn't work. No one was giving anything away whatsoever, and Armitage, sick and tired of the whole episode, finally put an end to the matter.

Unceremoniously warning us that if we ever got into trouble in the future and had the misfortune to appear in front of him again, he'd come down on us like a ton of bricks, and we wouldn't know what hit us. Then, seemingly out of nowhere, he told us we were free to go on our way. He'd basically abandoned his poorly planned and executed detective mission, just like that, because he couldn't get any of us to crack.

Barking up the wrong tree, Beaky had proved himself to be a prize John Thomas, but he was indicative of the kind of people we had teaching us in those days. I get the fact he was only doing what he had to do as our Head of Year, after the school had received the complaint from Excelsior Coaches; of that, there's no question. Allowing himself to become so totally engrossed in it all, in such an angry manner, when he didn't know the full facts of what happened, was another matter entirely. I think Beaky was seriously getting off on a power trip.

It appeared that the man was on a personal undertaking to exact punishment on those he perceived to have brought Priestlands School into disrepute. In his mind, he'd taken on the role of crusader, to protect the reputation of the school. Filing out in front of him, I half expected Beaky to utter Colombo's signature catchphrase, 'Just one more thing.' I don't wanna keep banging on about these people, our schoolteachers, but at the time, they could be maddening. As it transpired, I never did find out who the chewing gum coach fiend was on that infamous July day back in 1978.

I used to spend a lot of time round Angus McDonald's house, at the top of Grove Gardens. He was quite a character, along with his younger sister Annika, with their carefree attitudes, infectious youthful smiles and long blonde hair. I remember them once showing me a photograph of their mother Eva and telling me that she had been crowned Miss Sweden back in 1956. Eva was a beautiful, lovely lady and had retained her classic Swedish accent. She also possessed a unique sense of humour.

I recall her admonishing Annika one day for doing something she shouldn't have. 'Annika, if you ever do that again, we'll send you away to boarding school, where they'll whip your bottom until it bleeds!' It was hilarious. On another, memorable, occasion, I was at the McDonald household with a few of my mates. I think Dave and Urk were there that day, and possibly Tinley and Kev Joyce.

After listening to some of his prize punk records in his bedroom, we indicated to Angus that we were hungry and asked him if it would be okay to have something to eat. Angus reluctantly led us downstairs to the kitchen and motioned towards a loaf of bread on the worktop. Suddenly, Eva appeared in the kitchen doorway and exclaimed 'Angus! Gosh, there are a lot of you! Only half a slice each!'

I remember Eva's husband, Angus and Annika's father, was a tall, imposing but affable man of few words. One thing I do recall him saying though, was 'No visitors!' when a few of us turned up out of the blue at his front gate one day. Holding up the palm of his hand, a solemn look on his face, he left us under no illusion that we weren't welcome at his house on that occasion.

At one stage, Angus formed his own gang. I'm pretty sure Chris

Shepherd was a member, and another boy called Philip Wilkinson, who was in the year below me. They named themselves the Lost Eyebrow Gang, with each of them shaving off one of their eyebrows and parading up and down the labyrinth of narrow alleyways surrounding the McDonalds' house, in Navarino Court.

My friends and I would often sit in Angus's bedroom for hours on end, playing music loudly on his stereo and listening to the likes of Adam and the Ants, The Rezillos, Alternative TV, The Skids, Angelic Upstarts, The Ruts, Stiff Little Fingers, The B-52's and Angus's favourite band of all time, the awesome Magazine. On one occasion, Roger and Tinley turned up there with electric guitars and amplifiers. Tinley was hitting the strings so hard, there was blood all over his fingers. I have brilliant memories of those days.

In October 1978, I went to my first proper gig: Buzzcocks and Subway Sect at the Winter Gardens in Bournemouth. My friend Erk English was an ace character, another one with a fine sense of humour. His dad John, a respected local dentist, drove five of us there that night. There was Dave Dutton, Urk and his girlfriend Rebecca Chester, David Powell and me. I'll never forget David Powell wore a pair of flared trousers to the gig. Not to look out of place, he attached cycle clips around his strides, so they appeared straight legged, would you believe.

After a fantastic night leaping about like Zebedee (the jack-in-the-box fire wizard from the animated kids 60's TV programme The Magic Roundabout), John arrived to take us home. Boing! I remember spewing up through his car window on the journey back to Lymington. I was only fifteen at the time, and didn't smoke or drink. I can only rationalize that the reason for my nausea must have been the pure excitement of it all. Boing! The next morning, I went back to school.

Sometimes we'd travel up to the King's Road in London on the train, to hang out and buy punk clothing and Crazy Colour hair dye. One day Urk dyed his hair canary yellow. It looked cool as fuck. He was hoping for a reaction from his father, trying to shock him. When John simply stood there laughing at him, it caught Urk off balance. He bleached the yellow dye out of his hair the very next day.

Roger Figgures had his hair dyed bright red at a hairdresser in Bournemouth. Worried about what his mother would say, he didn't go home for two days, hiding out in Rebecca Chester's flat down on Lymington quay called The Loft. Becca lived in the flat with her mother Sue and her younger brother Ollie, and our little gang of miscreants would often hang out there, getting up to all sorts and listening to the latest punk records on their stereo.

I'll never forget the alarming sight of Urk entering the living room one afternoon wearing one of Becca's precious antique dresses, with his dick flopped out through an opening in it for all to see. It was outrageous. When Roger finally summoned up the courage to return to his own house, his mother, who was stood on a ladder wallpapering at the time, took one look at him and nearly fell off it in a state of shock. Subsequently, Roger bleached the red dye out of his hair and ended up looking like a tortoiseshell cat, which we all thought was great.

One morning during half term, I decided to bite the bullet and stick a safety pin in my nose. Rather than pushing it straight through, I dithered about in front of the mirror in my bedroom for hours. Using ice cubes to dull the pain, I finally succeeded in piercing my nose. There were tears streaming down my face and my nose was already swelling up, turning septic. I wondered what my parents would say when they saw it.

Around midday, Mum called out, saying she was dishing up lunch. Apprehensive about how she'd react, I put on a bobble hat and pulled it down carefully over my nose. All you could see was my mouth and chin. Blindly walking into the dining room, I felt my way gingerly to the table. Upon sitting down, my sister asked what on earth I was doing, and leant across and yanked the hat off my head. My eyes were still streaming, and my hooter had turned bulbous, oozing horrible yellow pus everywhere. I looked like a crazed version of Sneezy from Snow White and the Seven Dwarves. Mum just stared at me blankly and said, 'Wait till your father gets home.' It was utterly insane. Dad never got to see me with a safety pin stuck through my nose, as I pulled it out an hour or so later.

The following year, 1980, I bought some bright orange Crazy Colour hair dye from a shop on the King's Road. After bleaching my hair sheet white, and leaving the product on overnight, I painted an orange streak down one side of it. I thought my new hairstyle looked quite cool, but Mum disagreed and warned me once more of what my father would say when he saw what I'd done.

For the next two days, I miraculously managed to hide the orange streak from Dad. Although we lived together in the same house, I succeeded in keeping it undetected by walking past him sideways on, with the coloured side of my head invisible to him. Ideally, if he happened to be in a certain room in the house, then I made sure I wasn't. Even at mealtimes, I somehow managed to avoid his gaze. He didn't really have a problem with me having bleached hair, but I knew he'd go mad when he saw the bright streak.

I kept up this ludicrous charade for the next forty-eight hours before the inevitable occurred, and I carelessly dropped my guard. We were in the kitchen, talking, and upon seeing what I'd done to my hair, in his broad south Wales accent, Dad let out a tempestuous response which has gone down in the annals of local folklore: 'It's a bit orange, innit?' It was a brilliant spontaneous vociferation, an absolute classic.

After the Buzzcocks gig, I just knew I wanted to be a singer in a punk band. I'd play records on the stereo at home and turn them up full blast. Using a broom handle as a microphone stand, I'd mime the lyrics to the songs, pretending I was Johnny Rotten or Joe Strummer. I had tunes swirling around my head constantly and started writing down my own lyrics. Sometimes, I'd spend the evening round my mate Geoff Neal's house. He played the drums and had a kit set up in his bedroom, where he'd beat the living hell out of them for hours on end.

When I look back now to when I was a teenager, culturally, my generation had it damned good. There was the punk movement, the disco scene, the mod revival, heavy metal and the 2-tone ska revival, all happening at the same time. Music wise, compared to then, what have the kids got going for them now? What real youth scene is there, that they can they identify with? The truth is, there isn't one.

There was a narrow sloping lane leading up into Priestlands school, known by the locals as the Bunny Run. It was so narrow that a path would be a better description. Boys would often go down there to skive off hated lessons, to smoke a crafty fag or to secretly meet up with their girlfriends for a snog under the shady trees. During the autumn months, some of them would play games of conkers there with their friends. Conkers, horse chestnuts, are now banned from school playgrounds in Britain; another prime example of Health and Safety gone mad. They could hurt a bit, for sure, if in a game, your opponent accidentally missed, and smashed their conker across your fingers, but they were hardly lethal weapons. Kids certainly didn't walk around the school grounds with conkers on strings, deliberately targeting fellow pupils and whacking them about the head and body with them, causing serious harm.

If two lads got into an altercation, for whatever reason, one might challenge the other with the words 'Right, Bunny Run four o'clock!' After school had finished, they'd face off in the lane to sort out their differences, which sometimes led to a scrap. When this happened, there would always be a crowd of excited boys and girls surrounding them, egging them on. Some kids even climbed trees and perched precariously on the branches to gain a better view. When the fight was over, the crowd would disperse, and everybody went home.

At the top of the Bunny Run was a tall, metal cylindrical litter bin. We were in our fifth and final year in 1979 when one day Scott Brynen happened to be innocently strolling by. A group of us encircled him, chanting 'Cylindrical bin, cylindrical bin!' We grabbed him and lifted him into the bin, feet first. We then we launched Scott down the slope. The bin rapidly gained momentum, rolling faster and faster. You could just make out the blur of his head, spinning into oblivion. The bin kept rolling until it came to a sudden halt at the base of an old oak tree, at the foot of the slope. After a few heart stopping moments, Scott crawled out of the bin, shaken, but otherwise unharmed. We all found it highly amusing, including Scott, who had a wicked sense of humour.

We certainly got up to some stupid things while at Priestlands. I remember Geoff Neal came over to our house for tea one afternoon after school. The next morning in class, he opened his briefcase and produced the small, carved, shiny brown wooden crocodile my grandfather had brought back from West Africa and given to my mother as a souvenir many years ago. He'd swiped it off the Ladderax shelf in our living room while I wasn't looking. Another time, Geoff secretly filled a classmate's brief case with bundles of dry leaves, leaving the boy stunned, after he'd reached inside to take out an exercise book.

There was a long straight concrete path running the whole length of the classrooms in the main school building, adjacent to the playing fields. We called it the Stretch. During Mr Brown's English Language lessons in the fifth year, either I or one of my mates would often deliberately turn up late for class. We'd position ourselves at the top of the Stretch before promenading the hundred or so yards down it in ridiculous fashion. We'd walk in great loping strides and sometimes spin idiotically like a top on the ground, much to the amusement of our fellow pupils, watching on from inside Mr Brown's classroom. We must have resembled the John Cleese character in the classic Monty Python TV comedy sketch the Ministry of Silly Walks.

One Sunday afternoon in late '79, Geoff called round my house to see me. He was riding his mother's Honda moped. I asked him if I could take it for a spin, but he refused to let me. I kept on at him for ages, and eventually he relented, but on one condition. He said I could only ride the moped if I wore the crash helmet back to front. Donning the helmet, I zestfully jumped on and rode off down Broad Lane, looking utterly ridiculous.

Just as I reached the end of the road, a police car suddenly appeared. The officer inside motioned for me to stop, but I ignored him and crossed the junction and hurtled off down Normandy Lane, towards Roger Figgures' house, hoping to get away from him. He caught up with me when I was halfway down the lane. Pulling me over, he asked angrily what the hell I thought I was doing, wearing a crash helmet back to front, and if I'd ever seen a smashed skull. I sheepishly told him that I hadn't. He enquired as to who the moped belonged to, and was I insured to ride it. I told him it was Geoff's mother's moped, and I wasn't insured. He walked back to the police car shaking his head, then returned with some paperwork.

It was obvious the officer was hellbent on securing a conviction. He pulled out a pen and placed the papers on the roof of the car and asked me for my personal details. Just then, a gust of wind came in and blew all the paperwork everywhere. Inside, I was pissing myself. Infuriated, he got right in my face and warned me that I hadn't heard the last of this. A few days later, Geoff told me that the copper had gone round to his parents' house and tried to pressure his mother into prosecuting me. She was having none of it, and I got away Scot-free.

Outside of school, my friends and I would sometimes hang around town, bored, with nothing to do. There was never a lot going on in Lymington and you had to make your own entertainment. One evening, Dave Dutton, Gary Webb and I were idly chatting amongst ourselves, and thought how funny it would be to throw a load of bangers (fireworks) through the letterbox of the local branch of the Conservative Club. Dave looked quite a bit older than he was at the time. He'd started drinking in the Old E when he was thirteen and often popped in there for a pint or two during school lunch breaks.

Anyway, we walked up to Sperrings newsagents, and Dave managed to fool the shop assistant into selling him a box of bangers. We then made our way to the Conservative Club in Ashley Lane. We lit a few bangers and chucked them straight through the letterbox. We could hear them exploding behind us as we ran off laughing our heads off. The powers that be at the Conservative Club quickly realised we were the culprits, and I got into serious trouble with my dad for that one when he'd found out what I'd done. A thick ear and an early night, if memory serves me right.

I seem to recall a similar incident occurring around the same time which involved Dave, Gary and myself getting hold of a boat signal flare from somewhere down on Lymington marina and firing it directly at the front wall of someone's expensive property in the town one evening. On lighting the flare, a blinding flash of orangey-red smoke erupted, and we sent it fizzing away towards our target, a short distance from where we were standing. I can't remember the repercussions of that little escapade, if indeed, there were any, but we all found the whole episode uproarious.

The weeks went by, and it was nearly time for us all to sit our final exams. One day, Tinley brought his electric guitar into Mr Brown's English Language class. The teacher was talking to us about something important when suddenly, Tinley stood up, plugged his guitar into a practice amp and started playing power chords at full volume. Scott Brynen, who was sitting at the table next to him, shouted out excitedly in his Canadian accent, 'I've got my very own fuzz box!' After rummaging around in his brief case for a moment, he fished it out and handed it to him. Mr Brown went ballistic.

One afternoon, I was standing in line with the other pupils in the corridor outside a classroom. We were waiting for the history teacher, Mr Barnes, to return from his break and let us in for the lesson. I'd earlier tied a padlock and chain tightly around my neck and started crazily jumping up and down in front of the other kids. Their laughter ceased abruptly when an irate Bopper Haynes suddenly emerged from the shadows. He lambasted me for acting like a buffoon and ordered me to remove the padlock immediately. Red-faced and embarrassed in front of my classmates, I fumbled about awkwardly in my trouser pockets for the key. It wasn't there, and I couldn't find it anywhere.

Bopper Haynes was becoming seriously annoyed by now and told me to go downstairs at once and go across to the metalwork room and get the padlock chain sawed off from around my neck. I did as I was told, and went down to the metalwork room, feeling stupid that I'd lost the fucking key to the padlock. I knocked on the door, entered the room and explained my predicament to the metalwork teacher, Mr Lloyd. He looked at me as if I was some kind of idiot, then sent me over to a boy with a saw in his hand. The boy got me to tilt my head while he smartly cut through the chain. Returning to my history class, it was hard for me to not burst out laughing at the whole situation.

Break times at Priestlands could be a lot of fun. One of my schoolfriends was a boy called Kevin Denham. He a was studious pupil and was always at the top of his class, excelling in all subjects. Kevin tended to shy away from the games of football or cricket other boys played in their free time. Every day, over the course of about a fortnight, when the bell rang for the pupils to return to their tutor groups before afternoon lessons, Geoff Neal and I would corner Kevin in the playground. We'd good naturedly usher him towards the front of Mr Visick's classroom, the school library.

Peering in through the window, we'd wait for the teacher to return from his lunch break and unlock the door to the library. In an instant, we'd slide open the window and hoist Kevin in there, before ducking down and disappearing. Mr Visick was understandably baffled as to why Kevin was just standing there, saying and doing nothing, in his classroom each day. The shenanigans couldn't continue forever, though. The finally ended abruptly, when Mr Visick, in cracking good humour, posted up a picture of a guard dog wearing a sailor's hat, smoking a cigarette, in the window.

During the spring and summer months of 1979, I'd spend a lot of time round the houses of my mates Mike Case and Brent Jones. Brent was a superbly talented cross-country runner, who went on to represent his country with distinction in the sport. He was also an original member, and enthusiastic participant, of our tent-raiding party a year or so previously. Brent was a veteran of those irresponsible military style operations Mary, Mungo and Midge, and commanded the utmost respect from his peers.

One evening, Brent, Mike and I were sitting on the pavement outside the Jones family's house, chatting with a guy called David Perry. He was in the year above us, and had a pinhead, a wiry frame and a rather cynical outlook on life. He was the son of a local farmer and another talented cross-country runner. I remember Brent accidentally treading on a garden snail in the road, much to David's disdain. 'What did you go and do that for? He ain't done no harm, you. How would you like it if a gert great snail fell out of the sky and landed on your head, eh? Eh?' he exclaimed to Brent. What a ridiculous thing to come out with.

On my final day at Priestlands School, all the pupils in my year were gathered in the sports hall. The headmaster, Eric Platt, was standing in front of us, along with Bopper Haynes and Beaky Armitage. Unknown to them, and to most of the pupils, for that matter, Dean Lancaster had hidden a cassette player in the roof of the boys changing room. Dean had earlier recorded the Generation X song King Rocker and had set the tape up so it would come blasting out of the school's speakers fifteen minutes after he pressed play.

While Platt was waffling on about what about a model year we'd been and how proud he was of most of us for doing so well in our exams, the drum intro to King Rocker suddenly erupted through the speakers. Platt, Bopper and Beaky didn't know what to do with themselves. They just stood there, looking completely bemused. They weren't in a position to punish anyone for the prank, as it was our last day at the school, and we'd all be out of there for good in a few hours. We were all virtually untouchable now.

When the time arrived to say goodbye to Priestlands once and forever, Dave Dutton and Urk English headed off down the Bunny Run and lit up two fat Cuban cigars. Bopper was standing there watching them, shaking his head in frustration, and acutely aware that he was now powerless to have any measure of control over their actions. He must have wondered what the future held for boys like Dave, Urk and me. He probably thought to himself that we didn't stand the slightest chance of making a success of ourselves out there in the big wide world.

Looking back on my days at Priestlands, we certainly had our fair share of characters in our year. I recall a simian-looking smallish boy with shiny straight black hair called Sean Prendergast, who lived at a residential home in Milford On Sea at the time. He was an unfortunate soul, relentlessly picked on by some of the other boys, and I felt sorry for him. I wonder whatever happened to Sean. The last I heard he spontaneously combusted while on vacation in Alaska, but that's obviously bullshit.

Another, quietish, boy I remember, was Timothy Hamblin. One day, just before we broke up for the end of term Easter holiday, Timothy brought one of those tiny fluffy yellow plastic Easter chicks into school with him. He was sitting at his desk playing about with the chick when the teacher, Mrs Allberry, walked over to him and said 'Come on Timothy, hand that thing over. Now! What on earth do you think you're doing bringing it into the classroom? Don't be so silly. Honestly!'

Timothy looked absolutely mortified and was loathe to let go of his little chick. Replying to the teacher, appearing visibly upset, he stuttered out the words, 'Oh no, not Chicky! No, no, not my Chicky! Please let me keep him!' Mrs Allberry leant over and snatched the chick out of Timothy's hand and said, 'Don't be so ridiculous. How old are you? Come on, pull yourself together and stop being so childish.'

As the teacher turned and walked back to her desk at the front of the class, holding the chick, Timothy burst into tears, before spluttering 'Please Mrs Allberry, take good care of Chicky for me. Oh no Chicky. Poor Chicky! Oh my God, what am I going to do without my Chicky? He's my world!' It was extremely bizarre behaviour from a schoolboy in his teens, who should have known better. Exit Chicky, exit mind.

In September 1979 I attended Brockenhurst College of Further Education on a year's course. Dave was supposed to be there with me, but for some reason or another, the powers that be split us apart. They obviously thought we were a bad influence on each other. Dave ended up going to Southampton Technical College, and I have a sneaking suspicion that Bopper Haynes was ultimately behind the decision to separate us. Even though we were no longer pupils at Priestlands school, the spectre of Bopper continued to hang over us.

We were allowed to wear whatever clothes we fancied at Brockenhurst College, and initially it felt great walking into the car park in the mornings with our dyed spikey hair, fuck off T-shirts and bondage trousers. Unfortunately, some of the male college students in the year above us didn't share our enthusiasm for all things punk. They'd sit there on the grass staring at us in an unfriendly manner. They were dripping in acne and patchouli oil, looking just like the pseudo-hippies they undoubtedly were. They had horrible long hair and wore flared jeans and would throw stones at us as we'd walk past them. They were a pathetic bunch of individuals – cowards that hunted in packs.

The one who appeared to be the ringleader was a loud-mouthed bully, whose name I can't even be bothered to mention. He was a horrible, ugly-looking rugby type who didn't get it at all. He had far too much to say for himself and was one special kind of tosser. He really was a sorry cheesedick of a human being. I remember him threatening me one day, just because of the way I looked. Screaming in my face that he and his mates hated punks with a passion, he promised me he'd have me by Christmas. I recall wondering whether he intended to beat me up or give me one up the ass.

Ironically, the cretin zeroed in on me on my final day of college, pissed up on the concrete tennis courts in his rugby kit, muddy boots and all. Slurring his speech, he half-heartedly apologised to me for hating punk rockers. I mean, what sort of person would say something like that? An idiot, I suppose. A few years later, I went to a party in Lymington with my mates, and a couple of our tormentors were there. As soon as they saw us, they were like mice cowering in front of a cat.

For me, the best things about my year at Brockenhurst College were the gigs the Student Union used to put on in the main hall. I saw Crass, The Piranhas and Southampton band Catch 22 all play storming shows there. Two of the members of Catch 22, Phil Odgers and Paul Simmonds, later formed the band The Men They Couldn't Hang, who I've written about in detail later in this book.

Being afforded the freedom to dress as you pleased at Brock College was an obvious bonus, as was being able to drink alcohol in the Rose and Crown pub, just outside the college campus, when you were clearly underaged. Once or twice, I returned from the pub half cut and would sit there vacantly in the classroom, struggling hard to concentrate, or even keep my eyes open.

At some point in '79, Tinley's younger brother, Adam, who was eleven at the time, formed a kiddie-punk act called the Stupid Babies. Adam and Dominic, who was the youngest of the four Tinley brothers, recorded a song for the Fast Product label called Babysitters. Legendary alternative radio DJ John Peel played the song regularly on his show and the Stupid Babies even had write-ups in Smash Hits and Melody Maker.

The mod revival was in full swing at the time, and it was at Brock College I first encountered Richard Wallace, now sadly deceased and much missed. Upon introduction, his opening words to me were 'Hi, I'm Wallace and I'm a mod.' Another, insane, character I met there was Mark Ibbotson, who was also a mod. He was an extremely funny guy, with a unique sense of humour, who'd have you in stitches constantly.

Mark once lent me his whole collection of punk singles. There were hundreds of them: classics by the likes of The Adverts, Generation X, Alternative TV, Johnny Thunders and the Heartbreakers, Eater, The Saints, Pork Dukes, Sham 69, Menace, The Cortinas, The Vibrators, The Boys, X-Ray Spex, The Drones, Slaughter and the Dogs, Chelsea, Johnny Moped, The Maniacs and the Snivelling Shits. Add to these, the usual suspects, such as the Pistols, The Clash, Buzzcocks and The Damned, then you pretty much get where I come from musically.

Wallace and Ibbotson would ride into college each morning on their Lambretta scooters, whip aerials on the back, wearing Union Jack helmets and fishtail parkas. Ibbotson was constantly on Wallace's back, needling him at any given opportunity. For example, he fabricated a story about how he once visited the Wallace household in Sway one evening and found a penis enlargement kit in the drawer of Rich's bedside cabinet. On another occasion, Ibbotson reckoned he was over at the house, sitting up in the bedroom, when Wallace's mum called out from downstairs in the kitchen, 'Richard, your tea's ready. It's your favourite. Dead air gunner, egg flip and a whizzy milk!' I think this is what Ibbotson's own mother used to make him for his tea when he was a child, and he evoked these memories in an innocent but misguided attempt at humiliating Rich. For anyone who's interested, a 'dead air gunner' is basically Spam in batter.

One summer's day in 1980, Wallace was in the garden at Ibbotson's home in Hythe when he got stung by a wasp. Apparently, he panicked and ran into the house screaming 'Mrs Ibbotson, Mrs Ibbotson! I've been stung! I need Wasp-Eze!' This incident probably happened, but so much shit poured out of Ibbotson's mouth you needed wings to stay above it. Deep down, I believe in his heart of hearts, he genuinely adored and admired Wallace.

In reference to the tutors at Brockenhurst College, I can barely remember any of them, to be honest; they made that much of an impression on me. Their names I've long forgotten, and their faces will forever remain a blur. However, one springs to mind. His name was Mr Meredith, and he taught Geography, and was your classic old school type of teacher;

likeable enough, but authoritative, and didn't suffer fools gladly. One day, he admonished a mod called Martin Forsyth for having embroidered military insignia sewn onto his parka coat. Meredith had once served with distinction in the British Armed Forces and took umbrage at what he believed to be Martin's perceived lack of respect. He appeared genuinely offended, as I recall.

Addressing him in front of the rest of the class, in a serious tone, he asked, 'Why have you got those decorations on your jacket, boy? Did you earn those stripes? Are you in the Army? Have you ever fought in a battle? Have you witnessed first-hand the horrors of war? No, I thought not.' Martin meekly replied that of course he'd never been in the Army or indeed seen any action. Apologetically, he tried explaining to Meredith that the insignia was purely for show, and he honestly didn't mean to cause offence to anybody, least of all, military veterans. Meredith stared at his parka suspiciously for a moment, then quickly changed the subject.

Rich's great-great-grandfather, Alfred Russel Wallace, was a famous 18th century explorer, naturalist, geographer, anthropologist, collector and political commentator. He is best known for having the revolutionary idea of natural selection, entirely independently of Charles Darwin, and my wife Michaela is fascinated by him. She used to have many discussions with Rich about this intriguing man, due to her love of nature. Alfred Russel Wallace's adventures took him to the Amazon Basin with his friend and fellow naturalist, Henry Walter Bates. Their aim was to investigate the origin of species. Later, he travelled to the Malay Archipelago in the Far East, now Malaysia and Indonesia. It was here that Wallace noticed a striking pattern in the distribution of animals around the archipelago. He proposed an imaginary line dividing the region in two parts. Later known as Wallace's Line, this marked the boundary between the animal life of Australia and that of Asia. During his eight years in the Malay Archipelago, he collected over 125,000 natural history specimens, mostly insects, but also birds, molluscs and reptiles. Five thousand of these specimens were completely new to science.

On his return to England, Wallace published a travel book, *The Malay*

Archipelago, which is a vivid account of beautiful and undisturbed islands. Highlights of the book include his colourful descriptions of birds of paradise, orangutans, bay cats, striped possums, Sulawesi dwarf cuscus, tufted ground squirrels and common tube-nosed bats. He also chronicles his encounters with local inhabitants.

It was at Brockenhurst college that I first met Bill Trehearne and Dave Peden. They were punks, and we bonded straight away. They'd formed a band, and their singer was Phil Sheldrake, who'd been in the year above me at Priestlands. At lunchtime, they'd head over to their drummer Marcus Cotton's place to rehearse, just up the road from the college, and I would tag along with them. I'm not sure if the band even had a name, but I remember Phil in his silver catsuit catapulting around the room, giving it his all. We'd then head back to college, idly discussing topics such as the impending release of the Dead Kennedys' debut single, 'California Uber Alles.'

One night around this time, Bill, Dave and I went to Southampton to watch the band Catch 22 play at a small venue in the city. After the gig, the three of us walked back to the train station together, to make our way home. While crossing over a footbridge to the platform on the other side of the station, we came face to face with a small group of loud, pissed-up local trendy lads. Ibbotson used to call these kinds of people 'wedgy boys', due to the way their hair was usually cut and layered. However, this bunch were different. They had permed mullet hairstyles and moustaches, and wore drawstring shirts and denim dungarees, like many young blokes of that period. They were typical blind followers of the latest conventional fashions; sheep who weren't intelligent enough to think for themselves.

One of them, your stereotypical dim loudmouth, was trying to appear hard in front of his mates. Slurring his words, he started insulting us, saying stupid things like 'Whoa, have you seen this lot? Hah, hah, hah! Look at their hair, eh? That one there looks like a fucking hedgehog, and him, he looks like the Jolly Green Giant! Bloody punks, I shit on you! You want some, do yer?' The idiot suddenly picked up a traffic cone from somewhere and hurled it forcefully at us, narrowly missing our heads. We just ignored the cretins and carried on walking, and thankfully, they didn't bother following us.

Over the course of the next couple of years or so, me and my mates would occasionally encounter similarly aggressive males, in pubs, or out on the streets; generally intoxicated and looking to pick a fight with somebody. Most of them were gobby, obnoxious young lounge lizards, overdosed on testosterone, but sometimes we encountered older, boisterous, drunken rugby types who also presented a problem. Fuelled by alcohol, and full of ignorance and bravado, these people would hurl abuse at us, for no apparent reason, other than our appearance.

One Saturday morning in Lymington High Street, a local brain-dead moron who I vaguely knew of came lumbering towards me. I think his name was Ambrose, and he looked like a cross between a great ape and the Looney Tunes cartoon character Porky Pig. Bristling with unbridled vitriol, he grunted, 'Oi, I want a word with you! I was in a pub in Southampton the other night, and a load of your lot started having a go at me. They were bogging me out, then they laid into me. It was six against one! Fucking punks, I hate them all! I'm telling you now; you better watch out, coz sooner or later, I'm gonna get you, for what your lot did to me!' I remember thinking, he's that thick, I'm amazed he's got the capacity to even string a sentence together. Gazing deep into his wrathful eyes for a moment, it felt as if I was in the company of the missing link.

The bloke was almost certainly lying, but even if what he said was true, it was a ridiculously dumb thing to come out with. The narrow-minded fool had tarred a whole subculture with the same brush and placed us all under one convenient gigantic umbrella. What a total retard. Unfortunately, this was the mentality of some of the people we had to deal with at the time. Not long afterwards, Ambrose did indeed 'get me,' running up from behind unexpectedly when I was walking down the High Street one Friday night and thumping me hard on the back of the head. Proud of himself, he grunted a few indecipherable words at me, then trotted back across the street to where a couple of his mates were stood waiting. The oaf had exacted his revenge, as promised. From his perspective, it was job done, mission accomplished.

In the summer of 1980, I went on a family holiday to France. Bill and

June Wagland owned a property in the Auvergne region, in central France. and invited us over to stay. I had a great time out there, listening to punk albums with their son Gareth in the converted loft where we slept. Between the two families there were six kids, and Gareth and I were the principal mischief makers. We had a lot in common. We were into the same music and shared the same sense of humour. We got on like a house on fire.

One Sunday lunchtime, both families went out for a meal at a restaurant in a village not far from where we were staying. Altogether, there were ten of us. The four adults sat at a table with some of Bill and June's local French friends, and the six kids were seated on a separate table, on the opposite side of the restaurant. I remember it was busy in there that day, and the adults were engrossed in conversation with the French people. The wine was flowing, and they were all clearly having a good time.

Gareth and I decided to see if we could get away with ordering alcohol without our parents knowing. I called the waiter over and enquired if it was possible for us to have a bottle of wine. He replied 'Bien sur monsieur' and asked us to choose one from the drinks list. We selected a bottle of red, and he brought it over to our table a couple of minutes later. I can't recall if my sister Gail drank any of it, and my brother Rich was only nine years old at the time, so it's almost certain he didn't partake. As for Gareth's sister Nicola, and his brother Kelly, I have no idea.

All I remember was that Gareth and I made short work of the wine and quickly ordered another bottle. We polished that one off in no time and my head started to spin. I called the waiter over, and slurring my speech, asked him if we could possibly have a third bottle. He glanced over at the table where our parents were sitting; after all, they were the ones who'd be footing the bill. I was annihilated by this stage, and he politely said, 'Je suis désolé. Non, monsieur.' He must have thought we were juvenile delinquents, which I guess we were.

It was the first time I'd ever got drunk, and I couldn't even function properly as a human being. When it was time for us all to leave the restaurant, I had to get carried out of the place. In Bill's car on the way back, I was sick all over the seats. What an introduction to the demon drink. Sure, when I was a young kid growing up in Hythe in the 1960's, I'd minesweep the leftover cans of Woodpecker cider the morning after my parents had hosted a dinner party, but that was relatively weak stuff. This was different, and I was reeling.

I offered to clean up the mess, but Bill said he'd sort it out and suggested I went and got my head down for a few hours. Feeling embarrassed the following morning; I apologised to Bill. His response was 'These things happen in life Shaun. You're still young, and if you can learn from this experience and don't let it happen again in the future, then it shouldn't be a problem. Anyway, I'm sure you'll be all right.' What a top man. In hindsight, I didn't learn from that experience one iota, as you'll discover later in this book.

In October 1980, a month after leaving Brockenhurst College, Phil drove a few of us up to London to see the Dead Kennedys at the Music Machine in Camden. It was only the second ever DK's gig in the UK, following Middlesbrough the night before. UK Decay were the support act. I remember talking with the actress Helen Wellington-Lloyd, also called Helen of Troy, before the show. She was an original fan of the Sex Pistols, attending most of their gigs before they split up. She appeared in the films *Jubilee* and *The Great Rock 'n' Roll Swindle*, among others.

Anyway, post-punk/ Gothic Rock band UK Decay took to the stage, and they were right bang on it. Ploughing through their repertoire of songs, they finished the set with the superb *For My Country*. We then wandered around the venue taking in the atmosphere. Drinking pints of lager, smoking cigarettes and chatting to people, we were having a roaring time, it had to be said.

The Dead Kennedys came on to rapturous applause, and tore into their set with *Kill the Poor*, if I remember correctly. They smashed through classics from their recently released album *Fresh Fruit for Rotting Vegetables*, frontman Jello Biafra frantically winding up the crowd and going berserk onstage.

The band played *Let's Lynch the Landlord, Chemical Warfare, Drug Me, California Uber Alles* and all their other songs, ending the night with the monumental *Holiday in Cambodia*, possibly my favourite song of all time. As the band left the stage, Phil climbed up onto it, and whipped Jello's Shure SM58 microphone from the mic stand and handed it to me as a souvenir. I used this mic for Peeping Toms gigs for two years or so. It was truly an awesome gig on an epic night.

CHAPTER 3

ROCK 'N' ROLL PEOPLE

At some point in 1980, I'd started drinking and socialising in the local pubs. There were as many as twenty-five pubs in Lymington at the time, and I managed to get myself barred from twenty-three of them, mainly because of the way I looked. I'd spend ages in the bathroom, bleaching my hair and spiking it up with soap, and smearing on the eyeliner. The first establishment I drank in was Ye Olde English Gentleman, known as the Old English, or Old E, as we called it. In those days, pubs would shut at 3pm, then reopen again at 6pm. I'd been drinking in there with Dave one Saturday afternoon, and after leaving the premises, we agreed to hook up later and went our separate ways.

When I arrived home, I let myself in with my door key and went and sat down on the sofa in the lounge. There was obviously nobody else in the house, and I remember thinking Dad was probably off playing golf at the course in Brockenhurst, where he was captain at the time. Mum had most likely gone shopping. Where my brother and sister were, was anyone's guess. Anyway, I turned on the TV, and thinking I was completely alone in the house, rolled down my trousers and pants and idly started to... well, do I need to spell it out? I was young at the time and bored stupid and there was nothing else to do, I suppose.

The sofa was right next to the French windows, and just as I was really giving it some, I heard a noisy mechanical sound coming from somewhere in the back garden. Then, to my horror, Dad went past pushing a lawnmower, a look of utter bewilderment on his face, staring directly through the glass at me, literally inches away from my face. He'd been there all along and had been taking a breather from mowing the lawn as I'd arrived home.

Caught red-handed, I remember I kept on going, thinking I might as well be hung for a sheep as a lamb. Moments later, Dad went past again with the lawnmower, coming in from the opposite direction this time, peering in through the window at me once more. Baffled would be an understatement of what he thought of the situation at that moment. To say it was awkward for the both of us at the dinner table later that day was an understatement of epic proportions.

Thoroughly embarrassed by my actions, I attempted to compartmentalise the whole matter, put it to the back of my mind and move on with my life. However, try as I might, I just couldn't shake off the unsettling memory of that Saturday afternoon. I decided it might help to unburden the guilt I was feeling, somewhat, if I told a couple of my close friends what had happened. Upon hearing the sordid story, they struggled to contain themselves with laughter, and one of them even christened the affair 'the Lawnmower Incident'.

Another pub I'd drink in was the Monkey House. The landlord was my mate Barry Hilliard's father, Robin. There was a biker called Peter O'Sullivan who regularly drank in there. Sully, who is no longer with us, unfortunately, was completely mental. He'd crunch up shot glasses with his teeth and swallow them. He'd push drawing pins through his foreskin and nail it to the table, and staple beer mats to his forehead. He was total fucking nuts. He was an animal. Sully once took me out on the back of his motorbike. It was mental. He'd ride full throttle at oncoming vehicles, swerving aside at the last possible moment.

The band I was in at the time, Peeping Toms, played some of their first ever gigs in the Monkey House, and the pub's still going strong today. There was another place in town called the Old Bank House. The landlord, Mike Halliwell, was as cool as a cucumber when it came to dealing with the likes of us. He couldn't give a toss about the way you looked and treated you in the same way he treated everybody else. I remember he had these tufts of hair on his cheeks. Amusingly, he called them his bugger's grips. We played a few Toms gigs in the Bank House and Mike was always good for a lock in.

One of the regular drinkers in that establishment was a Lymington guy called Roger How. Roger was into making homemade bombs, and I remember he once got prosecuted for blowing up the telephone box at the bottom of our road. During one bombmaking experiment, he had the misfortune to blow off one of his thumbs. Roger's mother, Mary Gernat, was a famous children's book illustrator and designed the covers for many of the paperbacks written by such illustrious authors as Enid Blyton and Frank Richards. Roger and his four siblings were the inspiration for Enid Blyton's *Famous Five,* a series of children's adventure novels and short stories.

Other notable pubs were Long's Wine Bar, the Railway Inn, the County Bar, the Crown and Anchor and the Red Lion. The landlady of the Red Lion was a right old bag, and we called her the Woman of a Thousand Chins. One evening, Dave and I went in there for a beer. Glancing up at us, while pouring someone a pint, she said coldly, 'If my sons looked like you, I'd disown them.' From that moment on, as far as we were concerned, she was public enemy number one.

Another place in town we used to frequent was the Angel Tap Bar, which doubled as an off licence. The man in charge there was a volatile, skeletal old boy called Ernie. He always kept a baseball bat close by him behind the bar and wasn't afraid to use it. He wouldn't stand for any of your nonsense, that's for sure. Most of the locals simply referred to the Angel Tap Bar as 'Ernie's.' 'What are you up to tonight mate?' someone might ask. 'I'll probably go for a few pints in town, then finish off at Ernie's,' would often be the reply.

I remember an especially naff adaptation to the chorus of the well-known Benny Hill song I mentioned earlier, doing the rounds in the early 80s: 'Ernie, Ernie, and he pulled the fastest pint in the west,' was how it went. It was cakey, for sure. When I and a few mates got together in the bar one night and sang our version of the song to him, Ernie merely stood there in silence, unmoved, looking at us contemptuously. He didn't find it funny at all. Then again, I don't think he ever saw the funny side in anything, come to that matter. I honestly believe Ernie didn't like people, full stop. 'Was that the trees a-rustling? Or the hinges of the gate? Or Ernie's ghostly beer bottles a-rattling in their crate? They won't forget Ernie, Ernie, and he pulled the fastest pint in the west.' Dear oh dear.

I was on a six-month government training scheme at the time, at Lymington Community Centre. They called it work experience. The warden there was a lovely man called Bruce Halliday, and his daughter Jane was in the same year as me at Priestlands. It was basically a cushy number, which mainly involved setting up the rooms for adult education classes.

At first, the old ladies attending these classes were wary of my spiky hair and eyeliner, but they gradually came to appreciate me over time. They had a great little lounge bar in the Community Centre, which Dave and I would often frequent on Friday evenings after we'd both finished work for the week. It was there, in December 1980, that we learned of John Lennon's untimely death.

Lymington Community Centre had, and still has, a quaint little cinema within its walls called The Malt. I used to go there in the early 70s to watch Saturday matinees. During my time on the government training scheme at the Centre, in 1980 and 1981, the cinema was run by a short, dumpy humourless man with multiple chins called Jack Phillips. Jack never used to say a lot. All you ever got out of him was '35 mil, 35 mil,' in reference to the cine film reel cannisters he was always carrying about with him. 'Hello Jack, how's it going?' you'd ask when you encountered him. '35 mil, 35 mil,' would be his customary reply. The man was obsessed with those reel cannisters and held onto them as if his life depended on it. I wouldn't be at all surprised if he took some of them home to bed with him at night and stored them underneath his pillow. I dare say he probably drove his wife mad by keeping her up half the night, tossing and turning, shouting '35 mil, 35 mil' in his sleep.

I recall Tony Hayter, and another couple of older lads he used to hang about with at the time, sometimes gaining entry to the Malt Cinema without paying. When there was a movie showing there that they wanted to watch, they'd craftily sneak in through a back door behind the screen.

This was all well and good, but it meant they had to watch the images of the film in reverse.

Speaking of cinemas, there's a building on the High Street, now the site of Marks & Spencer, that used to be called the Lyric Theatre. The Lyric was managed for a while by my wife Michaela's great grandfather, Walter Mouland, and closed in 1963. The Lyric, in addition to screening movies, hosted a considerable number of stage productions, among other events. When Walter died in 1962, the great Walt Disney himself, a personal friend of his, sent the family a card expressing his condolences.

In March 1981, I enrolled in another six-month government training scheme, this time at a printing facility on an industrial estate in Stem Lane, New Milton, called Bradprint. The owner of this place was a man called Wilf Bradley. He'd work twenty-four seven to keep his ailing business afloat. His hair was a mess, his skin was yellow, and he had monstruous dark grey bags hanging under his weary eyes. He looked like a zombie in a horror movie and appeared to me as if he was perpetually knocking on death's door.

Wilf rarely spoke to me, or anybody else, come to think of it. Funnily enough, Fiona Johnson, a good friend of mine from my Priestlands schooldays, had a job in the office there at the time, and Stuart Durrant, a mate from Brockenhurst College, was the company's main printer. Apart from Wilf, Stuart was the only person qualified to operate the printing machinery in the factory.

Wilf's wife, a dowdy disconsolate woman with zero personality whose name was Christine, took care of the administration side of things, and the couple employed this weirdo from Dunstable called Roger. He had a hunched back, stuttered his words, and had greasy straight black hair and wore thick-rimmed glasses, which used to steam up whenever he drank a cup of tea or coffee. I think Roger was related to the Bradleys in some way.

I'd originally turned up for the interview for the placement with my hair flattened straight down on my head, trying to the best of my ability to appear as respectable as possible, hoping to impress my would-be employers. When I arrived for my first actual day of work at Bradprint, I sported spikey bleached blonde hair and thickly smeared eye makeup and wore a heavily studded leather jacket, red leopard print T-shirt and a pair of multi-zipped bondage trousers. Wilf simply couldn't deal with it at all. I recall him looking at me with his tired saggy eyes and shaking his head in vexation. To quote Johnny Rotten, onstage at the end of the last ever, ill-fated Sex Pistols gig at the Winterland Ballroom in San Francisco in January 1978, 'Ever get the feeling you've been cheated?'

The Bradley's had a shop at the front of the factory which sold various printing industry accessories. Wilf banned me from going in there, in the event I might frighten off the customers. 'I think we need to keep you hidden well away at the back of the factory in case any of our clientele see you,' were the words he said to me one day.

Years later, I wrote a short song for my current band, Bamboo Vipers, called *Chemical Castration*, in memory of my time working at Bradprint. It's on the band's debut album *Dangling the Bait*, released in 2014, and the lyrics are as follows: '*Chemical castration, or a day in Dunstable. Chemical castration, or a day in Dunstable. I chose chemical castration, no more ejaculation. But if that's what it takes. Coz I never ever wanna go there.*' As far as I'm concerned, Dunstable can fuck right off.

The conditions set in place were that I was required to pay for my own train fare, to travel from Lymington to New Milton and back each day, and Wilf would reimburse me at the end of the six months. But he never did. When I look back on it, I was only getting paid around twenty quid a week, and half of that went on train fares. Without a shadow of a doubt, Wilf was taking the piss out of me. Work experience? It was more like modern day slavery.

I'm not entirely certain, but I believe Bradprint went under not long after I'd finished working there and ceased to exist as a company. Throughout the following year or so, every time I watched a horror film on TV, or a video of one, I fully expected Wilf to suddenly appear there in front of me on the screen. Movies such as *Cannibal Apocalypse, The Thing, Jaws of Satan, House of the Long Shadows* and *Death Warmed Up* seemed made for him.

I used to go to the Gaumont Theatre in Southampton to watch bands, and I remember some cracking gigs at that venue. I saw Adam and the Ants, The Damned, Stiff Little Fingers and The Wall play there. I was right into Crass in those days and saw them loads of times. One Crass gig I went to was at La Babalu, a club in Ryde on the Isle of Wight. I travelled over on the ferry from Lymington to Yarmouth, then took the bus from there to Ryde, around fifteen miles away. I knew I'd never make it back to Yarmouth in time for the last ferry, so I was hoping I might meet someone at the gig who'd put me up for the night. Unfortunately, that didn't happen, and after the show I resigned myself to whiling away the early hours walking the mean streets of Ryde alone. There were a lot of punks from Portsmouth there that night and they'd all missed their last ferry home as well.

I got talking to the Pompey punks and we wandered about aimlessly in a group, looking for something to do. I remember heading off to Ryde pier with them. We arrived at the pier and noticed this monorail track and engine. We got hold of the engine, and with all our combined strength, pushed it into the sea, creating an almighty splash of water before it sank without trace. Just then, I looked back and noticed a uniformed nightwatchman standing in a tall, illuminated tower on the pier, staring at us. He was on the telephone engaged in animated conversation, and obviously talking to the police. As one, the whole group turned and made a desperate run for it, hoping to reach the end of the pier before the cops showed up. Alas, we weren't so fortunate. When we got to the shore, there they were, waiting for us. Loads of them.

In the event, we all got arrested and thrown into the cells at Ryde police station. I was put in a cell with a punk from the Isle of Wight called Deano and I recall him stumbling about, urinating all over the walls and floor. Nothing ever came of the monorail incident; no one got charged with criminal damage or anything, and after a few hours of incarceration at the police station, they let us out back onto the streets. In hindsight, pushing that engine, an expensive piece of machinery, into the sea was an extremely stupid thing to do, and something I'm not proud of.

Killing Joke are a band I was into right from the beginning. Their early stuff is their best, in my opinion. Dave and I would often catch the train up to London to see them play live. I saw Killing Joke many times during the early 80s, at venues such as Hammersmith Palais and the Lyceum, just off the Strand. They were on fire in those days, and the gigs were fucking ace. The energy that band put into their live shows was incredible.

It became a regular event, taking the train up from Lymington to London to watch bands. Most of the gigs we went to were at the Lyceum on The Strand on Sunday nights. Theatre of Hate, Discharge, UK Subs, Anti Nowhere League, The Exploited, Anti-Pasti, The Meteors and Chron Gen were just some of the many bands we saw play there.

In 1981, we were still only eighteen years old, and I remember one night, after leaving the Lyceum, there were a load of evil looking skinheads stood up against the wall outside the venue. They were a lot older than us and really intimidating. One of them shouted 'Get the fucking punks!' and they charged right into us, looking for a fight. Everyone scattered and legged it down the Strand, towards Charing Cross tube station, the skins in hot pursuit. I recall punks with brightly coloured Mohican hairstyles leapfrogging over the ticket barriers at Charing Cross in a desperate attempt to get away that night. Scary shit.

Whenever we went up to London to see a band, we never made it back to Waterloo Station in time to catch the last train home, which departed long before midnight. We had to spend the next six hours or so stranded there before we could get on a train. It was a real pisser. Every shop and café would be closed, and there was nothing for us to do apart from stretch out uncomfortably on a bench and try and get some sleep. Even today, the last train back from Waterloo to Lymington leaves at around 11pm; unbelievable in the modern era. We'd finally arrive home, knackered, about 7 o'clock the next morning.

It was in a pub in New Milton that I first met a guy called Melvin Cope, nicknamed Hash, another one who's gone too soon. He was a punk and played guitar. We got talking and hit it off straight away. He introduced me to a couple of his mates, Dave Edwards and Richie Morant, and after a few pints, we decided to form a band, with Dave on bass and Richie as the drummer. We called our band The Condemned but changed it to The Screws after learning there was already a band with that name, based up in the Midlands.

A friend of mine, Steve Carpenter, who was a regular drinker in the Old English pub and now lives in Thailand, rented a room in a house near Grove Gardens. He'd set up a shebeen with his landlady in the basement and invited the band to rehearse there. The only song I can remember us playing from those days was 'British Rail Intelligence,' influenced by my recent negative experiences of train travel, which I'd written a few weeks previously. The Screws obviously had more songs than just this one, but it was all such a long time ago, I struggle to remember the names of them. After rehearsals were done and dusted, we'd all go down the pub and get pissed out of our heads.

The first ever Screws gig was a memorable occasion. It took place one night in the hall at All Saints Church in Lymington. The audience consisted of mostly younger kids, who sat in rows of chairs in front of the stage. I remember Richie didn't even have a pair of proper drumsticks, using wooden spoons instead. I'd asked Dave Dutton to join the band, more for visual effect. He couldn't play the guitar, but we strapped one over him anyway. During the gig, Dave just stood there vacantly staring down at the stage. As I recall, we put on a good performance and received a positive reception from the crowd. The Screws only played a couple of more gigs before eventually disbanding.

In the spring of '81, I decided it was time to say goodbye to my family and leave home in search of new adventures. I caught the train up to London and moved into the Station Hotel on the Caledonian Road, in King's Cross. It soon became clear to me that most of the hotel's residents were unemployed and claiming benefits. Their rent cheques were sent directly to the manager of the hotel. I was determined to get a job in London, but to survive in the meantime, I first had to sign on at the Department of Social Security. This was a long-drawn-out process and meant walking for miles across the city to the DSS office.

After I'd completed all the necessary paperwork, I set out looking for employment. I ended up applying for loads of jobs but was always unsuccessful. The money I'd brought up to London with me was rapidly dwindling, and I remember not being able to afford to buy food and going without eating for several days. At long last, the dole cheque arrived, and things became a little easier from that moment on.

Many of the hotel's residents were older Scottish men and I'm pretty sure a few of them were involved in criminal activities; not that I gave a shit. I didn't have anything to do with them, and they never bothered me at all. Every other Thursday, we'd receive our giro cheques in the post.

While I was staying at the Station Hotel, the management had a habit of moving people about from one room to another without a moment's notice. You might have a room to yourself one day, then the next, be told you had to vacate the room and move in with a complete stranger in a different one. It was like musical chairs.

I remember one particularly horrifying experience. The hotel manager knocked on my door and informed me I had to leave the room immediately, and that I'd be sharing another room with a middle-aged Scotsman called Jimmy. What he didn't tell me at the time was that we'd also be sharing a bed together that night. It was giro day, and apparently Jimmy would blow all his money getting hammered in a pub down the Caledonian Road, after he'd cashed in his dole cheque. How the man survived from day to day, I'll never know. It was a mystery.

Anyway, that night, after getting into bed, I kept a sharp ear out for Jimmy returning from the pub. It wasn't long before I heard him come staggering down the street, coins falling out of his pockets, singing aloud drunkenly in his broad Glaswegian accent. Worried about what this bloke would do when he realised he was sharing his bed with someone else, I turned off the lamp, hugging the pillow in fear and trepidation, pretending to be asleep.

I could hear Jimmy, obviously blind drunk, slowly climbing the hotel stairs to the landing. He eventually reached the top and managed to find the room, fumbling with the door handle. Opening the door, mumbling incoherently to himself, he collapsed on the bed and fell straight into a deep sleep, or more like a coma.

I didn't get a wink that night, wary of what might happen if he awoke to find me lying there right next to him. Thankfully, nothing unspeakable occurred, and I left the room early in the morning, Jimmy still fast asleep on the bed, fully dressed in his clothes. He probably never even realised I was there in the first place. That was it for me after that. The following day, I packed my bags and checked out of the Station Hotel for good. I jumped on a bus to Waterloo, then took the train back to Lymington.

In December 1981, the other members of The Screws, Phil Sheldrake and I, travelled up to the Queen's Hall in Leeds for the Christmas on Earth punk festival, in Phil's van. We met up in the Bank House the night before and drove through the early hours of Sunday morning. I remember it was snowing heavily and freezing cold. I didn't lay down to sleep in the van on the journey to Leeds in case my spikey hair got flattened.

In the end, it was a pointless exercise staying awake all night because the moment I stepped out of the van, the falling snow rinsed the soap right out of my hair, and I looked like one of the characters in the 60s sci-fi horror movie, Children of the Damned. After Phil parked the van, we all headed to a nearby café for a hot drink. While we were in there, this weird dwarf-like girl came up to me and pointed at the Dead Kennedys logo on my leather jacket. She appeared smacked out of her head, and started ranting, 'That band, the Dead Kennedys, they're not real. They're just a front for Margaret Thatcher. She's their manager and controls everything they do. I hate them!' What the fuck was she going on about?

Appearing on the bill were The Damned, The Exploited, Black Flag, UK Subs, Chelsea and a host of other bands. The water main in the men's toilets had burst, and the place was flooded. Someone had kicked in the pipes, apparently. Everyone wandered about the hall, ankle deep in water. After the festival was over, we headed outside, and it was snowing harder than ever.

It was now 1982, and me and my mates seemed to be living in the Old English pub permanently. We could be found there drinking every night, daytimes as well, and it had become our second home. At the time, the landlord and landlady were a young couple called Roger and Fran Fayers.

I remember the bottles of Viking lager they sold there and the off licence at the rear of the pub. All manner of colourful people would frequent the Old E. It was here that I first met Cobert Cook, who would become The Cropdusters' fiddle player four years later. At the time, I believe Cob played in a local band, The Wrath of Zeus.

Regular drinkers in the pub at the time included Tony Hayter, who by now was utterly convinced he was a Viking and had changed his name by deed pol to Hagar, after the American comic strip character Hagar the Horrible. There was also Steve Carpenter and his brother Barry, John McWilliams, the ex-Hornets footballer Richard Cooper, Tim Colwell, Stuart Gates, Paddy Woolford and his younger brother Neil, John and Sue Rose, Mark Webster, Trevor Gale, nicknamed Tromper, Ginny and Mike Hobson, and Peter Frape.

A mate of mine called Steve Mould was another regular customer and had been drinking in the Old E since he was thirteen years old. There were many others, obviously, young and old, but there's no point in referring to them in this book. The reason why I've mentioned all these people in the first place is because they were the ones there when I first started drinking and socialising.

There was a small, pasty-faced bloke called Toby, who'd been in our year at school. He was a petty thief, and a bit of a waste of space. A horrible small furry thing, to be honest. One hot summer's day, he was caught red handed with his hand in the Old English till. Roger the landlord was understandably furious. Calling a few of us over to the bar, he asked our opinion on how best to deal with him. Someone suggested pulling down his trousers and pants, stringing him up to the lamp post outside the pub, and rubbing honey on his testicles, the idea being that the honey might attract any wasps buzzing about.

Roger and a couple more of us dragged Toby out the pub, pinned him on the ground, and pulled down his jeans and underwear. As he struggled to free himself, Roger and I locked eyes for a moment and shook our heads. We concluded it probably wasn't in everyone's best interests to continue with this. We let Toby off the hook. Quickly grabbing his clothes, he scurried off down the road like a mouse. He got the message and never set foot in the pub again.

Roger and Fran used to let us bring our records to the pub and play them loudly on the stereo behind the bar. They were very laid back and didn't mind how you dressed if you didn't make an ass of yourself and annoy the other customers. Roger had a great sense of humour. One New Year's Eve, he walked around the pub, which was packed to the rafters, collecting empty glasses, stark bollock naked. He was always up for a laugh and the Old English started gaining a great reputation. At weekends, people would come down to drink in there from as far away as London.

Another friend who used to drink in the Old E was Colin Insole, who was an English teacher at a comprehensive school in Southampton. Colin's brother Jim was an interesting character who'd neck pints of the evil scrumpy cider they sold there as if his life depended on it. The cider Jim drank was so acidic it would take layers off the concrete when it spilled out of the barrels onto the floor in the pub's basement. God knows what it did to his stomach lining. The more scrumpy he drank, the more boisterous he'd become. It often got to the point where Jim would conjure a mandolin from somewhere out of nowhere, leaping up onto a table, stomping his feet and singing loudly. He'd strum the instrument in furious fashion, regaling us with medieval tales of old, sweat dripping, froth pouring from his mouth. He came across as some kind of deranged travelling minstrel.

The Old English was a genuine spit and sawdust establishment. There was a dartboard in the main bar, and at weekends bands would set up their gear and perform in front of it. Rox Off always put on a great show in the pub. They were a blues rock band from Southampton and led by the charismatic Bruce Roberts. He was a brilliant guitarist, and a legend in his hometown. Bruce had been a member of the Jess Roden Band during the mid-70s. The original drummer was Pete Hunt, later replaced by Roger Pope, who'd once played with Elton John and Darryl Hall, among other well-known artists. Wally Phillips was the bassist and Ronnie Taylor played saxophone.

I was in the Old E one night, having a pint with Tinley. We decided to get together and form a duo and try and get some gigs booked in various pubs around town. There was a pub by the train station called the Railway Inn. I went in there one day to speak to the landlord, John Bull, about the possibility of us playing there. John was a cheerful, larger-than-life character and booked us without hesitation. Tinley and I had written a few songs together, but we needed substantially more material to fill out our set, ready for the gig, on a Wednesday night in two weeks' time.

We managed to write some new songs and rehearsed them in Tinley's bedroom. The only equipment we had at the time was a combo guitar amplifier and a vocal mic, which I plugged directly into the amp. We wanted to sound hard and raw, and to achieve the desired effect, Tinley would turn his guitar amp up to full volume and use a fuzz box, creating maximum distortion. It was certainly an unconventional set up, to say the least, but we were happy with the sound we were creating.

I don't know if we even had a name for our duo at the time. We must have been called something because I remember sticking up posters with wallpaper adhesive in the High Street, advertising the gig. Our act eventually morphed into a four-piece band, a month or so later, which we named Peeping Toms. This line up featured me on vocals, two guitarists, Tinley and Roger Figgures, and Kev Joyce on drums. To begin with, we didn't have a bass player on board.

Anyway, the night finally arrived, and we prepared to play our first gig. We got our equipment together and pushed it down the High Street in a wheelbarrow, heading towards the Railway Inn. With only one guitar amp and a microphone stand, it didn't take too long to set up and soundcheck. Halfway through proceedings, I noticed the pub was getting busy. It wasn't a bad turnout for a Wednesday. Quite a few people had come along to see us perform that night.

When it was time for us to get up there, Tinley turned on his amp and we hammered straight into our set. We played *Don't Wanna Die for Hampshire County Council*, *British Rail Intelligence*, *Jump for Joy*, *Born Without Freedom* and *One Arm Press Up Manoeuvres in the Dark*, along with several other of our musical creations.

The songs we'd written were fuzzed- up, punk influenced affairs with biting lyrics. I recall us getting a great reaction from the crowd after we'd finished our set. They genuinely appeared to like our music, as did John the landlord. After an hour or so, and a few pints of beer, we packed up our equipment, put it in the wheelbarrow and went home. I think we got paid £50 that night.

One day not long afterwards, my parents informed me that a good friend of theirs, Tony Leahy, had got me a job at the Rank Hovis McDougall flour mill facility, where he was the general manager. A vacancy had suddenly opened up in the cleaner/packer section there. As Tony lived locally to us, I assumed the job would be at the Rank Hovis mill in Southampton. I was stunned when they told me it was at the one on Felixstowe docks in Suffolk, 200 miles away. Incredibly, everything had already been arranged, and without my knowledge. The plan was, Dad was going to drive Mum and me there the following Sunday, and I would be staying in a self-contained bedsit, in a private house, the owners of which were total strangers to me. I was gutted. All I kept thinking was, my parents were desperately trying to get rid of me, and what had I done to deserve this? Surely, I'm not that bad a person, am I?

In hindsight, I think they'd grown frustrated with me not making any real attempt at gaining meaningful employment   a 'proper' job, if you like. In their eyes, singing in a punk band wasn't what they had in mind for me as a lifelong occupation. Then again, you can't mould someone into the image of what you conceive you want them to be, family or not. Ultimately, it must be that person's individual freedom of choice which counts. In all fairness though, I can't really blame my parents for wanting me to make something better of myself, but Felixstowe? Even the name didn't sound right.

We arrived at the coastal town of Felixstowe in the early afternoon, and I immediately sensed an air of foreboding. The weather was overcast and blustery that day, and the town looked bleak beyond words. In fact, it looked like a complete and utter shithole. I recall thinking, God, what is this place? What the hell am I doing here? Little wonder, Felixstowe was twinned at the time with an obscure town somewhere in France, called

Ennuyeux, which ironically, translates into the word 'boring.'

After getting something to eat in a poxy, rundown café in the town's crappy-looking shopping precinct, Dad drove me to the bedsit, which was situated down a nondescript little road. When the car finally stopped, I grabbed my rucksack from the backseat, and without further ado said goodbye to my parents, wondering what life had in store for me next.

I walked up the path and knocked on the front door of the house. A short, mousey haired, miserable looking middle-aged woman opened the door and reluctantly beckoned me inside, and I followed her into the hallway, and then the living room. I was immediately struck by the inordinate amount of glass there was in the room. There were glass doors, glass tables, glass shelves, glass lampshades, glass mirrors, glass cabinets housing drinking glasses, glass vases, glass ashtrays and an assortment of glass ornaments. A safety hazard, and a potential threat to life and limb, if ever there was one. Any illusions I'd harboured about moving into this godforsaken place were quickly shattered, as surely as all that glass would be someday.

She introduced me to her husband; a gruff, balding and bearded lumbering hulk of a man of very few words, who wore glasses. Well, he just had to, didn't he? I half expected him to be made from glass himself. He reminded me of a cross between the Bullet Baxter character in the children's TV programme *Grange Hill* and the British shot putter and strongman Geoff Capes. I became acutely aware of a large, growling, intimidating Boxer dog he was restraining, immediately behind him. We left the living room, and looking me up and down in the hallway, the woman said 'Right, I suppose I'd better show you to your room.'

She pointed to a flight of stairs, directly ahead of us, and we climbed up them together in silence. Opening the door to the bedsit, she begrudgingly handed me the key. As I put my rucksack down on the bed, she started speaking again. 'The rent is £50 per week, paid in advance. This is a nice respectable house, and we expect you to behave accordingly. There'll be no loud music played in here and you're not allowed any visitors. We're doing you a favour letting you stay here. Any trouble, you're to leave here immediately, and never come back.' She then closed the door behind her and walked back down the stairs. My reputation had obviously gone before me.

I decided I'd go for a wander and check out the local nightlife. There wasn't any. Eventually, I found a pub up the road called The Grosvenor. I walked inside and sat down at the bar and ordered a pint of lager. There weren't many customers in there. I got chatting to the bar staff and they seemed friendly enough. The Grosvenor was typical of the pubs operating at the time. There was a pool table in the back and a jukebox on the wall. After a couple of beers, I said my goodbyes and headed back to the house of horrors. I had to be up early the next morning for my first day's work at the flour mill.

Initially, I had to make my way to Felixstowe docks on foot. It was about a 40-minute walk to get there. The Rank Hovis mill had stood at the port's Dock Basin since the early 19th century and was a fine example of an Edwardian building. It was also a death trap. Anyway, I arrived in good time for my day's shift and was immediately handed a set of white overalls and a pair of wellington boots. Then I was shown around the mill before being introduced to my workmates in the cleaner/packer section.

There were ten separate wooden floor levels in the mill and our job mostly entailed sweeping up any flour spills and packing 25 kilo bags of flour and loading them onto pallets. It was dangerous work. For example, there was a vertical conveyor belt, with small foot platforms, running up through open hatches in the centre of the building. It operated constantly, enabling workers to hop on and off at the various floor levels. If you needed to go up to the highest floor, you'd have to jump off the foot platform, freeing yourself, before the conveyor belt looped around at the top of the building. The space between the belt and the roof was far too small for a person to fit through, so if you didn't jump off the foot platform in time, you'd be mangled to death in the rafters. There were no lifesaving emergency buttons to press; no safety measures in place at all.

There were many other ways to die in that flour mill. We didn't wear safety helmets, and occupational hazards included electrical fires, falling out of upper floor windows or into gigantic storage silos, being dragged by your overalls into dangerous rotating machinery, and developing serious respiratory problems through the inhalation of flour dust, as we never wore face masks.

Forklift trucks operated on the ground floor without mirrors and there was the risk of a dust explosion occurring at any time when a source of ignition is introduced into the right mix of dust and oxygen. The mill was constructed entirely out of wood, and incredibly, we were allowed to smoke on the premises. It beggars' belief, when I think about it now.

Jim Collins was the foreman on the cleaner/packer gang. He only had one eye and was a grumpy, hard drinking, chain smoking son of a bitch who lived at home on his own. We called him Cyclops. He could be a right difficult bastard, and I had a couple of proper run-ins with him during my time at the mill. I recall another, older guy, working there as part of our gang, an effeminate Welshman called Ken. Ken was so far up the foreman's ass, it was unbelievable. 'I've made you a round of your special sandwiches first thing this morning Jim. It was Spam on white bread, buttered on one side only, and cut into quarters, you asked for; as it's a Tuesday, wasn't it? I've got your flask of tea, bar of chocolate, and your morning newspaper. Here, have one cigarette for now, and another couple for later. Oh, and here's a lighter, and don't worry about giving it back to me, I've got another one in my pocket. Would you like me to gently massage your cock Jim, and give you an erection, so you can ejaculate all over my overalls? And don't worry about cleaning up the mess, I can see to it myself when I get home later.'

Seriously though, it was mental stuff, indeed. However, I guess it was relatively common for people of a certain generation to behave in that way in the workplace. Ken was obviously terrified at the prospect of losing his job, and creeping to the boss was his idea of keeping Cyclops onside, thereby protecting himself from possible dismissal. It was sad, and it was pathetic, but there you go.

Cyclops would take the sandwiches, flask, chocolate, paper, fags and lighter from Ken, grunt a few unintelligible words, then look at him disdainfully with his one eye, before walking away. He was one ungrateful schmuck. Ken lived in a house with his sister in the town and was a man with a naturally pale complexion. When he was at work, covered head to toe in flour dust, he resembled the Pilsbury Doughboy.

After a couple of weeks living in Felixstowe, amazed that I was still living and breathing, I bought a pushbike off one of my workmates. This shortened the journey to the mill by half. On the way home from work, I'd nip into the Grosvenor for a few beers before heading back to the bedsit. I didn't want anything to do with the wankers who owned the house and never socialised with them in any shape or form. I'd get a takeaway meal and wolf it down in the bedsit as quickly as possible. As far as I was concerned, the less time I spent in that place, the better. As soon as I'd finished my takeaway, I'd hurry out the door and head straight to the pub.

One day in the bedsit, I bleached my hair then dyed it bright red. I left the house and walked off to the Grosvenor. Upon returning, a few hours later, I noticed the old bag standing in the doorway. She'd seen a flash of red going past her window earlier, and looking out, saw me. She was not amused. 'How dare you! We welcome you into our home and you disrespect us like this. My husband's the secretary of Felixstowe Bowls Club and we're upstanding members of the community; I'll have you know. What on earth will the neighbours think? We knew you'd be trouble as soon as we set eyes on you!' Bigoted and judgemental, she and her husband were just the kind of people I despise.

During my time in Felixstowe, the Falklands War was in full swing, and I'd keep up to date with what was happening, watching the live coverage on the TV and reading about it in the papers. As the Falklands War ended, the 1982 Football World Cup, being held in Spain, got underway. A Scottish woman called Maggie worked behind the bar in the Grosvenor, and I'd go round her and her husband John's house to watch the games. I remember a guy called Alex, a pub regular, would be there. He worked for an international shipping company on the docks.

The best thing about working in the flour mill was Thursday lunchtimes. We'd get paid our weekly wages in cash in little brown envelopes, then hot tail it over to the pub on the docks and try and get as many pints down our necks as possible in an hour, before returning to the mill for the afternoon shift, half cut. This made the job even more dangerous. Being unaware of your surroundings could prove fatal. Not long before I started working there, an employee, clearly inebriated and unalert, had slipped and plunged to his death down one of the silos.

In July, my time in Felixstowe ended abruptly. Without a face mask for protection, I'd been inhaling an unhealthy amount of flour dust into my lungs. One night, I suffered my first real asthma attack. I wasn't hospitalised, but it was a horrible experience not being able to breathe properly. The next day I phoned the mill and explained to them what had happened, and that I wasn't coming into work again; I was moving back down south.

When I told the woman at the house the news, she instantly changed her attitude towards me. It was the first time I'd seen her smile during my stay there. In a patronising voice, she said 'Oh, that's a shame, we've really enjoyed you being here, but we understand your reasons for wanting to leave.' I mean, what a fake person. You could see it in her eyes that she was delighted I was moving out. The feeling was mutual.

One I'd returned to Lymington, I set out to find Dave Dutton. He was glad to see me, then told me he was moving up to Hackney in London, and that I must get up there to see him sometime soon. A couple of my friends, Urk English and Becca Chester, had already relocated to Hackney, immediately after we'd left Priestlands, in 1979. I wasted no time at all in tracking down Tinley, and the pair of us carried on from where we'd left off with the music. At some point not long afterwards, we got Rog and Kev on board and became a four-piece band, officially called Peeping Toms. We wrote a whole batch of new songs and rehearsed them regularly.

We played one gig with this line up, at the Railway Inn in Lymington. It was on a Saturday night, and the pub was packed. It was a great night all round, and I remember Tinley picking up a police radio transmission coming loudly through his amplifier. It went something like this: 'This is PC Braithwaite reporting on the frequency. We're currently sat in our patrol car outside the Railway Inn public house in Station Road. There's a lot of noise coming from inside the building. There seems to be some sort of punk rock band playing in there.' The band broke into hysterics, and we immediately launched into our song Twistgrip, which was written about PC Alan Mills, a notorious local motorcycle cop. Twistgrip was out to make a name for himself and would do everything in his power to bust people for even the most minor of infractions. He'd snidely lay in wait on his motorcycle at stop signs or at a crossroads, ready to ambush unsuspecting passers-by. Motorists, motorbike riders, cyclists, kids on go-karts, skateboards, sledges, roller skates and space hoppers – no one was safe from Twistgrip's all-seeing eye. He was a tenacious bastard. With his police crash helmet, goggles and walkie talkie, he really was a proverbial pain in the backside.

A short while later, Tinley made the decision to move up to Hackney, joining Dave, Urk and Becca there. That meant we had to find someone to take his place in Peeping Toms. Ideally, we needed a bass player. Enter John Bodley-Scott, Priestlands schoolboy at the time, and local doctor's son. Bod, as he was known, was an enthusiastic lad, and he fitted into the band straightaway without any problem at all.

Tinley went on to enjoy a prestigious musical career, playing in some well-known 80s London bands and writing the tune to his brother Adam's number one hit song, *Killer*. He was also the keyboard technician for Duran Duran for many years. Tinley now lives down in Glastonbury, in Somerset, where he works at a music shop called The Beach. We still see each other from time to time.

Rog and I were coming up with new ideas for songs. I'd write the lyrics, and he'd work out melodies for them on his guitar. We wrote a whole load of new songs around this time: *Never Gonna Be a Star, Big Nose, Brainless, Indecent Exposure, We Are Peeping Toms, Get Lost, Another Good Man Gone, Simon Snakebite, Cyberman, Out of Order, Wet Dreams, Bombay Blues* and *The Ballad of Nogger Sprockett* were just some of them. We covered *Tension* by Killing Joke and even worked out a rousing version of the Scottish folk song *The Wee Cooper of Fife*.

Peeping Toms rehearsals would normally take place in a shed at the bottom of Roger's back garden, on an evening in midweek. Rog had soundproofed the shed and laid down some carpets. Kev would set up his drumkit and Rog and Bod would plug their guitars into their amps. My microphone was plugged into a PA mixer. When we were all happy with the sound levels of the various instruments, we'd crack on and rehearse the songs for the next few hours.

The band was now ready to get out there and start gigging. Rox Off were playing up the Old English one Saturday night, and all the Toms were in the audience. During their break, Bruce Roberts asked us if we'd like to get up and play a few numbers. Jumping at the chance, we bashed through three or four of our songs, and the crowd really loved it. Later, Roger the landlord said he wanted us to play our own gig in the pub. He was enthusiastic about our music and gave us a lot of encouragement.

Over the course of the next two years, the Peeping Toms played loads of gigs in the Old E: Thursday nights, Friday nights, Saturday lunchtimes, Saturday nights, Sunday lunchtimes. Sometimes at the drop of a hat. They were loud, subversive and always a lot of fun, which I guess was the vital ingredient. The band loved every minute of it, and so did the people who came to see us. I'd like to think Peeping Toms were a massive part of the fabric of that pub, at that time in our lives. Even my brother Richard, then only ten years old, would come and watch us play. Fantastic memories.

In the spring of 1982, the band played a couple of gigs at the Joiner's Arms in Southampton, supporting Rox Off on a Saturday afternoon. The next one we played there, we were headlining. We hired a coach, and half the Old English bought tickets. Someone in the band got hold of a load of granny hats from a local jumble sale to wear onstage. We must have looked ridiculous up there, but we didn't care, and it was great fun. At the end of the gig, we threw the hats into the audience, and some of the punters put them on their heads and wore them on the coach journey back to Lymington.

Dave Dutton and Urk were now sharing a flat together in Powerscroft Road in Hackney. They'd organised a Saturday night party at their flat and it was high time we paid them a visit. I can't remember exactly who went up to the party from Lymington, but certainly Mike Case and a mate called Tim Cox were present. Richard Wallace, maybe.

We arrived in Hackney in the afternoon, completely hammered. I recall us drinking in a pub down by the canal when Buster Bloodvessel, the lead singer of Bad Manners, walked past. I think their new single had just gone to the top of the charts. Ironically, The Cropdusters played a few gigs with Bad Manners some years later. Buster, real name Dougie Trendle, used to bully our roadie Max at school in Stoke Newington in the 1970s.

Buster's a man of many different faces. At the first gig the Dusters played with Bad Manners, I think it was at Egham College in London in 1988, he was all over us like a rash. When we were on the same bill as his band at Manchester University several years later, he didn't want to know us at all. Indeed, he fucked me right off when he kept chucking whiskey down our drummer Krish's throat before we went onstage. We had people from the music agency Blast Hard, the same one that represented the Happy Mondays, coming to check us out that night. During our set, Krish was struggling to hold it together at times on the drums, although overall I think he just about succeeded in doing so somehow.

After getting shitfaced in the pub, we all ambled over to Dave and Urk's place for the party, which was evidently already in full swing. The music being played on the stereo was at full volume and it sounded like there were a lot of people in there. As we entered through the door of the flat, we were immediately greeted with the sight of an enraged biker guy called Mick the Dog throttling somebody, holding his head down the bathroom toilet and giving him a bog wash.

When Mick hauled the bloke out of the urinal, we realised straight away that it was the little thief Toby from Lymington. He'd been caught stealing someone else's dope and was now getting punished for it. Toby, soaked to the skin, was whimpering, and kept pleading with Mick. 'I'm really sorry mate; I promise you I won't do it again! Honest Mick, I didn't realise that gear belonged to somebody else, I thought it was mine! Please don't...aaahh!' Down into the toilet bowl went Toby's head once more.

Mick turned towards us with a glint in his eye, and said casually, 'Hello boys, nice to meet you. I hope you enjoy the party,' before ramming Toby's head straight back down the toilet and flushing the chain. We never saw

Toby again that night. It seemed he'd evaporated into thin air. The next morning, when he still hadn't reappeared, we thought Mick and his biker mates must have buried him under a patio somewhere in Hackney. Either that, or he'd been flushed away down into London's vast labyrinth of underground sewers; forever in the shit. Unfortunately, he re-emerged in Lymington a few weeks later.

Life went on. One Saturday night, a few of my friends and I headed off to the Bank House for a drinking session. There was a party going down in Pennington that night, and we'd been invited to it. No one was in a fit state to drive, so we walked across the road and phoned for a taxi. All the taxis were booked up at the time, but one company told us to hang on and wait, and someone would be with us shortly.

We were standing outside the post office, waiting for the next available taxi, when this pygmy of a police officer appeared on the scene, got right in my face, and told me to move off the pavement at once. His whole attitude stank. I politely explained to him that we were waiting for a taxi to take us to Pennington, but he was having none of it. 'I'm out on patrol in the High Street this evening, and if you're still stood here on the pavement when I come back, then you're nicked, sonny.' I just looked at the clown then instantly forgot about him.

Around ten minutes later, there he was again. 'I told you to move off the pavement, why are you still here?' he shouted at me. He was seriously getting on my tits by now. So much so that I thought about having a go at him, but I remained calm and diplomatic. Composing myself, I said to him 'I'll tell you what mate, I will get off the pavement' and proceeded to climb a lamp post a few feet away from me. The irritating policeman screamed 'You're under arrest! and climbed up the lamp post trying to grab hold of me. It was a pathetic sight to behold.

I was sitting on the top laughing at him, when he suddenly lost his balance. He came sliding down the lamp post, landing awkwardly on the ground and losing his helmet in the process. Pissing myself, I went for a role reversal. 'I told you to get off the pavement, officer!' I said to him with great delight. It was zero respect on my part, but the idiot brought it all upon himself.

While the policeman was writhing about helplessly, a couple of my friends, Barry Hilliard and Barry Cave, came running over from the other side of the street. Shouting 'Leave our mate alone!' they threw his helmet away and rubbed chewing gum into his hair. He radioed for assistance and more coppers quickly arrived on the scene. I was arrested, along with Barry Hilliard. Barry Cave somehow managed to avoid being apprehended. They locked us up for the night and charged both of us with the crime of being drunk and disorderly.

The policeman responsible for causing all of this in the first place claimed I had kicked him when he climbed up the lamp post after me. He was determined to get me in as much trouble as possible and was prepared to lie about what really happened that night. Appearing at Lymington Magistrates Court a few weeks later, the judge dismissed the officer's allegations, and we were fined around £50 each for being drunk and disorderly.

There was a place in Christchurch called the Jumpers Tavern. They used to put on bands at the time, and a friend, Mark Webster, would drive a load of us there in his green Ford Plymouth car. The Jumpers was where I first saw The Accused. The band was fronted by a bald, charismatic, dearly departed frontman named Mick Whitlock. We got to see a lot of Mick over the coming months, as he often rode his motorbike into Lymington, and pop in the Old English for a pint.

It was around this time that I bumped into a guy from New Milton called Lee Crocker. Crocker was a music-obsessed psychobilly nutcase. He still is. We hit it off straight away, mainly because we had so much in common. He was into punk rock, but his real love was 1950s Rock 'n' Roll music. Another personality I met for the first time back then was Rik Smith. Rick was nicknamed Rocket Pod, later shortened to Podders, and would become The Cropdusters' roadie in the late 80s.

Around the summer of '82, I began going out with a girl from Pennington called Tracy. By the autumn, we were spending a lot of time together, and it wasn't long before I'd virtually moved into the room she was renting, in a house down by the quay in Lymington. Tracy was a scooter girl, and her musical taste was deeply rooted in Motown and Northern Soul. This didn't stop her from going to Peeping Toms gigs, though, often accompanied by her brother Gary.

Around Christmas time, Tracy and I made the decision to bite the bullet and move up to London. Her sister Julie was already living there with her partner at the time. In January 1983, we said goodbye to our families and headed off to start a new life in the Big Smoke. Initially, we stayed at my Aunt Mary's house in Hampstead Garden Suburb in north London. After a week or so, we moved out of there and rented a bedsit at a house in Jerningham Road, New Cross, in the south-east of the city. It was tough going. As had been the case the previous year, employment was hard to come by in London, although Tracy eventually managed to find herself a barmaid job in a pub on New Cross High Street.

I remember we were living close to Millwall's football ground, The Den, and on match days, you could hear the roar of the crowd from our place. We spent a lot of our time over at her sister Julie's flat in a tower block in Greenwich, and looking back, that was probably the highlight of our stay in south-east London. Things weren't working out, for one reason or another, and we decided we'd had enough. Sometime during the spring, we packed our bags and headed back to Lymington.

Back in our hometown once more, it was business as usual as far as I was concerned. Hooking up with the Toms again, the band decided to go into the studio to record a ten-track album and release it on limited edition cassette. Kev came up with the idea 'Crotchless Bras and Peephole Panties', and that's what we called it. We booked a recording studio, Studio 95, for a Saturday afternoon session in Boscombe and knocked out the ten songs without any problems. The studio engineer, a strange, diminutive woman who kept saying the word 'rolling,' when she was ready to record, mixed the songs within our allotted timeframe, and bingo, we'd completed the whole thing in a day. A few days later, Kev turned up in the Olde E with a box of fifty Peeping Toms tapes. We kept them behind the bar, and they sold out rapidly. Legend has it that the Mayor of Lymington at the time bought up the last few copies of the cassettes, in a futile attempt at preventing their distribution among the town's inhabitants. According to him, people like us were to be seen and not heard.

One incredible, but true, incident happened around this time. The Toms were booked in for a Saturday lunchtime gig at the Old E, and after we'd sound checked, I wandered down the town to drum up some support. Saturday is Market Day in Lymington, and the High Street was busy. I saw Mike Case's younger brother, Reg, standing on the steps of Sperrings, looking a bit forlorn and shaken up, so I went over to talk to him, to check he was all right. He was only eleven years old at the time, and he told me that he'd just seen Simon Groom, who was a current presenter on the children's TV programme Blue Peter.

As Groom walked past on the opposite side of the street, Reg jokingly called out to him, 'Oi Groomy, where's your fucking tractor?' Groom charged across the street, a snarling look on his face, and screamed at Reg 'You what? You mouthy little squirt!' He then grabbed Reg in a headlock and proceeded to pummel him into the ground. When he'd finished laying into Reg, he quickly disappeared into the crowd of shoppers, no doubt praying his reputation wasn't in tatters, leaving Reg floundering on the Sperrings steps. What a thoroughly unpleasant individual. An absolute wanker, if ever there was one.

After a while, Reg went home and told his dad, Gerry, what had happened. Gerry, the steam pouring out of his ears, told Reg to jump in the car, and together they went searching for Simon Groom. Unfortunately, the quick tempered, bullying bastard remained elusive, and they never found him. I'd known Gerry Case and his wife Barbara since the early 70s, and I used to spend hours round their house in those days and occasionally stayed overnight there at weekends. They were a big part of my childhood.

Lymington is a small town sandwiched between the New Forest National Park and the sea. September in the New Forest meant only one thing to us: magic mushroom season. We'd go out there in packs, and usually, we'd find them. Thousands of them. There are many types of hallucinogenic mushrooms, but I'm pretty sure the one's we mostly came across are called liberty caps.

We'd spend hours foraging around the forest, our darting eyes constantly focused on the ground. If we discovered an especially large clump of them growing somewhere, we became ultra excited, gleefully scooping them up with our fingers and putting them into the carrier bags we'd brought along with us. When we thought we'd picked more than enough magic mushrooms, we'd head on home in eager anticipation of trying them out.

On several occasions on autumn evenings, me and my mates would sit in the Old English and mix the shrooms with packets of Worcester Sauce crisps we bought in there. After half an hour or so, we'd begin coming up and burst into hysterics at the slightest thing. I recall in 1985, when Dave Poore was the landlord of the Old E, a few of us munching away on the combination of magic mushrooms and crisps and literally rolling about on the floor in fits of laughter. Dave Poore, standing behind the bar, couldn't understand what was going on and kept glancing over at us, shaking his head with a bemused look on his face.

Another crazy incident, that occurred towards the end of '83, involved the biker Sully, who was at the very heart of it all. I'd met up with Crocker and another friend, Shaun Deering, in the Old English. It was a Friday night, and we'd taken a load of white lightning LSD tabs. At the time, Sully was squatting in a derelict house up the road from the pub. He nipped in for a quick pint and invited the three of us round to the house when the pub shut. We arrived at the squat late at night, tripping off our heads on acid. We noticed the place was all boarded up, but Sully soon emerged and beckoned us in through a secret gap he'd created. He looked absolutely fucking mental. Wearing only a loincloth, his long black, dishevelled hair all over place, he began waving his arms about like a madman. He appeared as if he was acting out a scene from the movie *One Million Years BC*. God knows what he'd taken that night.

Grunting and pointing, he once again urged us to follow him through the gap in the boarding and into the house. We crawled through, one at a time. It was pitch black in there, and the only thing you could see was the roaring fire Sully had lit in the hearth in the living room. Immediately he took on the role of caveman and began grunting and dancing about in front of the licking flames. At one point, I fully expected him to leap into the fire and get incinerated alive. It was like some kind of maniacal pagan ritual, and it was insane.

Sully had this crazed look about him, his eyes glowing with menace in the firelight. I remember thinking we needed to get the fuck out of there at once, before he burns the house down, with all of us in it. Sully must have read my intentions, for he suddenly proclaimed to us that he was indeed about to raze the whole place to the ground, and none of us would ever get out of there alive. He said he had a jerry can full of petrol somewhere in the squat and stomped off looking for it. He called out behind him, 'I wouldn't worry about it. Everyone's gotta die sometime!'

I recall trying to distract him, as we desperately tried to escape through the gap in the boarding. Sully attempted to stop us from getting away, but somehow, we managed to shake him off. In the driveway outside, I could still hear him howling and chanting incoherently as if he was lost in a bygone age, immersed in a deep prehistoric trance. Peter O'Sullivan RIP, what a loveable nutter.

Meanwhile, Tracy and I were looking for a permanent place to call home. After we'd returned from London, we stayed at my parents' house for a while, but we couldn't remain there indefinitely. However, an opportunity soon presented itself whereby it was possible for young couples to get themselves on the mortgage ladder. I didn't even have a job at the time, but amazingly, after going through the whole process of references etc, we suddenly had our own home, in a one-bed, self-contained property in Lymington.

We were both delighted, but regretfully, the honeymoon period didn't last long. Tracy was already in employment, and to make this work, I needed to get off my ass and get a job. Rock 'n' roll doesn't pay the bills. Cue Webb's chicken processing factory, a place I'd dreaded encountering for years. Tracy's brother Paul was a supervisor there and secured me a position on the packing line. It was a horrible place, but the mortgage had to be paid.

Rather than dwell on the negatives of working in that shithole, of which there were many, I'd rather focus on the few positives. For instance, some of my old schoolmates were employed there, and they were always good for a laugh. There was Bungle, Tash and Jake from East Boldre, and a few others I knew. You had to make the best out of a bad situation. Everyone was in the same boat.

The most powerful memory I have from my time working at Webb's chicken factory still makes me laugh today. Apart from the Lymington site, Webbs owned another one in Winchester. A big problem arose concerning the disparity in wages between the two factories; the Winchester employees were getting paid considerably more than we were. Our Trade Union representative, Butch, was an agitator, and he wasn't happy at all. I remember one morning, he shouted 'Right, everybody out!' Literally everyone on the production line stopped what they were doing, downed tools, and rushed to the exit. I was the first one out of the door. I was elated. It was totally ace. I'd only been working there a week or so, and my foreman, an old guy with a bald head and spider vein face, called Mick Borrie, couldn't get his head around what was happening. Catching up with me in the corridor, he tapped me on the shoulder and spluttered 'You've only been here five minutes, and now you're going on strike?' Fucking right I was.

Outside the factory, tempers were hovering at boiling point. The management were huddled nervously together in a group, in a remote corner of the car park, deep in animated conversation. They looked to me as if they just couldn't comprehend the situation developing around them. Most of them were as thick as mince. Anyway, Butch wandered over, and I'll never forget his words to me that day: 'I've had a quick chat with the boys, and we've all decided that you should be our leader on the picket line.' You couldn't make it up.

Picket line duty basically consisted of milling about in the road and turning away any lorries delivering chickens to the factory. The Railway Inn was nearby, and in shifts, one at a time, we'd nip down there for a couple of pints. The strike didn't last long, maybe a week or so. One day, the head honcho himself, Mr Webb, turned up and physically threatened Butch. Webb was an intimidating presence, and he was extremely pissed off. The upshot of it all was Butch called off the strike, and we returned to work. Unfortunately.

I remained at Webb's for two more years. The work was repetitive, and tedious beyond imagination. Sometimes I thought I was going out of my mind. The radio didn't help. It was on constantly, and the commercial crap the DJs churned out repeatedly, would keep you on edge all day long. The radio's tinny sound would screech above the noise of the clunking machinery on the factory floor, and it was unbearable.

On the production line each day, bored out of my mind, I'd scribble down lyrics on pieces of cardboard, whenever I got the chance. When the working day was over, my nerves would be shredded. I knew I had to get out of there before I went totally insane. In early '86, I handed in my notice, and a week later, breathing a huge sigh of relief, I walked out of the factory gate for the last time. I'd served my sentence.

Returning to 1983, the Peeping Toms were gaining a notorious local reputation. We'd worked out a punked-up rendition of *Rupert the Bear*, and we'd smash it out at gigs in the Old English, Monkey House and Bank House. I remember knocking up a poster for a gig at the Old E, featuring an image of Rupert with his dick hanging out. I plastered a load of them around town, on walls, lamp posts and electricity boxes.

A good friend of ours was a guy called Mark Hayter, nicknamed Spud. I would sometimes take a break midway through our set, for a breather and a pint. Spud would get up on the microphone and sing two or three songs. I remember him singing a song he'd written himself called *How Dark is the Night?* The man had a great voice and nailed it to perfection when the band covered 999's *Homicide*. We were all extremely saddened to hear of Spud's untimely death many years later in the 1990s.

Another person who'd rise to the occasion and strut his stuff in the interlude was an old mate called Paul Hawker, who was known by his nickname, Beagle. He was a comedian and would crack the whole pub up with his impersonations of Douglas Bader, among other well-known people. My friend Colin Insole wrote a blinding review of a Toms gig in the Old E and sent it to the *New Musical Express*. Amazingly, it got printed and we were all as chuffed as nuts.

Around this time, Tracy and I decided we'd grown apart over the last few months and went our separate ways. I suppose we were just too young. We'd shared some great experiences together, and I certainly won't forget them. In the end, it was an amicable split, and we remain good friends to this day. Indeed, we accompanied each other to a recent Priestlands school reunion at the social club in Pennington. I couldn't envisage going with anybody else.

I recall one night in the autumn there were a few of us drinking in the Old English: Pete Golden, Neil Woolford and Graham Cullen. There was a party happening in Pennington that night, and Pete offered to drive us there in his Ford RS 2000. We said we'd walk to the party as it wasn't far away, but Pete insisted upon driving.

At closing time, the four of us jumped into his car and we headed off to Pennington. Pete put his foot down on the accelerator, and as we reached the top of Highfield Road, he turned sharply to the left. I saw a lamp post looming directly in front of us and remember thinking this was the end. At the last possible moment, Pete swerved the car to the right, and it rolled over on its roof before spinning down the hill and coming to rest at the bottom.

Neil and Graham had been thrown out of the rear window with such force that they were now lying motionless, ten yards up the hill. The car seats had been ripped out and there was shattered glass everywhere. It didn't look good at all. Pete and I crawled out of the upturned car in complete shock. Just then, an old woman came charging out of her house, waving a broom about. She began shouting at us. 'I heard you coming from miles away, you were driving much too fast! It serves you right! I hope you've all got nasty injuries; it'll teach you a lesson. I'm calling the police!'

As she ran back inside her house, we went to check on the other two. Luckily, they weren't that badly hurt. At that moment, the woman reappeared and began frantically sweeping the broken glass from her driveway with her broom. She screamed at us 'I've called the police and they're on their way. I hope you all get arrested!' The four of us immediately started running towards the other end of the road, in the direction of the party. We didn't want to be hanging around there when the cops showed up.

As we reached the top of the road, we glanced back and saw a police car arrive on the scene. We kept on running until we got to the house where the party was. Once inside, we got our hands on a bottle of brandy, and between us, swigged it down neat. We were all in shock, and the brandy helped take the edge off. I don't remember whether Pete ever got charged over the incident. The car was a total write off, and we were lucky we never sustained serious injury. Apart from a few cuts and bruises, we were otherwise okay. We had got off lightly, all things considered.

It was now 1984, and the Peeping Toms were still out there playing several gigs. I can remember supporting Mick Whitlock's new band, Prima Voice, at Bournemouth Town Hall, which was a great night. A couple of months later, we decided to call it a day and split up, for various reasons. We wanted the band to go out with a bang though and booked the Regency Centre in Christchurch for our last hurrah. We hired a coach for the occasion, and it departed from the Old E in the early evening with all the usual suspects on board.

It was an ace gig, and a fitting way to say farewell. The only negative was this retard from Lymington happened to be there. At the end of the night, clearly looking for trouble, he grunted to a couple of us, 'I know. You need to get hold of a cage and put it up on the stage. We can get some of the local blokes in there, and I can go in and beat them all up!' Unfortunately, we'd sometimes have to deal with neanderthal twats like this at our gigs. They were out there then, and they still are.

Lee Crocker was now living in Boscombe, with his mother and her boyfriend Terry, who was a proper old school rock 'n' roller. A few of us would often go and visit him, turning up at his house on Saturday afternoons. We'd go on drinking sessions around the pubs during the daytime, then return to his place in the early evening. After listening to Crocker's vinyl records, and consuming more alcohol, we'd take a taxi into Bournemouth and head straight for the Third Side nightclub up on the Triangle. We had some brilliant times in that nightclub. At about 3 am the next morning, we'd leave the club and take a taxi back to Crocker's house and try and catch some sleep before heading home later that day.

Another club we'd often frequent was The Riverside in Woolston, Southampton. I saw some great gigs in that venue, most notably Folk Devils and Peter and the Test Tube Babies. At the Test Tubes show, some mates from the Bournemouth area were there, Tim Potter, Jon Bruce and Richard Strange. Del, the Test Tubes guitarist, had forgotten to bring a plectrum with him, so Tim gave him a 5p coin to use instead. There was a bunch of skinheads at the gig, and they asked if Tim and the other two were from Lymington and were fans of The Cropdusters. They had to do some quick thinking to avoid getting their heads kicked in.

I remember being at The Riverside one Friday night with my mate from Pennington, Bobby Ryan. When it was time to leave the nightclub, at around 2 am on Saturday morning, we realised we had no way at all of getting home from Woolston. We were stranded there. Talk about planning in advance. In the event, Bob and I had no choice but to walk the twenty miles or so back to Lymington.

After the Peeping Toms folded, our bassist John Bod joined another local band, called the Rib Joints. They were a psychobilly group, and my mate Mike Case played in it. So too did Tinley's younger brother Adam from the Stupid Babies, who would find fame in the early 90s as Adamski. In May 1990, I was flying back from Australia, after visiting my parents in Melbourne, and picked up a music paper that was lying around on one of the seats on the plane. Turning the pages, I was stunned to see Adamski had made number one in the charts with his song *Killer*, a collaboration with the singer Seal. I thought that was fantastic and was really pleased for him.

A real tragedy occurred in '84, when Roger Fayers, the landlord of the Old English, died suddenly, at the age of only thirty-two. His wife Fran left the pub soon after, and everyone was devastated. It was the end of an era. Roger and Fran had been great to us, allowing us to be ourselves and virtually giving us the freedom of their pub. The gigs, the lock ins, the camaraderie they shared with us. They weren't ever judgemental or opinionated. They were wonderful people, and I'll never forget them. Roger's funeral in Southampton was packed, and I remember a biker's club, who used to meet up in the Old E once a week, gave him a full guard of honour, riding in procession on their motorbikes behind the hearse.

Around Christmas time, Mike, Wallace, Crocker, Shaun Deering and I travelled up to a party at Paul Gray and Jim Raylor's flat in London. Paul and Jim were good friends, and we knew it was going to be one heck of a do. When we arrived at the flat, the group split up. Shaun and I took the tube up to north London to watch Arsenal play against Watford at Highbury. The others headed off down the pub, and we arranged to hook up again later at the flat, ready for the party. The football match ended in a disappointing 1-1 draw, and we couldn't wait to get back to Paul and Jim's. When we arrived, it was obvious the party had already started. Everyone was well on their way. We had a bit of catching up to do.

Soon, people were turning up from all over the place, and it was rammed in there. The music was good and loud, and everyone was getting trashed. Late into the night, somebody decided to put on the recently released Band Aid single *Feed the World*. They must have played the damned song thirty times on repeat, and I can remember it was driving us up the wall. The party continued well into the early hours, and it was about 4 am when Wallace turned to one of Paul and Jim's friends, and uttered the immortal words 'Don't worry about us, we're rock 'n' roll people.' Merry Christmas everybody.

CHAPTER 4

WAR AND PEACE

The winter months of early 1985 were bitterly cold ones, and there was snow and ice everywhere. One Saturday night, in mid-January, I was drinking with several of my mates in the Londesborough Hotel in Lymington High Street. As we left the premises at closing time, we started getting pelted with snowballs from the opposite side of the road. A large group of pissed-up youths, most of whom I knew, were gathered on the pavement, hellbent on causing trouble. I remember the Maidment brothers, Bob and Pete, were right in the thick of the action. We began throwing snowballs back at them, and before long, loads of other blokes had joined in the mayhem.

Our mate Richard Wallace was out on a date that evening and had taken the girl for a meal at one of the restaurants in town. Wallace and his date were sitting at their table, just getting ready to tuck into their starters, oblivious to what was happening outside in the street. Wallace later told us that a snowball came smashing through the restaurant window and landed right in the middle of the table. Soon, chunks of ice were being hurled through shop windows; I remember somebody chucked one through the glass at Midland Bank.

It was inevitable someone would eventually call the police. Sure enough, they soon arrived, making their way up the hill at the bottom end of town. It was slow going. They began floundering on the ice, as we all laughed at them. Soon we were throwing lumps of ice at the cops and taunting them. They tried arresting some of us, but kept slipping and falling over, although they did manage to nab Pete Golden for mooning at them. Someone lobbed a piece of ice at one of the police officers, hitting him squarely on his helmet and knocking it clean off his head. As he slid helplessly down the street, everybody cheered. We moved on up the High Street in a large group, before finally dispersing and going home.

Not long afterwards, Mike Case, Crocker and I were out on the town celebrating my 22nd and Crocker's 20th birthdays. In addition to Mike there were two guys from the French Foreign Legion drinking with us that night, although I have no recollection of their names, and no idea what on earth they were doing in Lymington at the time. After a pub crawl in the High Street, we thought it would be a great idea to go back to Mike's place to carry on partying.

As we were walking along Stamford Hill, near Priestlands school, a police van suddenly appeared on the horizon, hurtling towards us. It pulled up alongside, and one of the coppers shouted, 'That's them, get them in the van!' Two or three cops then jumped out of the van and told us all we were under arrest for being drunk and disorderly. They grabbed hold of us, and one by one, threw us in the back of the vehicle and drove off to the police station. By now, the French blokes were in tears, terrified of what might happen to them. So much for being hardened Legionnaires.

Upon arrival, the driver of the van punched me in the back of the head and another copper walked over to me and ripped the sleeper earring from my ear. They then threw the five of us into the cells. We hadn't done anything wrong that night, but it was obvious the police were looking for some payback for the snowball incident. They'd been made to look foolish that night, a laughing stock, and wanted to exact their revenge. Seeing us walking down the road earlier, they had seized the opportunity with open arms.

We appeared soon after at Lymington Magistrate's Court. Mr Baker, who'd been the principal at Brockenhurst College while I was there, was the senior magistrate on duty that day. Whilst he was reading out the charges,

Crocker suddenly burst into a fit of hysterics, tears of laughter streaming down his face. Baker was apoplectic with rage, shouting 'Do you think this is funny, eh? Who do you think you are? Pull yourself together, you're in a magistrate's court for heaven's sake!' The upshot of it all was we were found guilty of being drunk and disorderly and received a paltry fine.

Two weeks later, Mike Case came round to my parents' house. My brother Rich had a batch of homebrew beer on the go, and I recall us eagerly drinking the stuff, even though it was nowhere near ready for consumption. After listening to some music by bands such as Joy Division, Gang of Four and Half Man Half Biscuit, we headed off to the Crown and Anchor in town for a sesh. It was in this pub that I first met my future wife Michaela's younger brother, Martin. Mike and I got suitably leathered in there, then made our way up to Long's Wine Bar in the High Street. We walked down the flight of stairs, went up to the bar, and I ordered two pints.

The landlord, who'd only recently moved down to the area, point blank refused to serve us, and told us to leave immediately. When we asked him what the problem was, he angrily said 'We saw you two the other night, out on the High Street, instigating a riot. My wife and I were watching from our bedroom window and saw the whole thing. The pair of you were at the forefront of it all. It's abhorrent behaviour, and completely unacceptable. People like you are not welcome here. Now get out of my bar, before I have you thrown out!'

We both refused to leave, and the landlord was becoming seriously riled. He asked a bouncer standing nearby to escort us off the premises, up the stairs and out the door. The bouncer was a small, bearded, insipid looking chap, and he appeared to be reluctant to get involved. The landlord, who'd clearly had enough by now, shouted 'Right, come on, get out!' and started shoving me from behind, up the flight of stairs, towards the exit.

He was being way too heavy handed, and when we reached the top, he grabbed me forcibly by the back of my neck. I managed to break free from his grip and head-butted him, sending him tumbling down the stairs, which, I'd like to add, is totally out of character for me. On the pavement outside, I was talking to someone when the landlord came flying out the door behind me and put me in a headlock. Wrestling me to the ground, he tried to smash the side of my face into the pavement. I succeeded in getting him off me and walked down the road. Meeting up with Mike again, we headed back to the Crown and Anchor.

We went up to the bar and asked the landlord for a bottle of Teacher's Scotch whisky. He said he'd sell us one at cost price, providing we kept it hidden well away, underneath the table. We sat down and began secretly drinking the whiskey. After an hour or so, we decided we were hungry, so we left the pub and walked to the chippy at the bottom of town.

There was a short, chubby lad who worked in there behind the counter, who we vaguely knew of, called Scotty, who for some reason, reminded me of a young Alfred Hitchcock. Scotty was wearing your classic fish 'n' chips shop workers' blue and white striped apron and wore the silly white hat that went with the job. After ordering a cod and chips for each of us, we hung about, waiting for Scotty to serve us our meals. As he passed us the food, Mike decided he wasn't going to pay for it and walked out the door with the fish and chips. For good measure, I swiped a jar of pickled onions off the counter and trudged off up the High Street eating them.

It wasn't long before we found ourselves outside Long's Wine Bar again. A red mist descended over me, and in a flash of downright stupidity, I hurled the jar of pickled onions straight through the front door, shattering the glass. I tore across the road, running past the Conservative Club, before reaching the top of Grove Gardens. I then doubled back on myself and watched all the fallout from a safe distance. There were coppers everywhere, taking statements from people.

Several days later, I was walking along the High Street with Mike when a police officer approached us. Turning to me with a disparaging expression on his face, he asked if I was the person responsible for throwing the jar of pickled onions through the wine bar window a few nights previously. I replied to the officer that it wasn't my style, and after looking me up and down for a moment, he let the two of us go about our business. Glancing back, I noticed the copper standing there staring after us. It was then that I realised I hadn't heard the last of the matter. Something told me I was going to pay a heavy price for the pickled onions incident.

A fortnight later, a well-known local police officer called Chris Sawyer showed up at my parents' house and informed my father that they knew all along I was the guilty party, and that I should do the right thing and hand myself in at Lymington police station as soon as possible. I walked to the station and confessed to the crime.

It turned out that it was that bloke Scotty from the chippy who'd grassed me up. I don't blame Scotty for what he did that night; he was young, naïve and harmless enough, it must be said. Ultimately, he had little choice in the matter; well, supposedly so. Beam me up Scotty, or as I wrote in the chorus to a Bamboo Vipers song many years later, called *Spacewaster*, 'Beat Me Up Scotty', a reference to Star Trek, the classic 60s sci-fi television series people of my generation grew up with. As a young kid, I was mesmerised by that programme.

In court, some while later, I was charged with criminal damage and fined £250. I was also fined £5 for the theft of the pickled onions. The following Friday, the headline in the local newspaper, The *Lymington Times*, read 'Wine Bar Reject Took His Revenge.' A quote from someone who'd been drinking in Long's that night was printed in the report in the paper: 'I was sitting at a table in the bar with my friend, when suddenly, there was the sound of breaking glass and three pickled onions came bobbling down the stairs before settling on the bottom step. We were quite scared, you know.'

It was in 1985 that Mike Case, Crocker and I caught the train up to London to watch The Prisoners and The Sid Presley Experience play at the Klub Foot nightclub, in the Clarendon Hotel ballroom, on Hammersmith Broadway. I remember we were drinking bottles of Merrydown cider and cans of lager on the train and were in a right state when we got off at Waterloo. That night largely remains a blur, but I do recall the police turning up at the gig, with an arrest warrant for The Prisoners' drummer. As soon as he saw the cops, he bolted through the back exit and managed to evade capture.

It was time to get the music out there once more. Mike and I formed Dr Monroe's Office (DMO), an experimental band, if ever there was one. I put some lyrics down on paper, and they were completely unlike anything I'd written before with Peeping Toms. I approached the whole aspect of songwriting from a different angle. Three of the new songs I wrote for the band were *Berlin in the 1930's, Mickey Mouse is Dead* and *Wagbeat*.

I was the frontman and Mike played guitar, using loads of effects to create the basis of the band's sound. Gary Webb was brought in on keyboards, and his friend Mike Harrison played the bongos. We'd forgiven Toby a long time ago for his thieving at Dave and Erk's party back in '82 and allowed him to join on bass guitar. He could never be completely trusted though, and we had to keep an eye on him. We used a drum machine to underpin our mechanical wall of sound. It was an unconventional line up, but DMO were a band ahead of their time.

During DMO's brief existence, we only played a few gigs, maybe half a dozen or so. At the one's we did play, something bad always seemed to happen. We only ever played 30-minute sets, but our music seemed to bring out the devil in people for some reason. For instance, I remember fights in the audience at the Stateside Centre in Bournemouth while we were onstage, which carried on outside in the car park at the end of the night.

Maybe it was our ferocious, uncompromising sound, coupled with the fact that we'd always have a strobe light flashing through the whole duration of our set. We used to play a cover of Cabaret Voltaire's *Nag Nag Nag* as our last song, and I would lie there on the floor convulsing and stick my head directly into the strobe light for a full ten minutes. When I think about it now, it was a mad thing to do, really, but it was part and parcel of what the band was all about at the time.

One DMO gig that'll live long in the memory took place at a private party at the Abbey Hotel in Romsey. Yet again, a coachload of miscreants from the Old English were present. During our set, a full-on fight broke out on the hotel dancefloor between several of the locals and a few of the blokes that had travelled up on the coach from Lymington. At the end of the night, we were loading our gear out of the back door, into the car park, as the coach left the venue. Suddenly, we were surrounded by a group of about twenty irate and highly agitated Romsey guys. They demanded to know whether we were from Lymington. We tried explaining to them that we were in the band, and we were the entertainment for the night, and hadn't been involved in any way in the fight. They were having none of it.

One of them, a horrid, antagonistic little trendy type, lurched towards me with a vengeful look in his eyes. He had a ghastly shaggy perm and a sorry attempt at a moustache, and was wearing a white buttoned-up shirt and one of those skinny ties that were popular in the mid-80s. He was a complete bell-end and reminded me of a shrimpy version of the North American mythical creature Bigfoot. We had a name for those sorts of idiots back in the day: Spide. Species of spide. The bloke got right in my face and screamed 'Come on then, fight me, you fucking bastard! What are you waiting for?' I remember looking over his shoulder, searching for any possible avenue of escape, but on seeing how high the walls around the car park were, realised we were in a hopeless situation.

One of them, a horrible little trendy fucker wearing a buttoned-up shirt and one of those skinny ties that were popular in the mid 80s came right up to me. We had a name for those sorts of idiots back in the day: Spide. Species of spide. He got right in my face and screamed 'Come on then, fight me, you fucking bastard! What are you waiting for?' I remember looking over his shoulder, searching for any possible avenue of escape, but on seeing how high the walls around the car park were, realised we were in a hopeless situation.

One of the Romsey boys suddenly walked over to Mike Harrison and without warning, punched him in the back of the head. I was waiting for them to start attacking all of us, but at that very moment we could hear police sirens, getting louder, heading in our direction. The local dickheads panicked and legged it off down the street and we all breathed a huge sigh of relief.

A friend of ours, Del Hempstead, had driven the band up to Romsey that evening. As the two Mikes, Gary and I climbed into his car, we heard a squeaking sound coming from underneath. Earlier that day, I'd had a lump surgically removed from my arm, and as I rushed to take off the seatbelt, the stitches ripped apart. There was blood all over the place. Anyway, we went to investigate the squeaking sound, and lo and behold, there was Toby, peering up from under the car, whimpering, 'Have they gone yet? Have they gone yet?' He'd been hiding there all along, the coward. It was a pitiful sight. He crawled out and said 'Well, I'm afraid it's every man for himself!' As he opened the car door, expecting a lift home, we made our feelings abundantly clear to Del that we should leave him there to his fate. Toby started pleading with us, 'Come on lads, you can't abandon me here on my own; those blokes might come back and get me. Come on, it's me, your old mate Toby you're talking to here!'

The yellow-bellied little weasel ended up getting a lift back via Lymington Hospital, where I had my wound restitched. Straight after the next DMO gig, at Southampton University, we sacked Toby from the band on the spot.

Around this time, Kev Joyce, the original Peeping Toms drummer, decided to drive to Ipswich in Suffolk to see our old mate Jibber who had recently moved there. Funnily enough, Ipswich is not that far away from Felixstowe, the town where I lived and worked in 1982. While he was there, he somehow managed to set fire to his hair. Kev had previously bleached it, then died it with red henna, resulting in a fabulous luminescent orange colour. He'd crimped his hair up and Jibber passed him a joint while they were both sitting on the sofa. He grabbed a can of hairspray to keep his hairstyle in place and the moment he pressed the trigger, his hair burst into flames.

Fortunately, he succeeded in quickly putting out the fire on his head, but not before the flames had burnt away large patches of his hair.

Not long after Kev's little episode with the can of hairspray, he made the decision to emigrate to Australia with his girlfriend Sarah Tosswell, known as Toz. She was in the same school year at Priestlands as Michaela. Kev and Toz had experienced more than enough of the confines of little towns like Lymington and New Milton, and honestly, who could blame them for wanting out? The petty quarrels and gossiping associated with such places would drive any sane person round the bend. Meanwhile, I was still living there, trapped in a never-ending cycle of getting smashed out of my mind in local boozers, constant hangovers and the comedowns. Something surely had to give.

Not that I regret these times during the mid-80s at all. I had an awful lot of fun, to be truthful. Those experiences shaped the person I am today. In retrospect, it was simply the frustration of being a young man, albeit one with a very different take on the perceived norm, in his early 20s, and thinking, was this really my lot in life? Surely, there had to be something better than this.

I used to lie awake in my bed at night listening to alternative music at full volume through the headphones on my tape recorder and asking myself if there was something seriously wrong with me. It took me years to finally realise that there wasn't. It was everybody else, of course. In my mind, certain other people I knew were the true nutters in this world. The overall perception of madness is a crazy thing to behold. Just when you think you're so far out there that there's no coming back, someone you know well will do something that blows your head clean away. It's mental.

I remember a coach trip up to London, one Saturday, to watch Arsenal play against Queen's Park Rangers at Highbury. I'd recently met a guy nicknamed Goo, whose real name was Martin Gourlay. He was a good mate of Adam Tinley's, and was a total nutjob, if ever there was one. Goo was there on that occasion, and so was Tim Cox, but I can't recall who else was present.

We left Lymington quite early in the morning, and the coach dropped us off at King's Cross around 11am. We immediately made a beeline for the nearest pub. Anyway, we must have been in there for a good two hours, drinking as much alcohol as possible before the match kicked off. There was a good atmosphere in the pub. The jukebox was blaring, and the landlord, who was from New Zealand, was extremely friendly towards us. Goo loved a game of pool and was enjoying taking on all comers.

We'd been buying rounds of beer between us and must have been on our fifth or sixth pint when all hell broke loose. Goo was just about to play a shot with his pool cue, when he suddenly keeled over on the table, and began throwing up all over it. It was mental. The landlord went completely batshit, and screamed out 'What the fuck do you think you're doing, you fucking drunken idiot?' He leapt over the bar and lurched towards us. We instantly grabbed hold of him and literally had to carry him out of there. The man was on his knees. Dragging him up the road, he started babbling incoherently and spewing up again. There was vomit all over his clothes, and he was in a right state. It was barely 1 pm.

We eventually reached the tube station at King's Cross, and collectively hoisted Goo over the turnstile and onto the platform. On the tube up to Arsenal, Goo slowly started coming out of his stupor and began demanding more alcohol, from us, and from total strangers. I told him to hang on a bit longer; he could get beer at the ground, and we were almost there.

We arrived at Highbury in good time for the game and made our way to the terraces on the North Bank. In those days, you could buy three-pint cardboard buckets of beer from the bars inside the ground, and that's exactly what we did. It was an uninspiring game of football, and everyone was bored to tears. At one point during the second half, Goo simply plonked himself down on the terrace steps, swigging his bucket of ale, and started complaining. 'What a load of shit this is. It's one of the worst football matches I've ever seen in my life! I fucking hate Arsenal. Come on you Celtic!' His father, Jim, was Scottish, and they were both avid supporters of all things green and white hooped.

There he sat, beer bucket in hand, slagging off the Arsenal on the North Bank, slap bang in the middle of some of the club's most fervent and violent fans. You couldn't make it up. We had to get him out of the ground pronto, before we all got beaten to a pulp. Carrying him shoulder high from the terraces, while he was still mouthing off, we hurried towards the exit and stumbled out of the ground and onto the street outside.

Unbelievably, we then went on an impromptu pub crawl around north London, before finally managing to get ourselves back to King's Cross in one piece, just in time for the coach journey home. As a footnote, Arsenal won the game 1-0, via a fortunate 67th minute scuffed effort from Tony Woodcock. It was a scrappy game of football, not that anybody cared that much anyway.

Saturdays always seemed to be the day of the week when something insane happened. I was with Goo one afternoon, walking down Lymington High Street, when he started pissing in the doorway of one of the shops. Suddenly we were approached by a Special Constable police officer, a hobby-bobby, as they were known, whose sole intention was to apprehend Goo for what he'd just witnessed him doing. I knew the man from back in my days at junior school. He always came across as a bit weird, but was another one who was harmless enough, to be fair.

Grabbing Goo by the arm, he shouted, 'Right, you're under arrest!' Goo yelled back at him, 'Get your hands off me, I don't know where you've been! In fact, I'm gonna arrest you for assaulting me! You're under citizen's arrest!' The constable, looking flustered and taken completely by surprise, backed off for a moment and stammered, 'Uh, okay, we'll leave it there for now, shall we? But I'm telling you. Don't do it again, or you'll be in big trouble. Do you hear me?' With that, he turned away and carried on walking up the High Street. What a spectacle.

On another Saturday afternoon around the same time, Crocker, Goo and I caught a bus from Lymington to Bransgore, near Christchurch, just over ten miles away. We were heading to a birthday party in the village hall there, after Goo had been invited by the sister of the guy whose party it was. On the bus journey to Bransgore, the three of us were sitting on the back seats drinking bottles of Merrydown cider and cans of lager, and when we arrived at the village hall, we were suitably inebriated.

The birthday boy was a local lad who was nicknamed Tetley, and when he came out of the hall with a group of his mates to introduce himself to us, Goo immediately launched into a loud, drunken rendition of the classic Tetley Tea TV advertisement ditty: 'Tetley, Tetley. Tetley, Tetley, Tetley make teabags. Tetley make teabags make tea.' The bloke completely lost the plot, and boiling with fury, screamed at Goo, 'You what? Are you taking the piss out of me? Eh? Do you want some? Eh? Come on then, I'll smack your fucking head in, mush!'

Goo attempted to appease Tetley by apologising to him profusely and said he honestly didn't mean to offend the man, and that it was only meant to be a bit of fun. Tetley had to be restrained by a couple of his mates, and it took him a long while to calm down. When he finally did, he told the three of us we were not welcome at his party, and to basically fuck off back to where we came from. As it transpired, we ended up getting on the next bus to Lymington and headed straight to the Old English for a few pints, Goo with his tail between his legs. I must admit I was looking forward to that party but never mind.

Goo was certainly a party animal, of that there's no doubt, and probably one of the most mental people I've ever met in my life. I recall one hellraising all-night party at a house in Middle Road in Lymington. Mick Whitlock lived there at the time, along with a posh, eccentric older guy called Leslie Drummond-Rowe. I remember making my excuses and staggering out of there in the early hours of Saturday morning, annihilated. I was immediately confronted by the disturbing sight of Mick and Goo wobbling about all over the place on the pavement outside the house, frothing at the mouth and drinking neat washing-up liquid from out of a plastic bowl. They beckoned me to join them, and I shook my head in disbelief and told them they were fucking nuts, then headed on home. Looking back, I can't believe those guys did that. Where were their heads at? Then again, who am I to cast judgement?

I used to spend quite a lot of time round my mate Barry Hilliard's house in Harvester Way in Lymington. There would always be a load of us there, often partying until the sun came up. One Friday night, Barry, Goo, Hagar and I caught the train from Lymington to Southampton with the intention of getting off our heads. I recall we scored some LSD tabs from a pub in Derby Road, in the heart of the city's red-light district, possibly the Northumberland Arms.

After getting battered in Southampton, we somehow managed to get ourselves to the station in time to make the last train home. When we arrived back in Lymington, Hagar suddenly disappeared and went walkabouts. We eventually found him blindly stumbling around on the railway track near Barry's house, appearing very confused. When we had convinced Hagar that it would be a far better, and safer, idea to get himself off the track immediately and follow us back to Barry's, he managed to see right from reason and finally got his act together.

One album that will always remind me of those long-ago hedonistic gatherings round Barry Hilliard's is *Night Time* by Killing Joke, an absolute classic that we used to play constantly in those days. Anyway, after carrying on the party for a few more hours, Hagar decided in his head that it was time for him to go home. Mumbling incoherently to himself about something only he would know, he tentatively walked out of Barry's front door, and into the early morning light. It was around 9 am by this time.

When I got home myself, a short while later, I couldn't sleep at all. I kept worrying about Hagar, for some reason, and wondered if he was okay. Genuinely concerned as to his wellbeing, I decided to walk the short distance up to his house and check on him. When I arrived there, I could scarcely believe my eyes. Hagar's poor mother was sitting in the front seat of her car, which was parked in the road outside. She was wrapped in a woollen blanket and was fast asleep. Apparently, he'd gone inside the house, climbed the stairs to her bedroom, woken her up, and ordered her to get out of the house. What a scenario. You really couldn't make it up.

By this time, Goo and Mick Whitlock and a mate called Mark Pellow, who was nicknamed Toad, had moved into a house with two girls, in Samber Close in Lymington. Toad later became a roadie for the Cropdusters. Toad and Mick were another couple of friends who are now long gone. One Saturday, after being awake all night partying, several of us decided to head up to London to watch Arsenal play against Everton, in our last home game of the season. Mike had borrowed his dad's car, and we set off early in the morning. Apart from Mike and me, Goo and Tim Cox were present on this occasion.

We arrived in London in good time for the match, and Mike found somewhere to park the car. We then went drinking round some pubs near the football ground. The game itself was a disappointing one from my perspective, as the only Arsenal supporter in our group. We lost 1-0 and Everton scored the winner in the 86th minute, courtesy of a header from Adrian Heath; the smallest man on the pitch that day, would you believe.

It had been an underwhelming season overall, and the fans weren't happy at all.

After the game had finished, the four of us joined in a demonstration outside the ground, demanding the sacking of the manager, Don Howe. The streets were packed with angry supporters calling for his head, and at one point, the situation threatened to explode. Everyone was chanting 'Don Howe out! Don Howe out!' Suddenly, a police officer on horseback arrived on the scene, galloping along the middle of the street. Speaking through a megaphone, he ordered the crowd to disperse immediately. We trudged off to a nearby pub for a couple of drinks before returning to the car for the journey home.

Leaving Highbury that afternoon, we were soon caught up in a major traffic jam. It felt like we weren't going anywhere for hours; nothing was moving at all. Mike had finally had enough of it and drove his dad's car out of the queue of traffic, hitting another vehicle in the process. We managed to make our way out of London without further incident and were soon on the M3 motorway. After an hour or so driving, we decided to stop at Fleet service station for a break.

We'd brought a ghetto blaster along with us and were playing the Peter and the Test Tube Babies album, *The Mating Sounds of South American Frogs*, on tape at loud volume. After parking the car, we wandered into the services, carrying the ghetto blaster, the music going full bore. After we'd had a drink and used the toilet, we began heading towards the exit, to the car park outside. There was this big, drunken bloke standing in the doorway, and as I walked past him, he said, 'Are you looking for trouble?' and punched me in the side of the head. He then attacked Goo, whose arm was in a sling at the time, after he'd recently broken it.

I'll never forget the sight of Goo getting whacked around the face by this lumbering, pea-brained oaf, spinning about one-handed on the tarmac and singing his trademark anthem, *Surfin' Bird*, by the 60s American surf rock band, The Trashmen: *'Ah well a everybody's heard about the bird, a papa ooma mow mow, a papa ooma mow mow!'*

When we'd all got back in the car, I suggested to Mike that he should run that fucker over. He was still standing in the car park, lurching around and waving his fists at us; his mates were sitting in a vehicle parked up behind him. Mike replied that under normal circumstances he would have done, but it wasn't his car, it was his dad's. We drove off, and the idiot got in his mate's car, and they followed us for a few miles down country lanes before we finally managed to shake them off.

Goo sadly died on the streets of London in 2006. Another good man gone. Unfortunately, it was blatantly obvious he was on a downward spiral to self-destruction. Personally, I don't think he ever got over losing his best mate Toad, who was involved in a fatal motorcycle accident in Southampton in 1989. After that tragedy he certainly wasn't the same funny, carefree, mad Goo we all knew and loved. It was evident that he was an unhappy soul. He'd lost a lot of his natural vigour and vitality, and seemed to have withdrawn into himself.

It's incredible how many blokes have nicknames. In this part of the world, I know, or knew of, Erk, Stump, Jibber, Spud, Beagle, Nipper, Toz, Bungle, Jake, Tash, Frogger, Tibby, Ponce, Tromper, Nummers, Spotty, Twistgrip, Sully, Tootch, Nodrog, Dippy, Flash, Hagar, Tickle, Wilbur, Albert, Tigger, Chubbles, Papa T, Fuzz, Squiffy, Dinty, Rampton, Pumper, Toad, Swill, Gus, Nogger, Monkey, Gyp, Denzil, Percy, Spike, Bunders, Grizzly, Hash, The General, Springer, Mutley, Crash, Midge, Bunny, Pixie, Ginge, Bubsy, Mincer, Stig, Podders, Albie, Boomer, Squeak, Jonks, Wire, Tad, Nobby, Tunny, Swoop, Cosmic, Moey, Biff, Sweatie, Rocket and the distinguished Sir Tony Rumsey. The list goes on and on.

The day of my Christening in Hythe, Hampshire in 1963. There are too many of my relations in the photograph to name them all. In the forefront of the picture, Mum's sat down holding me, and Dad's stood directly behind us.

Yours truly as a baby, with Dadcu in his back garden in Cadoxton, South Wales in 1963.

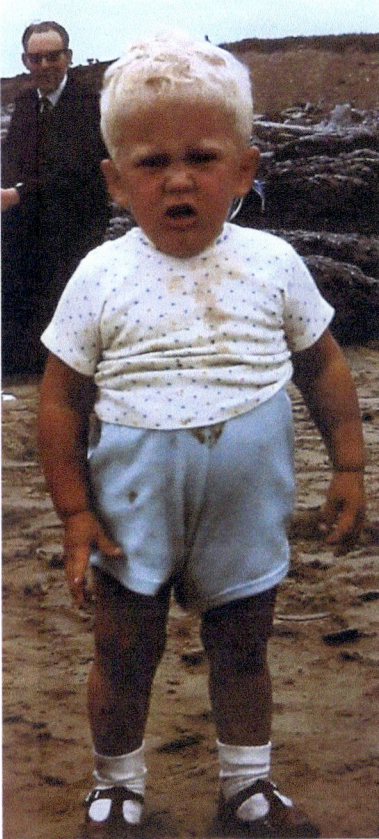

Testardo the hothead. Filthy dirty, and far from happy! As a toddler on a beach in South Wales in the early 1960's.

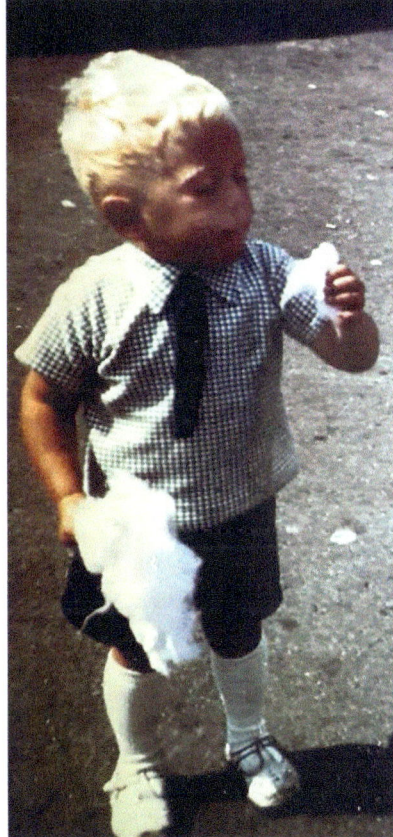

Munching on the candyfloss at an unknown location in the early 1960s.

The boy with the feather in his cap. Wearing the traditional lederhosen my
Grandad bought me. Hythe, Hampshire, 1968.

At a wedding somewhere in Wales in the mid 1960s. Left to right: Myself, Dad,
Nanny Nee, Mum, my sister Gail and Dadcu.

Out on the town. My parents with their great friends the Waglands, at the splendidly named Waterside International Rubber Club in Blackfield, Hampshire in the 1960s.
Left to right: Dad, Bill, Mum and June.

Sneering for the camera in the foyer of The Old Bank House wine bar in Lymington in the summer of 1980. Photo: Rick Cook.

My first band, The Screws, pictured in 1981. Left to right: Richie Morant, myself, Dave Edwards, Dave Dutton and the late Melvin Cope.

Peeping Toms gig at Ye Olde English Gentleman pub in Lymington in 1982. Note the red Jibber backdrop behind our drummer Kev Joyce.

Dinner jacket and fingerless gloves. Giving it some with Peeping Toms at Ye Olde English Gentleman pub, Lymington in 1983.

The last incantation of Peeping Toms, with guitarist Roger Figgures in the foreground. Onstage at Mr Kyp's, Poole, Dorset in 2018. Photo: Paddy Covey

The Cropdusters at Bampton's Farm, Lymington in 1986. Left to right: Roger Figgures, Mike Case, Cob Cook, myself and Bill Haley Photo: Ollie Butler.

Painting the first Cropdusters backdrop with Roger, Mike and Bill in the back garden of our house in Broad Lane, Lymington in 1986. Photo: Carole Morris.

The Cropdusters Hard Times EP was the band's first record, released in 1986. This is the colourised version of the picture that was used on the front cover. Photo: Ollie Butler.

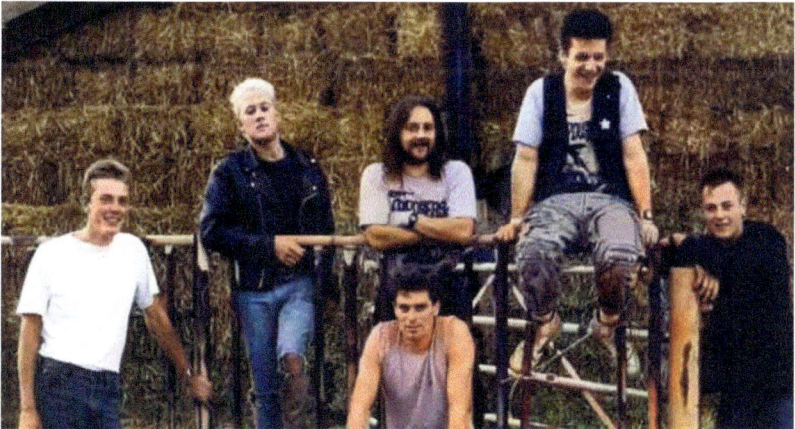

1987: the Cropdusters down on the farm again. Left to right: Bill Haley, myself, Cob Cook, Roger Figgures, Marcus Stott and Mike Case. Photo: Ollie Butler.

The Cropdusters and crew outside Seale Hayne Agricultural College, Devon in 1987.
Left to right: Bill Haley, Roger Figgures, myself, Marcus Stott, Mike Case, Rod Hamilton,
Cob Cook and Brian Goodall. Photo: Ollie Butler.

The Cropdusters onstage at a festival somewhere in Europe in 1992. During the band's
initial eight-year existence, we played so many gigs it's nigh on impossible to remember
the exact details of them all.

The Cropdusters at Castell Coch in Wales on the Just Poppin' Out to Fight a War tour in 1988.
Left to right: Cob Cook, Roger Figgures, Mike Case, myself, Marcus Stott and Bill Haley.
Photo: Ollie Butler.

Joe Strummer and the Latino Rockabilly War outside the coach the band hired from
The Cropdusters for the Rock Against the Rich UK tour in 1988.

The Cropdusters and crew at the U4 Club Vienna, Austria after the final date of the band's first European tour in 1989. Left to right: Cob Cook, Mike Case, Dave Bindon, Rick Smith, myself, Marcus Stott, Rod Hamilton, Bill Haley and Roger Figgures.

On tour with The Cropdusters in Germany. Marcus watches on as his brother Krish chisels out pieces of the Berlin Wall. December 1989.

The Cropdusters smashing the hell out of it onstage at a festival somewhere in Belgium in 1992.

This machine kills Cropdusters! In a hotel room in Amsterdam, Holland in 1991, after a banging show at the Melweg. Left to right: Steve Simmons, myself, Mike Case, Marcus Stott, Rampton, Rick Smith, Cob Cook and Roger Figgures. Photo: Krish Stott.

With my daughter Nancy when she was a tiny tot, in my parents' back garden
at their house in Sandy Down, Boldre, Hampshire in 1999.

At the King Guesthouse, Phnom Penh, Cambodia in 2005. The King and his wife are
standing to my left in the picture, and on my right are two of their female relatives.

Feeling all right with the crew! Drinking cans of Angkor beer with the locals in a bar opposite the Tuol Sleng genocide museum, Phnom Penh, Cambodia in 2005.

Old punks never die! My family on Dad's 80th birthday in 2013. Left to right: myself, my brother Richard, my sister Gail, Mum and Dad. Photo: Michaela Morris.

It ain't half hot mum! Relaxing with Michaela one evening at a restaurant in Columbo, Sri Lanka in 2015.

Michaela and I at an elephant sanctuary near Yala National Park in Sri Lanka in 2015.

Drinking cocktails with Michaela at my 50th birthday party in the Freebird Bar and Grill, Phnom Penh, Cambodia in January 2013. A manic night indeed!

Our wedding day at St John the Baptist Church in Boldre, 4th May 2013.
Left to right: Dad, Mum, myself, Michaela, Michaela's mum Maz and her dad Gordy.

Michaela with the late Kak Channthy of the Cambodian Space Project at the Hyatt Regency hotel, Phnom Penh, Cambodia on New Year's Eve 2011. A night I'll never forget! Photo: The author.

Sue Chester's wake at Chat's Palace, Hackney, London in October 2013. Left to right: Steve Elliott, Dave Dutton, Becca Chester, Marcus Stott, myself and Mark Tinley. Photo: Michaela Morris.

The centre of the universe. Lymington High Street as it was in the 1980s.
The Old Bank House Bar and Restaurant is visible at the left of the picture.

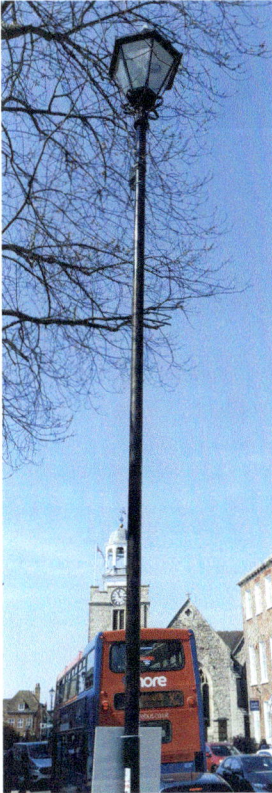

The infamous lamp post in
Lymington High Street, scene
of my arrest in 1982.
Photo: The author.

Dave Dutton's wedding reception at the Master Builder's,
Bucklers Hard, Hampshire in March 2019.
Left to right: Dave's dad Barry, Dave and myself.
Photo: Michaela Morris.

My daughter Nancy and I together at the Snakecatcher pub in Brockenhurst, Hampshire in 2023.

Michaela and I hanging out with the punks and a smiling policewoman at the 2012 Rebellion Festival in Blackpool. Photo: Marcus Stott.

My father and I at the annual summer fete at Birchy Hill Nursing Home in Sway, Hampshire in 2016.

Michaela and I holding endangered baby Tasmanian Devils at the awesome
Australian Reptile Park in Somersby, New South Wales in 2017.

Michaela and I at the stunning
Blue Mountains in New South Wales,
Australia, 2017. What a day that was!
Photo: Kev Joyce

In Le Tigre De Papier bar with Michaela on
Pub Street in Siem Reap, Cambodia, 2019.
Photo: Sarah Tosswell Joyce.

The original Bamboo Vipers line up onstage at the Hope and Anchor, Islington,
London in 2014. Photo: Paddy Covey.

Onstage with Bamboo Vipers at the Bandit Country Spring Smasher event at the Masonic Hall in Lymington in April 2024. Photo: Tony Jones.

The new Bamboo Vipers line-up outside Untapped Talent rehearsal studio,
Southampton, 2025. Left to right: Rich Bartram, James Jenkins, myself, Lee Duffel
and Steve Hayward. Photo: Ifelse Photography Agency.

Bamboo Vipers supporting Peter and the Test Tube Babies at the New Cross Inn,
London in December 2024. Photo: Sarah Rodriguez.

The wax model of myself on display at the Madame Tussauds Museum in London, 2024.
Photo: Sebastian Staveley.

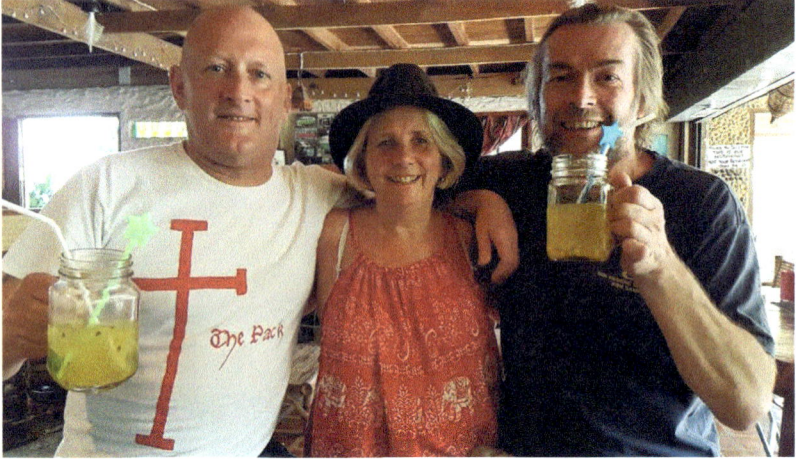

Michaela and I drinking gin with our great friend, the late Richard Wallace, in a bar in Pai, Thailand in 2016. That was an unforgettable day.

Tank as a very young puppy in our back garden in Pennington in the spring of 2020.
Photo: Michaela Morris.

The original shed that eventually became a pub, in our back garden in Pennington in the spring of 2020. The pub is named Ye Olde English Gentleman, in honour of the infamous Lymington establishment. Photo: Michaela Morris.

The bar area of the pub as it looks today, complete with optics and a whole lot more. April 2025. Photo: Michaela Morris.

Inside the pub extension we call The Snug, with Tank in the foreground of the picture. April 2025. Photo: Michaela Morris.

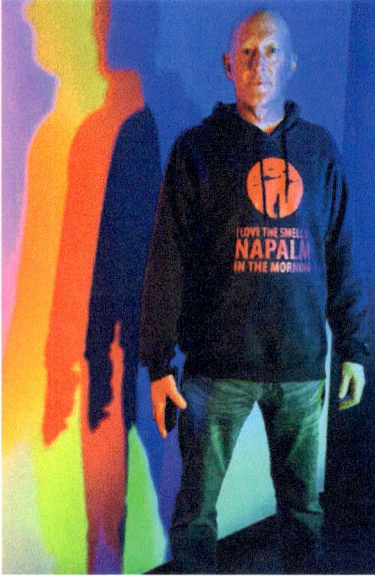

I'm at the Toronto Museum of Illusions in Canada in this picture, which was taken in December 2024. What a mind-bending experience that was!
Photo: Michaela Morris.

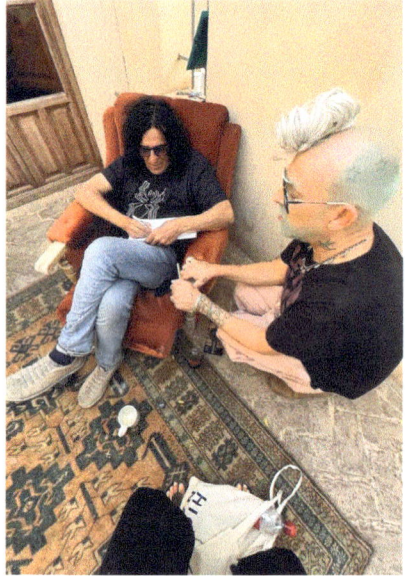

Adam Tinley (Adamski) getting Jaz Coleman of Killing Joke to sign my 60th birthday card at a music festival in Europe in 2023.

Drinking Singapore Sling cocktails in a restaurant in Ho Chi Minh City, Vietnam. March 2023. Photo: Nancy Quinn-Morris.

My good Cambodian friend Thol and I at the Freebird Bar and Grill, Phnom Penh, Cambodia in March 2023. Photo: Nancy Quinn-Morris

Michaela indulging her passion. Photographing wildlife at the Lymington and Keyhaven Marshes nature reserve. Photo: The author.

THE PEEPING TOMS
Lymington Old English

IN YACHTY Lymington, where most other musicians are bald, grey-haired or jolly sailor-boys at heart, The Peeping Toms are always good fun. Few weekend sailors and their pale, seasick girlfriends venture as far as 'The Old English' to drink snakebite and rough cider and boast of arm-wrestling and body-building.

The sound is fast, hard and never falters. Most songs mock or celebrate local heroes and local humbugs, the satire is good-humoured though, even affectionate. Ken Dodd cover versions are as likely as the admired Killing Joke. Who could fight during "*Nicknockynicknocknickynockynoo*"?

At their best, fact and gossip blur with fantasy as in 'The Ballad of Nogger Sprockett'. The gnarled old fisherman, greedy for flatties, is himself devoured by a legendary white whale, called 'Spunker', only to return, like Jonah, from the monster's mouth.

See The Peeping Toms; they're better than most.

Colin Insole

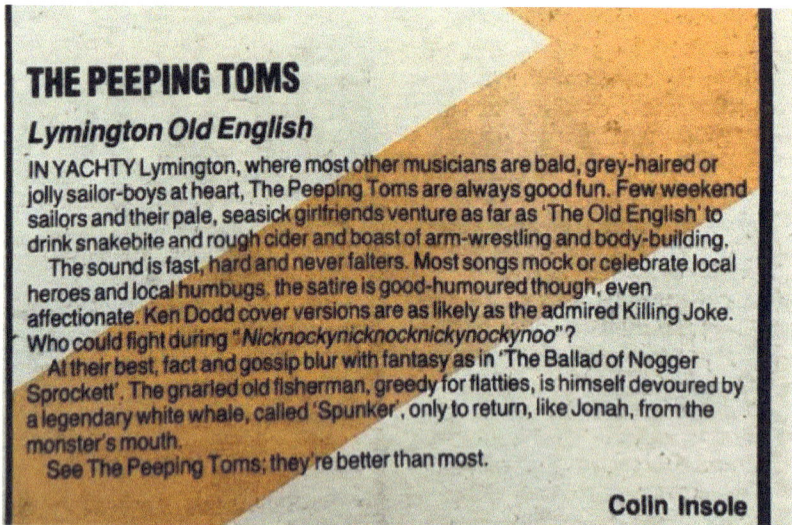

Colin Insole's review of a 1983 Peeping Toms gig at Ye Olde English Gentleman pub in Lymington, which was printed in the national music paper New Musical Express.

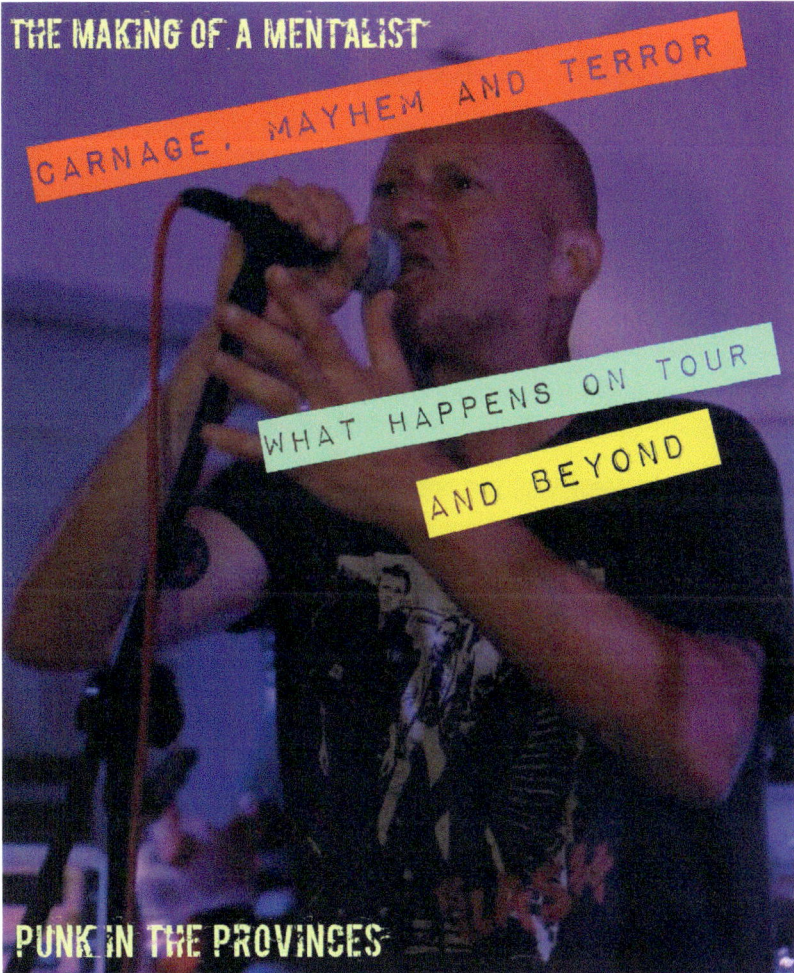

THE MAKING OF A MENTALIST

CARNAGE, MAYHEM AND TERROR

WHAT HAPPENS ON TOUR

AND BEYOND

PUNK IN THE PROVINCES

CHAPTER 5

THE CROPDUSTERS

It was now 1986, and high time we put another band together. Roger Figgures was up for it, and so was Mike Case. Ex Rib Joints drummer Graham 'Bill' Haley had been playing drums in the London-based rock 'n' roll/psychobilly band The Highliners, and bassist Mike had been involved with that band also. Deciding on what to call ourselves, we struggled for a while to find a name everyone agreed upon, before eventually settling on Beware Goroth the Transparent-Winged Wood Aphid. Looking back, it was an utterly ridiculous name for a band; although, I must say, it seemed funny as fuck at the time. During rehearsals in Roger's Garden shed, we'd periodically bring out the 'Beastie Bag', which contained various flying insects, either dead or alive, which we'd collected for some bizarre reason in and around the shed. The contents of the Beastie Bag included mosquitoes, midges, wasps, bees, hoverflies, moths, daddy-long-legs and an ichneumon fly, which Richard Wallace called a Nanette Newman fly.

We were all big fans of The Pogues and The Men They Couldn't Hang, and liked the way both bands used traditional instruments to complement their predominately rock sound. We decided to go down the same route. By the late spring of '86, we were up and running. The four of us had written several songs that we were more than happy with, and we thought getting a fiddle player in the band would be the icing on the cake. Enter Cobert Cook. Cob was a few years older than us, and a great musician. He was enthusiastic about what we were doing musically and couldn't wait to get on board.

One thing had to change though, and that was the name of the band. The keyboard Gary Webb was using in Doctor Monroe's Office had a single engine crop duster pre-setting. The Cropdusters. There was the band name staring us right in the face. It fitted perfectly with the music we were creating, which was a blend of American hillbilly and traditional Irish with a punk rock energy. In the beginning, a good friend of Cob's, a guy called Yanny, came in on saxophone with us. Yanny didn't hang around for long though and only played a handful of gigs with the Dusters.

The first ever songs we worked out for The Cropdusters were *Southern Life* and *Just Poppin' Out to Fight a War*. We got on a bit of a songwriting roll, and other early Dusters compositions included *God Damned No Good Coyote*, *Hard Times*, *Yesterday's Cakes*, *Stompin' Through Siberia*, *The Lady Next Door*, *Can't Slow Down on the Old Hoedown*, *Hillbillies on Moonshine* and *Jammit O'Reilly*. We also covered a couple of songs: *Chicken Train* by the Ozark Mountain Daredevils, and *John Henry*, an old traditional American tune.

I'd been living in a house in Southampton at the time, with Goo and Toad. After leaving that place, I moved in with Cob, his wife Sharon and their two young daughters, Lucy and Rose, in their house in Bay's Road, Pennington. I hadn't been living there long when it all went tits up. Cob took his family on a well-earned holiday to Portugal, and I was entrusted with looking after the house. One Saturday afternoon, a load of us hit the Old E and got battered. There was Crocker, Toad, a guy called Geoff Bloom, a girl called Donna Woodford and me.

We staggered out the pub and headed back to Cob's for a session. Everything was going swimmingly; the music was on, and we were all getting progressively pissed and royally stoned. Spirits were high, but all that changed when suddenly, there was an almighty smashing sound and Cob's twenty-gallon fish tank exploded into pieces all over the living room floor. One of the stereo speakers had vibrated off the shelf and fallen onto the tank. We just sat there, totally stunned, watching Cob's lounge rapidly filling up with water as tropical fish flipped around everywhere. Panicking, Toad went to pick up the soaking wet speaker and got an electric shock in the process. It was nuts.

After regaining our composure, we set about saving as many of the fish as possible and scooping up the water in buckets, which had now flowed into the kitchen and hallway. We were fighting a losing battle.

Just then, there was a knock at the front door. Everyone instantly became deathly silent, and Crocker peered through the curtains and whispered, 'Oh fuck, it's Cob's parents!' This was turning into a bad dream. In a low voice, I asked Crocker if he'd locked the door behind him when we'd returned from the pub, as he was the last one into the house. He said he was certain he had, and we closed the lounge door.

We sat down on the sofa with our ankles deep in water, praying Cob's parents would go away. The seconds felt like hours, and the tension was palpable. Then, we heard the door handle slowly turning, and Cob's folks letting themselves into the house. After an agonising few seconds, we heard them splashing through the water along the hallway, before tentatively opening the living room door.

There in front of us, stood Cob's dad Bob, with his wife Esme beside him, a look of horror on their faces. At that moment, a gush of fish tank water washed a frog towards Bob. I'll never forget it leaping onto his shoe and looking up at him and croaking adoringly. Esme then said to me 'They're coming back from holiday tomorrow.' They both turned away, and sloshed through the rising water, out of the front door, shaking their heads, the frog hopping speedily behind them. I don't blame the frog for wanting out of there sharpish; we were a nightmare in those days.

We managed to clean up all the carnage, although it was a long time before the waterlogged lounge carpet dried out properly. When Cob and Sharon returned home from Portugal the next day, I explained to them what had happened. They were genuinely cool about the situation, although understandably unimpressed. Crocker and I were determined to atone for the damage, although I accept sole responsibility for the disaster in the living room that day. Ultimately, it was me who was supposed to be looking after the house, and probably me who'd turned the stereo up to full volume, causing the speaker to fall crashing down onto the fish tank.

A week or so later, we bought Cob and Sharon a new tank and some brightly coloured tropical fish, plus a small green frog to go in it. As it turned out, Crocker had been wearing his Charles Manson T-shirt on that fateful day, and every time he wore it, something bad happened. That was the last time he ever donned that T-shirt; it was cursed.

Another mad Saturday incident occurred not long afterwards. A few of us had got pissed in the local pubs and had taken some LSD. I remember we went to Beagle, the local comedian's house, to pay him a visit. Beagle was obsessed with Second World War movies and had stacks of them on video. He would watch films like *The Dambusters, The Bridge on the River Kwai, Stalag 17, Dunkirk* and *The Great Escape* repeatedly. He knew every single word spoken in these movies and would march about the living room doing impressions of the various characters. It was funny as hell.

After a while, when we couldn't handle watching yet another WW2 film, we said goodbye to Beagle and headed off down the quay. I decided to take a running jump off the quayside onto a pontoon below. I missed the pontoon completely and plunged straight into the water. I was wearing a pair of heavy paratrooper boots that day and began sinking fast. I remember the weirdest thing about this was that I knew I was probably going to drown, but I couldn't stop laughing at my predicament. The acid had really taken hold by then. It was ridiculous.

Once more, somebody saved my ass; this time by reaching down from a boat that was moored in the harbour and pulling me up out of the water to safety. I thanked the person profusely, then walked to the Crown and Anchor pub just up the road. Drenched in seawater, I went straight up to the bar and ordered a pint. Someone later told me that after I'd fallen in, the only thing they could see was my black felt hillbilly hat floating on the surface.

Reminiscing about this incident recently with Roger Figgures, he said to me that when he turned up at the quay a short while afterwards, it was to a scene of utter carnage. Understandably, he wondered what the fuck was going on. Earlier, on the spur-of-the-moment, our mate Fitzy had stolen a dinghy from somewhere on the marina and was rowing it haphazardly towards the Wagon and Horses pub on the other side of the river, totally out of his face. It was complete bedlam. I'm not sure exactly what happened to Fitzy, but I knew he was okay when he materialised later that evening in the Old English, appearing his usual self, as right as rain. Me and my mates had a right laugh that day, make no bones about it, and yet again I'd lived to tell the tale. On reflection, some of the stuff we used to get up to back then was crazy beyond belief. It really was.

Things eventually returned to normal in the Cook household, although I'm not sure what I mean by the word 'normal.' The band often had songwriting sessions round there, which could go on for hours at a time and always turned out to be productive. Cob's younger brother, Rik, was periodically staying at the house, and he became the first official Cropdusters manager. I recall a prank played on Cob, that I'm pretty sure Rik was involved in.

Cob had a mate, a biker called Chris Harvey, who died recently, who lived in nearby East End in the New Forest. One day, while Cob, Sharon and the kids were out, Chris turned up on his motorbike. He walked into the house chuckling to himself, with an American bullfrog tadpole in his hand which he'd bought from a local tropical aquarium. He went over to the new fish tank and dropped the tadpole into the water. Chuckling even louder now, and with a devious look on his face, he said 'Don't tell Cob I put that thing in there. These bullfrogs grow to enormous sizes. In no time whatsoever, it'll be eight inches long!'

Somewhile later, after a hot knife session in the kitchen one night, Sharon, Cob, Rik and I were relaxing in the lounge, watching television. Cob suddenly leapt up off the sofa, gobsmacked, exclaiming 'What the hell's that fucking thing doing in my fish tank?!' There, sitting on a rock in the tank, was a massive American bullfrog, with the small frog we'd bought Cob hanging from its mouth. Only its legs and webbed feet were visible. I jokingly told him Chris Harvey was the guilty party, and luckily, he saw the funny side of it all.

Cob and Sharon's box-like downstairs toilet was a place to behold. From the moment I first moved into their house, the toilet was transformed into something I can only describe as a shrine. Over the course of the following few years, its walls were plastered with so much nonsensical graffiti it was staggering. Visitors to the house would add their own personal touch to the walls by drawing pictures and scribbling words on them with coloured marker pens. There was even a comic strip featuring the dubious exploits of Toby, who'd been a member of my old band Dr Munro's office, before being sacked. That little toilet was unique, if nothing else.

Most of the time I spent living at Cob and Sharon's was spent in their kitchen. I recall going through a strange phase early on after moving in with them when I couldn't help but read everything backwards. For instance, on a shelf in the larder there might be jar of sardine and tomato paste. In my mind, it was a jar of enidras and otamot etsap. A tin of Minestrone soup would appear as enortsinim puos, and to me, a packet of beef burgers in the freezer would be a packet of sregrub feeb. I wasn't the first person by any means to engage in this proclivity. Mick Whitlock used to call his Consulate cigarettes Etalusnocs. 'Hey, funnels! Has anybody seen my packet of Etalusnocs?' he'd ask.

It took me an awful long while to shake the overwhelming habit of reading things back to front. Whether it be labels on food products, road signs, billboard posters, book titles or whatever, I simply couldn't help myself. It became all-encompassing, compulsive and more than a little frustrating, and to a certain degree, infuriating. In retrospect, maybe I should have taken the time out to learn to speak the English language backwards properly, full-stop; or on another completely different level, lived my whole life in reverse, as Marcus Stott, the Cropdusters banjo player once suggested: Have my ashes scattered, get cremated, have a funeral, die, get married, buy a house, go to work, attend school, be born, be conceived.

Was I cracking up? Saw I gnikcarc pu? Thankfully, I realised soon afterwards that I probably wasn't. Discussing it all with my wife Michaela recently, I mentioned how brilliant it would be to have the ability to speak the English language back to front, fluently. People would obviously wonder what the hell you were going on about, but surely there might be scope to make yourself a fair bit of money in some way. An opportunity not to be passed up, maybe. In the long run, it really doesn't matter, because it ain't gonna happen.

We had some right laughs at Cob and Sharon's house in Bay's Road. One day, a local man known as the General – I never did learn his actual name – appeared out of the blue. He was idiosyncratic in anyone's estimation. Wearing a pair of National Health glasses and one of those tight-fitting, old-fashioned crash helmets, he arrived on his moped to deliver a package to the person living next door. Apparently, this person had lost the package, maybe having accidentally dropped it somewhere in the road. The General had obviously seen it there, and reading the address on it, had decided to deliver it to its rightful owner.

Cob and I were watching out of the lounge window when the General turned up with the package. Switching off the engine on his moped, he dismounted and knocked on the neighbour's front door. The person opened it, and appeared genuinely grateful, thanking him for his kind deed. As soon as he got back on his moped, he produced a walkie talkie from somewhere, and speaking into it, relayed the words, 'Control, do you copy? I say control, do you copy? Package delivered. Another successful mission completed. Beep beep. Transmission over.' He then rode off, no doubt on another Good Samaritan mission. I ain't joking, that man was barking.

Earlier in this book, I wrote quite a bit about the Morey family. Well, as it turned out, they didn't all live together under the same roof in a council house in Pilley. One of them lived in a place directly opposite to Cob and Sharon. He used to sit in his living room for hours on end, staring out the window, eyes keenly focussed on his immaculately cared for front lawn. If so much as a single tiny leaf happened to be blown by the wind onto the lawn, he was out there like a shot. He'd pick up the leaf, examine it for a second, then take it back indoors with him. Moments later, you would see him staring out of the window once more, waiting for the next leaf to land on his lawn, repeating the pattern over and over again.

Cob once told me about a plant called Datura stramonium (also known as Jimsonweed). He'd read somewhere that it caused intense, sacred, occult visions, and that tribes in Central America used it during initiation ceremonies. They would walk barefoot through fire and not feel any pain. I thought it sounded great, and he recommended I go down to a chemist in the High Street and buy some Potter's Asthmatic Remedy. Cob reckoned Datura stramonium was one of the main ingredients in the product, and if you put just one teaspoonful of the stuff in a cup of tea, and drank it, it would seriously fuck you up. And boy, didn't it just.

I foolishly took Cob's advice on board, and headed off to Smith's Chemist in town, and bought a tub of Potter's Asthmatic Remedy, which came in the form of dried, finely cut green leaves. The product was meant for people with breathing problems, and you were supposed to pour a small amount onto a saucer in an enclosed room. You then lit the leaves and breathed in the fumes. It was supposed to act like an inhaler and clear the chest. Taken properly, it was purportedly harmless, but the stuff is highly toxic when ingested.

There were three of us willing to take up the Potter's Asthmatic Remedy challenge; myself, Tim Cox and Goo, surprise, surprise. After putting a teaspoon of it in our cups of tea and slurping it down, we left Cob's house, and walked to the Old English pub. I remember thinking, there's no way the landlord, Dave Poore, was going to let Goo in there, as a couple of weeks previously, he'd caught him making faces at him in the mirror behind the bar. He'd banned Goo on the spot, and it was non-negotiable.

We were sat in the Old E Garden waiting for the pub to open at 6 pm when I suddenly felt the Datura start to kick in. The landlord then appeared outside the back door, and upon seeing Goo, told him he was barred, and that was the end of the matter. Goo then rose from the picnic table we were sitting at and lunged over and picked up a sign off the ground and attempted to hurl it through the pub window. Dave Poore asked Goo what the hell he was on, and then Goo's legs suddenly turned to jelly, and he collapsed into the bloke's arms.

I don't know what happened to Goo that night, or indeed Tim, but I recall sitting inside the Old English unable to even take a sip of my pint of beer. Gary Webb's sister, Lisa, was there, and she said, 'Come on Shaun, I'm driving you home.' The trouble was, although I now lived at Cob and Sharon's place, in my addled state of mind, I was convinced I was still living with my parents in Broad Lane.

Lisa helped me out of the pub and drove me to my folks' place, a short distance away. When we got there, I babbled something incoherently to her and staggered off looking for the key to the back door. Somehow, I managed to find it and let myself into the house. The next thing I remember was lying on top of my brother, who was fast asleep in his bed. I was so out of my head; it was just unreal. I don't know what happened next, but I then found myself crouching in the wardrobe in my old bedroom. I honestly cannot recall anything else from the rest of that night. Potter's Asthmatic Remedy was eventually withdrawn from the shelves in 1988.

I remember some of the earliest Cropdusters gigs took place in local pubs, in the early summer of '86. There used to be a place in Southampton called Maddos, which a few of us would travel up to on Friday nights to score. It was utterly insane in there. People would brazenly snort lines of speed off the bar, and the staff would do the same. Maddos was a biker's bar, but it attracted all kinds; Punks, goths, metalheads, ageing hippies, petty criminals, drug dealers, tramps, misfits and deviants. There was an atmosphere of danger lurking round every corner in that place. It was edgy, exciting and it was real. It had a great vibe, and we loved it in there. The music was always cranked right up, and at weekends, you could hardly move, it was so rammed. One Friday night, we headed up to Maddos to watch Fester and the Vomits. and Bruce Roberts asked the Dusters to get up and play a few songs during their break. It was on that night we first got talking to Gus, the band's bassist. He's a cracking guy, and I'm still in touch with him today.

Other early Cropdusters gigs included the White Horse Inn at Milford-on-Sea, the Speckled Trout and Stanley's Country Club in New Milton, The Cliff Hotel and The Angel in Southampton, and of course, the Old English in Lymington. The band played at a music festival in the grounds of the Shirley Holms Drug Rehabilitation Centre, in the New Forest. The festival was called Just Say No, and Fester and the Vomits also performed there. Another festival the Dusters played at was Party in The Park, in Hogland's Park, Southampton. There was a serious amount of people there that day, and we were gaining a reputation for our frenetic live shows. We were also building up a sizeable following.

In June, I attended Glastonbury Festival for the first time. I've only ever been there twice, in 1986 and 1987. Every member of the band went to Glastonbury '86 and we flew our ragged homemade Cropdusters flag high in the sky outside one of our tents in the camping area where we were staying for the weekend. I recall thinking that the festival was completely on another scale. The number of tents and vehicles on site, and the sheer volume of people attending the event was mind blowing.

Some of the acts I remember seeing at the 1986 festival were The Cure, Psychedelic Furs, The Pogues and That Petrol Emotion. For me, the musical highlight of the weekend was the Birkenhead, Liverpool post-punk band Half Man Half Biscuit, who were playing on Stage Two. Their frontman, singer/guitarist, Nigel Blackwell, is without doubt one of the greatest lyricists ever in my opinion, his clever play on words laden heavy with Scouse satire and wit.

HMHB smashed it that day. Tearing through a set of their early stuff, they brought the roof down. They played *Trumpton Riots, Dickie Davies Eyes, I Hate Nerys Hughes (From the Heart)* and *Time Flies by (When You're the Driver of a Train)*, among a host of other classic songs. They were on fire and lit up the stage. They really are a superb band; totally unique and still going strong today.

I'd travelled down to Glastonbury from Lymington in a transit van with some of my bandmates and a few other people on the Friday morning. We didn't even have to pay to get into the festival; we sneaked across someone's back garden and climbed through an unguarded gap in the perimeter fence.

On the Sunday afternoon, after an insanely hedonistic weekend at the festival, we packed away our tents and camping gear and prepared to go home. I remember the journey back to Lymington very well. It was the day England were playing Argentina in the World Cup quarter finals; the match in which Diego Maradona scored his infamous 'Hand of God' goal. We listened to it all unfold on a radio in the van, while drinking copious amounts of wine and cans of beer.

At the '87 festival, I once again got in without paying for a ticket. Like the previous year, I and several of my mates scaled the fence, and making sure there were no security people around in the immediate vicinity, we jumped down onto the site and quickly disappeared into the crowd. I recall watching New Order, Julien Cope and Husker Du. I don't remember much else about that weekend, most of it's a haze, although one funny incident sticks in my mind. The iconic radio DJ, John Peel, was standing chatting to a group of festival goers in front of the Pyramid stage on the Saturday morning. Mike walked over and introduced himself to the great man and told him he was the bass player in The Cropdusters. Mike then pointed towards me and informed him I was an Arsenal supporter. John looked at me and said drily 'Well, I won't be playing any more of your records ever again.' Mike and I cracked up with laughter before wandering off elsewhere. What a classic thing to come out with.

During the autumn of '86, the band played the first of many gigs at the Gander on the Green pub in Bournemouth. They were always great occasions, whether it was a Saturday night or a Sunday lunchtime, and we had some top hoedowns in that venue. At some point around this time, The Cropdusters entered the Southampton Battle of the Bands competition. There were twenty-eight acts taking part in this, and some of them were damned good. I remember we breezed through the heats and semi-finals; making it to the final, which was being held on a Saturday night in November, at the Guildhall in Southampton.

There were four bands vying against each other for the grand prize of £450, plus a considerable amount of free studio time at the Hell's Angels owned P&F recording, in town. Fester and the Vomits were one of the acts who'd reached the final, but I can't for the life of me, recall the other two. I don't really know why, but the Dusters were confident we were going to win the Southampton Battle of the Bands. In fact, so confident of victory were we, that we'd ordered a crate of champagne beforehand, from the off licence above Long's wine bar, to pick up on our way home from the Guildhall, later that night.

It was an unforgettable day. We'd hired two coaches in Lymington, to transport the band's mates and fans to the venue. It made for a wonderful sight, watching all these mainly inebriated people spilling out onto the Guildhall square in such buoyant mood. One of the Battle of the Band's organisers was a well-known guy everyone called Nodrog, Gordon spelt backwards. Nodrog also wrote gig reviews for a Southampton music magazine called Due South at the time.

To make sure it was fair to all the bands contesting the final, the organisers didn't have a pre-arranged running order in place. Instead, it was the luck of the draw whether you came onstage first, second, third or fourth. I pulled the number three out of the hat, meaning The Cropdusters would be performing second to last on the night. The Vomits drew number four.

The Guildhall was packed out that night and the atmosphere was electric. When it was the Dusters' turn to take the stage, there was a huge surge forward of bodies from the back of the hall, and the hoedown began. With Cob driving us on with his manic fiddle playing, we certainly gave it our best shot. By the second or third song, there were 250 odd people going utterly mental directly in front of the stage. The more songs we played, the crazier it got. I'd never experienced anything like it, in any of the bands I'd played in, up to that point.

When we finished our last number in the set, *Southern Life*, the whole place erupted in a cacophony of deafening applause. It was an exhilarating feeling as we walked off stage that night. In the dressing room afterwards, we all agreed we'd given it everything we had, and had done ourselves proud.

The band certainly had some catching up to do on the drinking front, but it wasn't long before we were in the same state as most of the other people in the building. I remember watching the Vomits set, and thinking it's between them or us who wins this competition and takes the prize. They played an excellent gig on the night.

There was a small group of judges who ultimately decided who the winner was for the Southampton Battle of the Bands 1986, and I think Nodrog was the head of the panel, so to speak. At the end of what had been an unbelievably hectic night, by all accounts, he came over to inform me the Dusters had won the competition. I was ecstatic, and so were the other members of the band when I told them the news. We'd only being going a few months and hadn't played that many live gigs up to now. It was incredible what we'd achieved in such a short space of time.

This victory gave The Cropdusters immeasurable confidence in what we were doing, and the necessary belief in going forward with our own brand of music. Of course, the element of fun of playing in a band was a crucial part of our DNA, but we wanted to take the Dusters as far as we could professionally, and honestly believed the future was ours. In jubilant mood, on the journey home, we stopped off at the off licence in Lymington to pick up our crate of champagne. We then headed straight to Cob's place for a celebration party which lasted at least a week.

Immediately after winning the competition, in November, the Dusters went into P&F Recording studio in Southampton to record the Hard Times EP. We recorded four tracks for the EP: *Yesterday's Cakes, Just Poppin' Out to Fight a War, Goddamn No Good Coyote* and *Hard Times*. The studio engineer and co=producer was a great guy called Rod Hamilton. His father, Richard, was a famous painter and collage artist; his innovative work was right at the forefront of the swinging 60s scene in London.

It was Richard who designed the artwork for the Beatles' *White Album*, released in 1968. He also provided the inspiration for the sleeve cover of the band's *Sgt Pepper's Lonely Hearts Club Band* album. The recording sessions were great fun, and we all put everything we had into making a success of our time in the studio. We would work long and hard into the night, and there was never a dull moment. In the long run, everyone got on so well with one another that it made the whole process an awful lot easier.

What I remember about the Hard Times recording sessions was initially the process of operating in a studio setting. None of the band had that much previous experience of recording, and we were always open to any guidance or suggestions that was offered to us. The rhythm section,

Bill, the drummer, and Mike, the bassist, laid down their tracks first. It took several takes before everyone was satisfied with the sound, and that there were no mistakes on the playing side.

Next, it was Roger's turn to lay down his guitar parts. After that, Cob recorded his fiddle. A guy called Deano then added harmonica to sections of *Just Poppin' Out to Fight a War*. When everybody was happy with how it was all sounding, it was time for me to record my vocals. The rest of the band were well happy with what they'd accomplished in the studio, and Rod had done a fantastic job so far. Listening back to the recordings repeatedly, well into the early hours, I thought they sounded fucking brilliant. It was now my turn, and the pressure was on. Cob had completed his work on the Saturday night, and I couldn't wait for mine to begin.

I woke up on the Sunday morning, excited at the prospect of the day ahead. An hour or so later, I was convinced I was going to die. I'd eaten some dodgy bacon or something, and I felt fucking terrible. Anyway, in the age-old spirit of rock 'n' roll, the band picked me up from Cob's house in Roger's transit van and literally carried me into the recording studio horizontally. For me, this was an absolute personal nightmare, but I had a job to do, and the band were working to a set timeframe.

After snorting enough whizz up my nose, I was soon able to function properly again. What you hear of my singing on the Hard Times EP is a combination of acute food poisoning and me speeding out of my head. It was a strange mixture, but somehow, I think it worked. I managed to get my vocals down in good time, and now all that was left to record were the backing vocals. Bruce Roberts and a good friend of ours, Paul Wild, aka the DJ Tony Who, were bang up for the task and sang on *Just Poppin' Out to Fight a War* and *Goddamn No Good Coyote*.

Next up was the drawn-out mixing process. Rod did an excellent job mixing the four tracks, with considerable input from the band members. Finally, after everyone was happy with everything, we had our debut record down on master tape. The *Hard Times* EP was released soon after on the band's own Total Hoedown Records label.

One Sunday morning, we went out to the New Forest for a band photo shoot. Ollie Butler, a mate of ours from Pennington nicknamed Chubbles, took loads of black and white pictures of us. There are photos of the Dusters standing under trees in the woods of the New Forest, strolling towards the camera out on the open plains, leaning against ramshackle rustic sheds, and some of us standing on top of a haystack. We wanted Ollie to capture the typical American hillbilly vibe with his camera that day, and I think he succeeded in doing that, without question. After Ollie had developed all the photos in his darkroom at home, we had the task of narrowing them down and cherrypicking which ones we wished to use on the Hard Times EP cover. For the front cover, we eventually opted for one of the pictures of the band standing on the top of a haystack. When it came down to designing the artwork for the back cover of the EP, Cob and I spent hours one night painstakingly twiddling around with tiny pieces of Letraset. I think in the end, we achieved the desired effect, and the Hard Times artwork has a certain DIY look about it, without a shadow of a doubt. Today, when I look at what's written on the back cover of the EP, I can't help but laugh at the words 'Arnold Cartwright's Nodding Donkey,' which was the name of a fictitious management company made up by a member of the band on the spur of the moment.

Initially, we had 2000 copies of the vinyl pressed. When the EP hit the record stores, it sold out rapidly. Incredibly, in the Southampton music charts one week, it outsold George Michael's *Careless Whisper*, which was sitting at number one in the national music charts at the time. It was totally unreal. People still say to me that out of all The Cropdusters' records the band released, the *Hard Times* EP is the best.

Looking back, I think because it was the first thing we'd put down on vinyl, and the fact that it's so raw sounding, it captures the moment perfectly. It felt great to finally have our musical creativity documented and tangible. As regards the many photos Ollie Butler took of the band that day in the New Forest, I don't know what happened to all the negatives. I did bump into Ollie a few years ago in Pennington Club and asked him if he still had them. Scratching his head and thinking about it for a moment, he said he couldn't remember for the life of him where they were, which is a crying shame, really.

Meanwhile, offers to play at live music venues were coming in thick and fast. After Battle of the Bands, many of the people who saw the Dusters that night, started turning up at our other gigs. I remember a particularly mental one at the Onslow pub in Southampton. It's where I first met a couple called Steve Simmons, nicknamed Flash, and his girlfriend Becky Grant. They couldn't get into the pub that night, it was so packed. The landlord told them the gig was sold out and closed the doors on them. There was no way he was going to let anybody else in. We eventually opened one of the toilet windows, and they climbed through unnoticed.

It was around this time that I began developing an unhealthy appetite for amphetamines. At first, I used speed to give me extra energy onstage. The Dusters music was intensely fast paced and frenzied, and I naively thought by taking it, it somehow enhanced the band's performances. However, it wasn't long before I was indulging in speed every day, gig or no gig. Like any drug, it slowly creeps up on you without you knowing. I'd be whizzing my head off at rehearsals, in the pub, and at home, and I was caught in a vicious circle. I never once injected speed; I always used to snort it up the nose. I found myself needing more and more of the substance, to achieve the desired effect. I'd go nights on end without sleeping, and I became hooked on it, without any shadow of a doubt. I'm a compulsive person by nature, and I guess, deep down inside, I have the addictive gene, like so many other people. Back in the day, we took drugs for fun; although, as I've just mentioned, you need to have your head screwed on properly, as they have the nasty habit of coming back to bite you on the ass.

My amphetamine use caused problems within the band, and looking back, it could easily have derailed everything we'd all worked so hard for together. I continued taking speed at a prodigious rate, probably for the next year or so, before I finally got a grip with the problem and confronted my demons. After that, I took the drug sporadically at the odd gig, or at parties, but never to the extent I was using it during late 1986 and '87. On reflection, it wasn't big, and it wasn't clever. As a footnote, I haven't gone anywhere near the stuff in well over a decade and feel all the better for it.

The Dusters were booked to play in the Borough Arms in Lymington on New Year's Eve. It's a night that lingers long in the memory, but not all for the right reasons. We turned up at the pub early in the day with all our equipment, and Roger began building a stage for the occasion. While the stage was being put together, I went over to the bar and ordered a pint of lager.

I got chatting to the landlady, Rose, and her other half, Dave. They seemed like friendly enough people and appeared genuinely positive about the evening ahead. The band stayed in there for hours, helping Roger build the stage and drinking and socialising with the other customers. It was still only mid-afternoon, but the atmosphere was great, and everyone felt excited about the gig later that night.

When the stage was completed, we began loading in the gear from the van, which was outside in the pub car park. Once we'd set up the PA, drums and guitar amps, we were ready to do our soundcheck. It was now around 6pm, and we blasted through a few songs without encountering any problems. The landlady didn't seem unduly bothered about the music being played at such loud volume in the bar, and we all thought we were in for a great night. We were really up for this gig and couldn't wait to get going.

As the evening progressed, more and more people started arriving at the pub. By 8 pm, you could hardly move in there. It became nigh on impossible to get to the bar, but punters were still turning up, trying to get in. I noticed Rose, the landlady, looking visibly anxious at the scene unfolding in front of her. Around 9pm, there were so many people in the bar, they were squashed together like sardines. At this point, we decided we'd better get onstage straightaway.

As it was New Year's Eve, spirits were sky high with the punters in the audience, and most of them appeared well on their way to oblivion. The Dusters hit the ground running and launched into the first song of our set. The place immediately erupted, and the crowd surged forward towards the stage en masse. People were falling onto the PA monitors and beer glasses were being smashed everywhere. By the time we'd began playing our fourth song, there was a rush of bodies from outside, and the window of the pub door went through. It was unmitigated havoc in there.

Suddenly, I could hear screaming coming from the bar. I looked over, and saw the landlady, her hands clasped tightly against her ears, shaking her head, and basically going berserk. Somebody managed to squirm their way through the crowd to the front of the stage and shouted at us to turn the music off at once, as Rose was having a complete meltdown. We carried on playing for a few more minutes, before finally stopping. Rose then started screaming at everyone, 'Get out! Get out! All of you, get out of my pub now! I can't take it anymore. You'll be the death of me. Get out, the lot of you!'

It was utter pandemonium in there, but gradually the disgruntled punters started leaving the premises, filing out through the door, and walking over a sea of broken glass in the process. When the dust had settled, a couple of the band went off to find Rose, but she was nowhere to be seen. We were all pissed off by now, as we'd put in a lot of time and effort into making this night a memorable one, and we'd only been allowed to play three whole songs, for fuck's sake.

Anyway, we broke down the stage and loaded our equipment into the van, parked outside. We'd agreed a fee for the gig with the landlady beforehand, but as we couldn't find her, decided to return the following morning so we could get paid. Mike and I said we'd come back and make sure we got our money.

Early in the morning of New Year's Day, Mike and I turned up at the Borough Arms and knocked on the back door. There was no answer, so we knocked again. Still no answer. After waiting around for a while, we started banging loudly on the door and shouting 'Come on Rose, we know you're in there. Stop hiding from us and pay us what you owe us!'

A minute or so later, Rose's wrinkled, ashen face appeared from behind the tatty curtain in the window of the door. She began muttering 'Go away, I'm not paying you anything. I should have never agreed to let The Cropdusters play in my pub in the first place. You're all a load of nutters. Now go away, or I'm calling the police!' She then pulled the curtain back across the door window and disappeared, forever. I certainly didn't see that woman about again, and you know what? We never did get paid for that gig.

We're now moving into 1987, and the Dusters have broken onto the London gig circuit. I remember playing at venues such as the Clarendon Hotel on Hammersmith Broadway, the Sir George Robey in Islington, the New Pegasus in Stoke Newington, and because of our friendship with Becca Chester, Chat's Palace in Hackney, as she was working there at the time. Before long, we were playing famous London venues like The Marquee, Dingwall's and the Mean Fiddler. Closer to home, there was the Joiners in Southampton, Basin's nightclub in Portsmouth and the Three Chuffs in Blandford Forum, Dorset.

The Mean Fiddler, in Harlesden, holds a special place in my heart. It was a brilliant venue, and the band played there numerous times. It was run by Vince Power, who had a soft spot for us, and in my mind, some of the best Cropdusters gigs of all time took place in that club. The way in which the venue was set up was ideally suited to a band like ours. It had a 700 capacity and was split into two separate levels. On the lower level, to the left of the stage, there was a bar running the length of the room, and in the centre was the dance floor. On the upper level, a wooden balcony ringed the whole area, and punters could look directly down onto the stage where the bands were playing. It was a truly wonderful venue. I saw the ace fuzzed-up rock 'n' roll trio Screaming Blue Messiahs in the Mean Fiddler one night in '87. They were razor sharp and it was one of the best gigs I've ever been to. I'd gone to the show with Marcus, Becca, Flash and his girlfriend Becky, and we all had a rocking time.

In May, we played at Del Hempstead's wedding at the Masonic Hall in Lymington. Supporting us on this occasion was Crocker's band, the Crunchie Tractors. Half the town must have been there that night, and it was a banger of a gig. The Masonic Hall has a unique resonance about it. It's a great place to put on a live music show, with its ambience and subtle lighting. The bar area out the back is special, and you could easily host a successful event in there. I believe the hall to be a jewel in Lymington's crown, but in relation to contemporary music, an underused one.

Lymington is a wealthy town, best known for its harbour and yachting fraternity, and the place certainly has its fair share of selfish, stuck-up, entitled wankers; just like anywhere else, I suppose. Many of them don't even come from the area; they're incomers. I'm not saying these people are all like it, by any means, and many of them are the total opposite of all that. However, if you go to certain pubs for a drink down here, there's a good chance there'll be some asshole loudly holding court at the bar with his fake accent, stereotypical pink Chino trousers and deck shoes. Some of these people give off the distinct impression they think they're better than you, for whatever reason, and look down on you as if you're something stuck to the bottom of their shoe, an inconvenience. I just shake my head and laugh to myself at their snobbery, because they haven't got a clue about real life. It's all about money with them; the accumulation of material possessions and one-upmanship. I can safely say I've had more meaningful life experiences than most of these fools put together. To an old punk like me, they come across as a bit pathetic, to be honest. At the end of the day, no one's superior to anyone else; we're all only one missed heartbeat away from vacating this planet forever.

Back in the early 80s, when I began drinking in the local pubs in the town, the grief I got from some of these people was unreal, and all because of the way I looked. It was never just the one bloke having a pop; they needed the security of their friends backing them up. If you stared them out, their eyes would invariably dart about nervously before they'd look down awkwardly into their glass of expensive champagne, or whatever else they were drinking.

It was now June 1987, and the Dusters were scheduled to play a gig at the Zap Club in Brighton. We'd contributed a track for a compilation album which was released on *Hag Records*. The song we'd chosen was *Southern Life*, and the purpose of the gig was to showcase all the bands that appeared on the album. We were headlining the event, and with a couple of hours to kill before we were due onstage, we wandered down to the Richmond Arms. There was a half-price tequila promotion in there that night, and I thought I'd neck a few to help fire me up for the gig. It was something I'd later regret, big time.

I recall we hooked up with our mate Podders in the pub, and after a few pints of beer and a load of tequila slammers, we all headed back to the Zap Club. I remember sitting in the van outside the club, drinking cans of lager, when an idea suddenly sprang into my head. Reaching for a tin of spray paint from under the passenger seat, I jumped out of the van and began spraying graffiti across the metal shutters of the closed shops along the seafront: The Cropdusters, Hillbillies on Moonshine, Total Hoedown; that kind of thing. I then got back in the van. Cob was sat in the driver's seat, smoking a brass prototype pipe full of hash and the rest of the band were inside the club, psyching themselves up for the gig.

The band were supposed to be ready to go onstage in about fifteen minutes, when I noticed two coppers walking directly towards us. Someone had obviously grassed me up. Cob immediately threw his pipe out of the driver's door, onto the pebbled beach. One of the cops came up to the passenger door and tapped on the window. I pretended to ignore him. He tapped again, and said 'Come on lad, give us the can.' I wound the window down and, laughing, handed him an empty can of Budweiser. He then shouted at me 'Right, you're under arrest for criminal damage!'

The two cops dragged me out of the van, as I protested to them that our band was due onstage in ten minutes. I suggested they allow me to play the gig, then arrest me immediately afterwards. Of course, they were having none of it. They handcuffed me, and bundled me into a police van, then drove straight to Brighton police station. They charged me with criminal damage and threw me into a cell. At around 2 am the next morning, they let me out and informed me I had to attend Brighton Magistrates' Court in two weeks' time.

I left the police station in a disorientated state of mind. I didn't know where I was, and the effects of the tequila hadn't yet worn off. I remember thinking, surely by now, the rest of the band were in the van travelling home. Trying to get my bearings right, I realised I could smell the sea and stumbled off in that direction. When I reached the seafront, I was amazed to see the Dusters' van parked just up the road. They'd been hanging about for hours, wondering what had happened to me. No one said a word on the journey back. The guys were obviously pissed off with me, and I could hardly blame them.

As it transpired, the lead singer of Flik Spatula, who were on the same bill, Justin Travers, replaced me onstage that night. It was the one and only Cropdusters gig I ever missed. A fortnight later, accompanied by the band's manager, Ashley, I took the train back down to Brighton for my court case. I pleaded guilty to the charge of criminal damage as I really didn't have any choice, and the magistrates fined me around £400.

Not long afterwards, Mike, Stuart Gates and I went on holiday together to Torremolinos in Spain. It was a week-long trip with glorious sunshine, healthy sea air, drinking to excess and debauchery in general. Beforehand, we'd booked ourselves a smart villa to stay in, up in the hills not that far from the town, and we arrived there in the early hours of the morning. Those were hedonistic days, and we certainly made the most of our time out there. During the day, we'd drink ourselves stupid in the villa and make full use of the communal swimming pool on the premises. I recall being completely hammered one afternoon and stripping off my clothes and diving into the pool fully naked. In the evenings, the three of us would walk, or should I say stumble, the mile or so into Torremolinos with the sole intention of getting even more annihilated than we already were. It was mental.

On a personal level, I didn't really like Torremolinos. In fact, I found everything about the place a tad banal, and it was overrun with idiots of all nations. With its naff ex-pat run cafés, bars and restaurants touting for business, the place did nothing for me. It was tacky. Years later, I used my experience of holidaying in that popular Spanish tourist destination as the inspiration for a Bamboo Vipers composition I'd written called *Mainstream.* The opening verse to the song goes like this: '*A timeshare in Torremolinos, Friday at Bill and Jean's. Dancing in the moonlight on cassette. From the Tufty Club to the Caravan Club. Take a stroll after dinner, robotic and regular. Rivers of normality, straighter than an arrow.*'

Around the fifth day of the holiday, we realised we'd nearly run out of money between us. To raise some much-needed funds, Mike and Stuart would play games of pool for cash with strangers in several of the bars in Torremolinos, in the hope of making a quick buck. I recall they were reasonably successful, winning most of their games. I didn't participate as I wasn't very good at pool and left it in the hands of the other two to try and win us some money. When the week was over, we caught a flight back to the UK, and Mike and I headed off straightaway to Wallisdown College in Poole, where The Cropdusters were booked to perform that night.

In July '87, the Dusters promoted a show at Southampton's Mayfair Suite, previously the Top Rank Suite, in celebration of the band's first birthday. It was intended to be one hell of a bash, and there were four bands booked to play the gig. Apart from ourselves, there were Edinburgh's We Free Kings, Fester and the Vomits, and local act Flik Spatula on the bill.

There were 1200 people in there that night, and when we hit the stage, it turned into one fabulous, banging, almighty hoedown. The walls were dripping with sweat, and punters were hanging off the upper-level balcony. It was manic and it was intense, and the band loved every minute of it. I remember Bruce Roberts joining us onstage for *Chicken Train*, and the roof went off. What a way to celebrate your first birthday. It was a belter of a gig, and we were all buzzing afterwards.

In August, the band enlisted the services of banjo player/ multi-instrumentalist and token northerner Marcus Stott. Marcus was in a relationship with Becca Chester, and they were living together in Hackney. The first Cropdusters gig with Marcus on board was at Wellworthy Social Club in Lymington, in September. The show had sold out well in advance, and there were no tickets available anywhere.

Midway through the evening, I opened the fire escape door and saw there was a queue of people stretching about fifty yards down the street. One of the punters complained to me that he couldn't get a ticket for the gig that night, so I let him in through the door. Upon seeing this, all the other people in the queue piled forward, and when the last one was safely inside the club, I closed the door. How the management didn't cotton on,

I'll never know. Maybe they were aware of what was happening and simply didn't care. Anyway, it turned out to be a hot, sweaty, night, and the place was rocking. It was epic.

In the meantime, the Dusters had worked out a batch of new material. Some of the new songs we'd written were *Banjo Hill, Gold Against the Soul, Luddites, Strange Olde Song of the Seas, Proverb* and *You Were the Pilot.* The gigs were piling up, and at one stage, we were playing up to four shows a week: at colleges, universities, nightclubs and pubs. It was relentless.

I remember shows in Winchester, Portsmouth, Bournemouth and Poole, and the band playing at the 1987 Dorset Steam Rally in Stourpaine. The Poole gigs took place at a great venue called Mr C's, and the band subsequently performed there many times. We also played a few shows at Wallisdown Arts College, which was part of the Bournemouth University campus. The band always received a wonderful reception whenever we performed there. We'd had a run of Cropdusters T-shirts printed up, and they sold like hotcakes. At one point in '87, if you walked down Lymington High Street, on any given day, it appeared as if one in ten of the town's inhabitants was wearing a Dusters T-shirt.

I can remember a gig we played in Hereford one Saturday night, just after Marcus had joined the band. I can't recall who was driving the van on this occasion, but I know it wasn't Roger. On the journey up there, he produced this realistic looking toy machine gun water pistol that he'd bought earlier, and was play-acting with it, pretending to shoot people from the passenger door window.

As we reached the outskirts of Hereford, the traffic slowed to a standstill. Suddenly, an angry looking police officer appeared at the driver's side of the van. He started shouting 'Who's got the gun? What the hell do you think you're doing with that? We've got royalty visiting Hereford today, and there are snipers positioned everywhere around here! You were lucky they didn't take you out, you idiots!'

A red-faced Roger admitted his guilt and apologised for being so stupid. He showed the officer the toy gun, explaining to him that it didn't fire real bullets, only water. Satisfied that we weren't hardened terrorists, he let us off with a verbal warning and waved us on our way.

The Hereford gig was a cracker, literally. While we were doing our stuff onstage, someone in the audience broke their leg badly. He'd been caught in the middle of a frenzied hoedown, where anything can happen, and often does. The paramedics arrived on the scene, and he was taken out of the venue on a stretcher, grimacing in pain, to a waiting ambulance.

The trip back down from Hereford the following morning was a memorable one. We'd decided not to travel on the motorway and instead drove across into North Wales. The scenery was beautiful, and at lunchtime we stopped at a pub for a beer. One drink turned into another, and eventually someone in the pub persuaded us to go and fetch our instruments out of the van.

We started playing acoustic renditions of Dusters songs, and the locals loved it. One of the customers bought us all shots of whiskey, then another one bought us more. In the end, people were dancing on the tables, having a whale of a time. We'd managed to turn this quiet idyllic pub into a hotbed of insanity, and it was barely two o'clock on a Sunday afternoon.

As the band kept playing, the landlord came over with a tray of whiskey shorts, one for each of us. He told us the whiskey was from his private stock, and it was only the best. We thanked him and downed them in one. Everything was going brilliantly, until Goo, who'd travelled up to Hereford in the van with us, started becoming lairy. He'd said something to a bloke in the bar which didn't go down too well. The man became irate and told Goo he needed to keep his mouth shut, because he was the local copper around these parts, and if he offended him again, he'd nick him. It was the cue for us to leave.

It was around this time we started realising who our real friends were. There were one or two people from my local area who I'd known for ages who expected to be on the guest list at every single gig. Half the time, they couldn't even be bothered to watch us play. They'd sit backstage in our dressing room while we were onstage, helping themselves to the band's rider, without asking anybody if it was okay. They were leeches feeding off The Cropdusters' name, and they brought nothing to the table. Basically, they were just a tiny group of hangers on. It used to piss me right off when we got back to the dressing room, after sweating blood onstage, to find there wasn't even one beer left in the fridge for the band. The parasites had cleaned us out. Their sense of entitlement was off the scale. Years later, when they couldn't rinse anything else out of me, they didn't want to know. Wankers.

There were even occasions when we'd get off stage and find total strangers making themselves feel at home in our dressing room, eating our food, and stealing our alcohol. If we weren't in a good mood, then it was bad news for these people. I remember a few times, immediately after a gig, where we had to forcibly eject these scroungers, who were taking the absolute piss. Microbes boring into our very soul would be a fitting description of them.

The future was looking great for the band, and things got even better when Mike announced to the rest of us that The Men They Couldn't Hang wanted the Dusters to support them on their upcoming nationwide tour in October. He said Paul Simmonds, the band's main songwriter and mandolin player, had seen us play a gig at the Solent Suite in Southampton, supporting That Petrol Emotion, and he'd been really impressed.

We were ecstatic. I knew Phil Odgers, known as Swill, and his brother Jon, TMTCH's singer/guitarist and drummer respectively, from when we used to go to punk gigs up in London. The Cropdusters had arranged their own 'Foot Stompin' Hoedown' tour for September, and the plan was to then join up with TMTCH to support them on their tour. It was one of the best experiences of my life, and when it was over, none of us would ever be the same again. The tour dates were as follows:

THE CROPDUSTERS FOOT STOMPIN' HOEDOWN TOUR

SEPTEMBER 18th ST. LEONARD'S, MR CHERRY'S

SEPTEMBER 19th CAMBRIDGE, THE ALMA

SEPTEMBER 21st LONDON, FINSBURY PARK, SIR GEORGE ROBEY

SEPTEMBER 23rd BRIGHTON, OLD VIC

SEPTEMBER 24th PORTSMOUTH, BASINS

SEPTEMBER 25th EXETER, BART'S TAVERN

SEPTEMBER 26th POOLE, MR C'S

SEPTEMBER 27th WINCHESTER, ART COLLEGE

SEPTEMBER 29th WENDOVER, WELLHEAD INN

SEPTEMBER 30th HOLBURY, OLD MILL

ON TOUR WITH THE MEN THEY COULDN'T HANG

OCTOBER 3rd MIDDLESBROUGH, TEESIDE POLYTECHNIC

OCTOBER 7th LOUGHBOROUGH, UNIVERSITY

OCTOBER 9th LONDON, GOLDSMITH'S COLLEGE (Dusters only)

OCTOBER 10th ESSEX UNIVERSITY

OCTOBER 16th WARWICK UNIVERSITY

OCTOBER 22nd FOLKESTONE, LEAS CLIFF HALL

OCTOBER 24th LONDON - BRUNEL UNIVERSITY, UXBRIDGE

OCTOBER 26th CARLISLE, STARS AND STRIPES

OCTOBER 27th STIRLING UNIVERSITY

OCTOBER 28th EDINBURGH UNIVERSITY

OCTOBER 29th GALASHIELS UNIVERSITY

OCTOBER 30th ABERDEEN UNIVERSITY

OCTOBER 31st STRATHCLYDE UNIVERSITY

NOVEMBER 1st INVERNESS UNIVERSITY

NOVEMBER 3rd LONDON, KILBURN, NATIONAL BALLROOM

NOVEMBER 5th LEICESTER UNIVERSITY (Dusters only)

NOVEMBER 6th NOTTINGHAM UNIVERSITY

Life on the road proved to be everything we had expected, and a whole lot more. Sure, it's not as glamorous as it's cracked up to be, but the good points overwhelmingly outweigh the bad by some considerable margin. From my own personal perspective, the only negatives were travelling long distances from gig to gig, couped up with six other blokes in a Transit van, day in, day out, for hours on end; although that's not a real negative, as the band always found a way to have fun, whatever the situation. Plus, we had the music playing constantly on the stereo, which I think is a vital component of being on tour.

Sometimes, if we weren't due to perform onstage until very late at night, or into the early hours, it could be draining. At some of the gigs the Dusters played, promotors would require us to be at the venue early in the afternoon, even though we weren't on until midnight, for instance. It didn't happen very often, but I remember us having to hang around for up to twelve hours, just so we could do a soundcheck. With boredom creeping in, and the easy availability of alcohol at these venues, it could be tempting to start drinking a lot earlier than you had planned to. The devil makes work for idle hands, as they say.

The other thing that could be a bit of a downer was not having very much money. We paid ourselves £10 a day – PDs (pay days) as they were called. This was usually enough to buy yourself breakfast and a packet of cigarettes, but not a lot else. Even that didn't really matter, because the promotor always provided the bands with something basic to eat and a fridgeful of beer, cider, and sometimes wine.

Before the tour started, we joined the World Service Agency, who represented us over the next few years. We also had the Hard Times EP re-pressed. Being in a position where we were able to sell them at the gigs on the tour kept the band afloat. We also had our T-shirts available to buy, so at least we had some merchandise on board with us while out on the road.

Fuel expenses ate most of the budget away, and we sure couldn't afford to stay in hotels. The Men They Couldn't Hang were signed to Warner Bros, a major record label, and they had the luxury of travelling and sleeping in a modern tour bus. For the Cropdusters, it was the transit van or bust. We never complained though, and in the long run, I think it toughened us up as a band.

On the Dusters' Foot Stompin' Hoedown tour, my biggest memory is playing at the Alma pub in Cambridge. The landlord of the Alma was an old friend of Cob's called Nick Winnington, a musician himself. It was a manic gig, and at closing time, Nick invited the band to stay for an all-night lock in. Quite a few of our mates had turned up to see us play, and they were invited as well. Everyone was getting hammered, and it was one hell of a party.

Around 5 am the next morning, Nick started feeling strange and asked if anyone had put something in his drink, drug wise. He said he was seeing all these different shapes and colours and wondered what the fuck was happening to him. As it turned out, someone had slipped a white lightning acid tab into his pint of beer while he wasn't looking. I didn't know who the culprit was and still don't until this day.

Anyway, when it was time for us to leave, he stood on the pavement outside the pub, waving us goodbye, a look of abject confusion etched on his face. Nick was a good guy, and some years later, his band the Culture Vultures supported the Dusters at the Town and Country Club in London. I was talking to him, and he mentioned that night in the Alma. He'd sussed out what had happened, but there was no bad feeling on his part.

The Cropdusters went down well with the audiences on The Men They Couldn't Hang tour. From our point of view, as the support band, the pressure was off. After we'd played our set, we were free to drink to our hearts' content and meet new people. I loved the university gigs, as there was always a decent jukebox and a table football in the student's union bar. When TMTCH came onstage, we'd usually be out the front, watching them play, or backstage in the dressing room, partying.

The Dusters shared some great times with TMTC on that tour. Apart from Swill and his brother Jon, the band consisted of Paul Simmonds, who was the main songwriter, on mandolin and charismatic singer/guitarist Cush, from Portsmouth. Cush had this tremendous booming voice that would fill a whole room at a large music venue. Watching him perform at the time, he made a real impression on me. Sadly, Cush is no longer with us.

Scotsman Ricky McGuire was the bassist and had once played in 80s Blackpool punk band The Fits. Ricky also played in the UK Subs, appearing on a couple of their albums and an EP. One of the Subs hilariously nicknamed him Plonker Magoo, and that's the name he's credited with on the record sleeves. The band's road manager was a lovable fruitcake called Spence, who was always up for a crack, and kept everyone thoroughly entertained and on their toes. I'm still in touch with Spence today.

I remember one particularly hilarious incident happening on this tour. At the Loughborough University gig, TMTCH were onstage, and the Dusters were in the dressing room. We'd had quite a bit to drink and were generally fooling around. Some of the band members suddenly grabbed hold of me and started pulling off my clothes. When they'd succeeded in stripping me naked, they rubbed a load of toothpaste on my bollocks and put a cardboard box over my head. They then pushed me straight through the dressing room door, and onto the stage. I started dancing about and waving my arms in the air. Apparently, Swill, and Ricky, the bass player, couldn't believe what they were witnessing. A couple of the Dusters blocked the doorway, so I couldn't retreat to the dressing room. I kept on prancing around for a good while before they finally let me back in.

At the Warwick University gig on the tour, a couple of members of TMTCH kicked a section of a low concrete wall on the campus so hard that it collapsed. Someone at the university complained to the band's record company, who were far from happy. To deflect the blame from themselves, TMTCH told them they were innocent, and it was The Cropdusters who were the guilty party. Being accused of something we didn't do was initially somewhat galling, but eventually we saw the funny side in all of this, and didn't harbour any ill feeling towards them.

When the band played in Manchester, on the penultimate date on the tour, we were delighted when TMTCH offered to put us up in their hotel for the night. After spending weeks on end travelling around the UK, sleeping in the transit van, rest assured, it was a welcome relief. After the gig that night, both bands returned to the hotel for a party. Things got a bit out of hand during the early hours of the following morning, and I recall someone smashed the glass door of the hotel bar and a load of wine glasses. Rock 'n' roll, eh?

A few hours later, I was rudely awoken by the angry voice of the hotel manager, who was kicking me in the head while I was lying in my sleeping bag. He started screaming at me in his broad Mancunian accent, 'What's going on here, then? Who the hell are you? You're not in The Men They Couldn't Hang, are ya? Get the fuck out of here now, before I physically kick you out!'

I remember thinking, I hope he hasn't seen the state of his bar downstairs, or he's gonna go berserk. Luckily, he hadn't yet checked the bar, and the Dusters managed to leave the hotel in one piece, jump into the Transit, and make good our escape from Manchester. We then headed down to Bristol for the final gig of the tour, at the Bierkeller, which is a cracking venue. The Cropdusters played a blinder that night, if I say so myself, and by all accounts, it was a fitting end to a brilliant British tour.

The gigs we played in Scotland were wild affairs, and the shows were always packed to the rafters. The Glasgow experience was typically insane. I drank so much that night, and got so wrecked, I could barely function. The next morning, travelling up to the Scottish Highlands in the van, I realised I was suffering from the effects of alcohol poisoning. I felt fucking terrible and was dreading going onstage in Inverness later.

The Highlands are incredibly beautiful, and I'm glad I wasn't so messed up that I couldn't appreciate the stunning views and scenery. The band arrived at the venue in the late afternoon, and I wasn't feeling any better. As we were getting the gear out of the van, Marcus asked me if I'd go and check the place out. I was smeared in extra thick black eyeliner that day, to try and cover up my hangover and disguise how bad I was feeling.

It was on that day that Sky TV broadcast their first ever game of live football, Celtic versus Aberdeen. I walked into the bar, and it was rammed solid with boisterous drunken Scotsmen, all watching the match on the television. I tapped one of them on the shoulder and asked him if he knew how Arsenal had got on that weekend. He turned round to me, and I'll never forget his response. In the broadest Scottish Highland accent, he loudly exclaimed 'Look at his eyes! My God, look at his eyes! Hey, Gordon, Hamish, come over and get a look at this bloke's fucking eyes! Hey, you lot, you've gotta see this. Look at his eyes. For fuck's sake, just look at his eyes!'

I was suddenly surrounded by a group of imposing, hostile, pissed-up Scotsmen, all wanting to have a good look at my eyes. In my addled state of mind, I was convinced they were going to beat the shit out of me, right there and then. I recall thinking, *what is this place? I really hope these nutjobs don't show up at the gig tonight, or it could turn into a serious fucking nightmare.* Fortunately, I never saw any of them again.

I walked back outside the bar and told the band what had just happened, and that it was mental in there. We hung around for a bit, until the football match finished. When the last of the punters had left the bar, we started loading the equipment into the venue. I knew I needed a beer, urgently, and after a couple of pints, I began feeling a whole lot better. The gig itself was a corker. Apart from TMTCH and the Dusters, there was another act on the bill; the superb Scottish bluegrass/psychobilly band Swamptrash, fronted by an enigmatic banjo player called Harry Horse.

After the live music was over, we all proceeded to get well and truly smashed. There was booze flowing everywhere, and my hangover felt like a distant memory. It's amazing how quickly you can go from thinking you're about to die of acute alcohol poisoning to feeling happy and relaxed and on top of the world.

My mate Toad was the Dusters' roadie on this tour, and like the rest of us, he was thoroughly hammered that night. The party was in full swing when Toad suddenly got up from his chair, his eyes half closed and unsteady on his feet. He unzipped his jeans, and after a bit of fumbling around, managed to get his dick out, and began pissing all over someone's leather jacket that was lying on the carpet. Everyone was howling with laughter, and I was probably laughing the loudest. That all changed when I realised to my horror that it was my leather jacket Toad was urinating on.

Overall, I thought that UK tour was brilliant. We'd gone down really well with the audiences at the venues and had got our name out there, which was the band's overall intention. We'd accomplished what we set out to do, and it was an amazing experience for all of us. It was hard work, without a doubt, but we had a lot of fun partying, and we were always professional enough to pull off the gigs.

Sometime in 1987, the Dusters played at Moles Club in Bath. It was a typical bonkers Friday night gig, with a great atmosphere, and the crowd going mental to us. After the gig, I was drinking with my old mate Richard Wallace, who'd come down to Bath with us in the van. There was a tall guy in a long black coat standing by a pillar a few metres away. He looked cool, and he was surrounded by young punters, eager to talk to him.

Wallace walked over and approached the man, and said, 'Hey, you look just like Hugh Cornwall from The Stranglers!' Of course, it was Hugh Cornwall. I nearly died of embarrassment on Wallace's behalf for that one. Hugh was living in Bath at the time and apologised to me for turning up late and missing our set. He said he'd been told by someone connected to the club who knew what he was talking about that the Dusters had played a blinder. What a true gent.

In December, the band ventured abroad for the first time, headlining the final night at the Trans Musicales Festival in Rennes, France. I think that was one of our best gigs. We were on top of our game and received an excellent reception from the crowd. The Los Angeles band Fishbone had come on before us, and after we'd finished playing, some of them came over, and one of them said 'That was a great show, no one ever goes on after us and lives!' High praise, indeed.

On Christmas Eve, The Cropdusters headlined a massive show at Southampton Guildhall. It was a crazy night. Towards the end of our set, punters stormed onto the stage, and at one point, I reckon we had nearly 200 people up there, dancing and leaping about. The staging began falling apart under all the weight, and the DJ, who was set up beneath the stage, was lucky to escape with his life. Large pieces of wood came crashing down on top of him, and he could have easily been crushed. It was a total hoedown, if ever there was one.

In February 1988, the band recorded a semi-documentary programme for TVS, which was aired nationwide. The television company set up a gig for us at a pub in Woolston, Southampton, and I recall the whole filming process being a lot of fun. The production team managed to persuade me to walk up Lymington High Street one afternoon while they filmed me, but only after I'd drank a load of Jamieson's whiskey, which they kindly paid for.

The programme is only eleven minutes long, but the TV crew filmed hours of footage of the band. I've never seen all the rushes; someone had them on a video, but I don't know where it is now. It could be anywhere. After the programme had been aired, we joined the production crew for a celebration party at a venue in Maidstone, Kent, which was a laugh, if I recall.

Apart from the Dusters, the programme also features a diminutive old forester playing the matchbox; strumming it as if it was a ukulele, yodelling, and neighing like a pony. His name was Maurice Cooper, known as Maurie, and you would often come across him in Lymington High Street, where he'd try selling you one of the two hundred or so fake wristwatches he'd have strapped to his arms. 'What's on then?' he'd ask, before whinnying away quietly to himself. He had squinty, darting eyes that seemed to act involuntarily, and a sporadic wrinkling of the nose, a nervous tic.

Maurice Cooper was certifiably bonkers. For instance, he'd tell anyone prepared to listen that he owned most of the ponies in the New Forest. 'That one's mine, and that one, and that one. Eh? That's another one of mine over there. See it? The brown and white one munching on the patch of grass by the heather, you. There he goes. Eh? Look, I tell ya! Here, see the black one over by that gorse bush? See it? See it? Eh? Mine, they is. Mine. Yep. They is. Mine. All mine.' God only knows what was going on in the man's brain.

Maurie once received a letter from Hampshire County Council. Because he couldn't read or write, he got it completely into his head that the letter was informing him that the HCC was paying him a large sum of money that they owed him. Maurie was ecstatic and couldn't believe his good fortune. What he didn't realise was that the letter was advising him that he owed this money to the council, and not the other way round.

In euphoric mood, he proudly dressed himself in his best clothing. This consisted of a tatty old flat cap, a scruffy moth-eaten suit jacket, floral shirt with a collar the size of Boeing 747 aeroplane wings, timeworn trousers held up with a piece of string, and a pair of ridiculously oversized wellington boots, peppered with holes. He then traipsed off to the Forest

Heath pub in the village of Sway, to share his welcome news and celebrate. Maurie took with him the letter he'd been sent from the council and was showing it to all the pub's customers while he happily bought everyone rounds of drinks. Pointing at the letter, eyes squinting and nose wrinkling, he excitedly proclaimed 'See this here? I got loads of money. Eh? Mine this is. It's not yours, it's mine. Mine.' Later, when it was explained to him what the letter was about, he was categorically speechless. Turning a deathly shade of white, he started trembling uncontrollably, and slunk back into a chair, incredulous.

I remember the Dusters kidnapping Maurie once. The band were booked to play at a music festival at the Three Chuffs pub in Blandford Forum, Dorset, and we turned up unannounced at his house en route. While his wife was in the kitchen making him a cup of tea, a couple of the band members snuck in through the front door into the living room, grabbed hold of Maurie, and chucked him in the van, which was parked outside in the road. I don't think he could believe what was happening to him, but the upshot of it all was he ended up having a rip-roaring time with us down in Blandford.

One day we took Maurie up to London with us, for a gig at the Mean Fiddler in London. Before the Dusters went onstage, we persuaded him to get up there and perform in front of the crowd with his matchbox. Anyone who witnessed it will surely never forget the sight of this rural Lilliputian strumming away and neighing under the full glare of the bright stage lights. There were 700 punters inside the venue that night, and the man went down an absolute storm. The whole thing was surreal.

Immediately after recording the TVS programme, the band entered the Giddyhouse studio in New Cross, London, to record the *Banjo Hill* single. In April, it was released on Scottish independent label DDT records. The single featured two other tracks, *You Were the Pilot* and *Gold Against the Soul* and went to re-press within a fortnight of its release.

After the release of Banjo Hill, the Dusters went on a lengthy UK tour to promote the record. For me, one of the highlights of that tour was the gig we played at Birmingham University. The Levellers were on the same bill as us that night, and after we finished our set, we got more than a bit pissed. Rather than watching The Levellers play, the band wandered off in search of some proper entertainment.

Backstage, Mike discovered a load of stage costumes stored in a large box. I can't recall exactly who wore what, but Mike put on one of those Roman centurion standard bearer's uniforms, complete with bearskin pelt. Someone produced a yellow rubber ball from somewhere, and what followed was mayhem in the corridors of Birmingham University. The band were wrestling each other for possession of the ball, and it got quite rough at times. The incident became known to us as The Battle of the Yellow Ball. We were all well drunk, and it was a great fun, and a much-needed release from the rigours of touring.

Laughing our heads off, we headed outside to the university car park to have a smoke and take a leak. We were standing by an embankment at the edge of the car park in a line, urinating, when we heard whimpering voices coming from the other side, complaining 'Urrgh, what's going on?' It turned out we were literally pissing on The Levellers, and not for the first time, either. They just happened to be taking a nap there. *Gloriose In Libratores Micturientes.*

The Dusters at the time were virtually unmanageable, and we took no prisoners. We lived so much in the here and now that we didn't even know if we'd be alive the next day. We meant it, man. Even now, at the ripe old age of sixty-two, I find it hard to deal with people in bands that pussyfoot around. It's either ingrained in your psyche or it isn't. You don't learn how to become a poet or a musician; you're either born with the talent, or you're not.

During tours around the country, if the band had a couple of days off and we weren't too far away from London, we'd often stay at Sue Chester's house in Mehetabel Road, Hackney. Sue lived there with her two children, Becca and Ollie, having moved up there from Lymington in 1979. Marcus was in a relationship with Becca at the time and lived there as well. I recall him once telling me an extremely funny story about Mark Tinley. I'm in frequent touch with Marcus, who now lives in Oswestry, Shropshire with his beautiful wife Jan. I've asked him to recount his memory of what happened that day in London with Tinley, and here it is.

The Joke Blue Dye

Now, the way I remember this one is as follows...

Tinley was living in a flat with Urk and Dave, a venue of, well, not particularly healthy pastimes in the world of 'recreational drugs. All residents were participants, some more enthusiastic than others, including Tinley (who it is probably fair to say wasn't really that suited to these sorts of 'substances').

Anyway, we were round at the flat for some reason or other and I had in my possession this joke shop blue powder that was touted as being great fun to smear in people's gloves, put on their hands etc. etc, as it would just spread and spread on contact with any form of moisture. It was the same principle as the joke blue sweets that you can still buy, but in a powder form that had the consistency of talcum powder. Anyway, it was suggested by someone that it would be a good idea to put a little in the brim of the battered Homburg that Tinley always wore. Tin was asleep (or, more specifically, fucked) at the time. The deed was done, and Tinley never did appear, so we forgot about it, left and went about our business.

Next day me and a couple of others were meant to be rehearsing somewhere or other and Tinley was the guitarist. He was well-aware of the rehearsal. We got to the space (can't remember whereabouts it was) and set up. Waited for the absent Tinley. Half an hour... an hour... two hours... a complete no-show. This of course was before the days of the mobile phone, so these things were often just shrugged off in the name of 'something must've cropped up'.

Later that night we were meant to be going to some club (can't remember which one... again. Maybe the Batcave?) Anyway, Tinley once again failed to materialize. This was getting stranger and stranger. Turns out that (after a couple of days had passed with no sight or sound of Tinley) he had emerged from his coma at the flat and popped his hat on. Obviously, he didn't know that it was booby-

trapped and, by the time he did realize, his entire face had turned a vivid shade of royal blue... He wasn't best pleased, to put it mildly. The way I remember it didn't come out for a couple of days, and he was absolutely fucking furious with me in particular. The stuff wouldn't come off at all and this is probably the reason you can't get it nowadays. I apologised profusely and was truly regretful about how it had turned out (and how effective the fucking stuff actually was!) and he finally deigned to talk to me again and, eventually, it was (sort of) forgotten. That said, here I am still talking about it some FORTY years later!

Marcus Stott

In July '88, the band travelled to a recording studio in Kent to begin work on our follow-up 12" single *Just Poppin' Out to Fight a War*, b/w *Jammit O'Reilly and Oliver Reed Goes to Salt Creek*. The single was released in September on DDT Records and again went to re-press within a couple of weeks. It was a wonderful weekend, as I recall, and we spent much of it outside, basking in the glorious sunshine. The studio was situated in a tiny, picturesque village, complete with its focal point, the local pub. We'd spend many an hour there drinking beer and fine-tuning elements of the songs we were in the process of recording.

There's an interesting story concerning *Just Poppin' Out to Fight a War*. Several years after we'd recorded this version of the song, my brother and a good mate of his called Tim Robertson travelled to the United States for a road trip around the Deep South. At one point, they were staying at a place called the Bluebird Hostel in New Orleans, Louisiana. It was a shady establishment; an old, decrepit townhouse, with a rickety bar and guests with secret pasts.

Unbelievably, *Poppin' Out* suddenly came on the radio. The proprietor of the hostel told my brother the radio was tuned in to a local college station. Considering the song is about one man's experience in the Confederate States Army during the American Civil War, it seems fitting that it was being played out there in the Deep South. The first verse and chorus to the song are as follows:

Many many years ago, there came the battle call

Brother fighting brother, in the name of civil war

Johnny was only 10 years old, but he had to play a part

From watermelons to Wilmington, he set off with a heavy heart

Just poppin' out to fight a war. Don't know what it's about, what are we fighting for?

Just poppin' out to fight a war. Don't know what it's about, what are we fighting for?

After recording the *Just Poppin' Out to Fight a War* single, The Dusters embarked on our third national tour to promote it. It was called The Awkward Cabbage Tour, in honour of a group of diehard Cropdusters fans from the West Country who used to follow us everywhere. The principal Cabbages were Richard Stirk, Pat Ireland, Paul Northover and a guy nicknamed Bunny. There was a flyer, designed by Marcus, with all the tour dates listed on it, and a drawing of a cabbage wearing an American Civil War Confederate cap. Next to the drawing, Marcus had written the words, 'Your Garden Needs You!'

On one occasion, when the Dusters were on tour in Germany, Richard Stirk somehow managed to succeed in munching his way through eighteen separate meals of bratwurst and chips in a single day. After that memorable feeding frenzy, the band nicknamed him Stirkwurst. The following year, in 1989, when the Screaming Blue Messiahs released their third and final album, the excellent *Totally Religious*, for amusement, we reimagined the title of the opening track, *Both Engines Burning,* to *Both Ends Burning*, as a tribute to Richard's incredible eating exploits.

I recall a couple of blokes from the Home Counties who were big fans of the band at the time and would turn up at venues all over the country to see us play. One of them was a guy called Ken from Croydon in South

London, who reminded me of the English comic actor Kenneth Williams. The other bloke, I think his name was Mark, was from Gravesend in Kent. We christened him Captain Stonewash, due to his questionable choice of denim jacket, which he seemed to wear to all the Dusters gigs he went to. I remember a show supporting The Men They Couldn't Hang at Brunel University in Uxbridge, West London, where Mike dedicated one of our songs onstage to him: 'Oi, Stonewash, this one's for you!' I recall the cowpunk band Blubbery Hellbellies were also on the bill that night.

Another bunch of dedicated followers of the band, in the early days anyway, were the Winchester Bovine Spongiform, a name given to them by Mike. The Winchester Bovine Spongiform posse consisted of five or six guys and got their name from the incurable and invariably fatal outbreak of 'mad cow disease' which swept across large swathes of rural Britain during the 1980s. This catastrophe resulted in the deliberate destruction by farmers of over four million head of cattle to contain the outbreak.

By now, the Dusters had long since ditched the faithful old Transit van and upgraded to a second hand 48-seater coach. Between us we ripped out most of the seats, and Cob, a joiner by trade, set to work on fitting out the rear of the coach with wooden bunk beds. Roger and Rod alternated as drivers, and unsurprisingly, it proved to be a far more comfortable way to travel.

When the band were on the road, it was a bizarre feeling, relaxing on one of the coach seats with my legs outstretched across a table, while the vehicle was stationary at a set of traffic lights. It might be eight o'clock on a rainy winter Monday morning, but with a can of beer in my hand, I'd occasionally look out the window at some disbelieving and obviously envious lorry driver in the lane next to us. Raising the beer can, I'd gesture to the man and mouth the words 'Cheers ears!' to him. I wasn't intentionally winding him up; I'd only do it to people who stared at us through the coach window presumptuously, with hostile or disapproving expressions.

That must have pissed the bloke right off, as he went about the eternal drudgery of his work. Being able to do what we loved, travelling all over the UK and Europe, performing in front of crowds of strangers at live music venues, colleges and universities, afforded all of us something the lorry driver probably didn't have. There's a good chance he was earning considerably more money than The Cropdusters were, but that didn't matter. I guess we were luckier than most in that respect.

That July, Joe Strummer from The Clash, no less, hired the coach from us for the Rock Against the Rich national tour. His new band were called Joe Strummer and the Latino Rockabilly War, and they'd arranged to play around twenty dates across the country. The Cropdusters were chosen to support them at Poole Arts Centre on the tour, and we were honoured, to say the least.

I remember meeting Joe for the first time before the Latino Rockabilly War sound checked in the afternoon. He said to me 'I've heard a lot about your band, you'd better be good tonight!' We smashed it onstage that night and it was a great gig. Backstage in the dressing room after the show, some people lit up cigarettes and started smoking them and inadvertently set off all the fire alarms in the building. Soon, there were firefighters swarming all over the Arts Centre. Joe Strummer and The Clash were big heroes of ours, and supporting the great man was a big deal for us at the time, and another milestone in the Dusters' history.

Boldre Working Men's Club, or Pilley Club, as it's more commonly known, is situated in a rural setting, a mile or so away from Lymington, on the dark side of the cattle grid. It's true bandit country out there and home to the indigenous Morey clan, who I mentioned earlier. The club hosted regular live music events back in the day; in fact, they still do, and The Cropdusters played numerous cracking gigs in that venue over the years. They were always packed to the rafters with hordes of locals, and people who'd travelled there from all over the surrounding area to see the band.

The club boasted a jukebox, a pool table, a dartboard and table football. Most importantly, the place sold cheap beer. The Pilley Club shows were always manic affairs. The audience loved the band and went completely mental when we were up onstage. Club regulars included Bruce Witt, Alan 'Albie' Wateridge and his brother Trevor, Keith Newman, Sean Hallett, Ally and Rachel Royan and 'Swoop' Saunders. They were some of our most ardent fans, and the words Total Hoedown seemed to be specifically written for them. Some of these guys were, or indeed still are, on the club's committee.

One memorable gig the Dusters played in '88 was the Oxford University Spring Ball. After we'd completed our sound check, Rod suggested we visit his father Richard Hamilton, the famous artist, who lived nearby. Richard was a lovely guy. He lived in a beautiful house and made us all feel very welcome. He was such a genuine, non-egotistical man, and at one point during the afternoon, he wheeled in a trolley full of expensive wines and spirits for us to sample. Richard really looked after the band that day. The gig itself was good one, although, if I recall correctly, the acoustics in the hall we were playing in, left a lot to be desired.

Other notable shows we played in 1988 were at Bournemouth Academy with the psychobilly band Guana Batz, and another sold-out Christmas gig at Southampton's Mayfair Suite. Salisbury Arts Centre was a wonderful venue, and a great place to perform, and we always brought the house down whenever we gigged there. The Town and Country Club, in London's Kentish Town was an awesome place to perform. The Cropdusters played there on a few occasions; most notably, supporting New Model Army and Fishbone. We shared the stage with New Model Army several times, the best gig being at Brixton Academy in London.

In the summer, we were on the bill for a music event at Falmouth Castle in Cornwall, along with The Men They Couldn't Hang and a Bristol band, the Blue Aeroplanes. It was a blistering hot day, and I'd bleached my hair the night before. I was boiling, and my skin was turning a deep dark brown colour. I must have looked utterly insane while I was up onstage. The dates for the Awkward Cabbage UK tour were:

SEPTEMBER 22nd WEST SURREY COLLEGE OF
ART & DESIGN- FARNHAM

SEPTEMBER 23rd BENEDICT'S, BOURNEMOUTH

SEPTEMBER 24th NEW PEGASUS, STOKE NEWINGTON, LONDON

SEPTEMBER 29th COVENTRY POLYTECHNIC

SEPTEMBER 30th MANCHESTER UNIVERSITY

OCTOBER 1st FROEBEL COLLEGE, ROEHAMPTON

OCTOBER 4th NORTH LONDON POLYTECHNIC

OCTOBER 6th MIDDLESEX POLYTECHNIC

OCTOBER 8th LEICESTER UNIVERSITY

OCTOBER 11th MAJESTIC, READING

OCTOBER 12th SOUTHAMPTON UNIVERSITY

OCTOBER 15th PORTSMOUTH POLYTECHNIC

OCTOBER 17th BRISTOL POLYTECHNIC

OCTOBER 20th TEESIDE POLYTECHNIC, MIDDLESBROUGH

OCTOBER 21st THE VENUE, EDINBURGH

OCTOBER 22nd GLASGOW TECHNICAL COLLEGE

OCTOBER 27th DUCHESS OF YORK, LEEDS

OCTOBER 28th POLYTECHNIC OF WALES, TREFOREST

OCTOBER 31st KENT UNIVERSITY, CANTERBURY

NOVEMBER 3rd KINGSTON POLYTECHNIC

NOVEMBER 4th MEAN FIDDLER, LONDON

NOVEMBER 5th BRUNEL UNIVERSITY, UXBRIDGE, LONDON

NOVEMBER 12th POLA CINEMA, WELSHPOOL

NOVEMBER 14th BOURNEMOUTH ACADEMY

Two days before the gig at Coventry Polytechnic, on this tour, the coach broke down. The engine had seized up, and for some reason, we ended up stranded outside Northwich Victoria's football ground, Drill Field, in Cheshire. We needed a new coach engine, and fast. Luckily Roger was bang on it and came to the rescue. '*Roger Ramjet, he's our man, he's our man, he's our man. Roger Ramjet, he's our man, good old Roger!*' He hired a van, and drove all the way back down to Lymington, picked up a new coach engine, then drove straight back to Northwich. It was a 450-mile round trip.

That man is something else. I remember the only people travelling on the coach at the time, were Roger, Cob, Bill, and myself. Because we had a two-day gap before the next gig in Coventry, the other members of the band had driven back to Lymington, for some reason or another. We all helped Roger take the old engine out of the coach and put the new one into the compartment. It took a long time, but when the job was finally completed, Cob slammed down the coach's hood in triumph. His jubilation quickly turned to despair, as he smacked his elbow in the process. He was in agony and was seriously worried about whether he'd be able to play fiddle at the forthcoming gig, at Coventry Polytechnic. At the Coventry show, the Dusters were billed to go on straight after Wilko Johnson, who'd been the guitarist with pub rock/rhythm and blues band Dr Feelgood during the 1970s. As it turned out, Cob somehow managed to complete the gig; but only after he'd drank a shedload of whiskey to numb the pain in his elbow.

The Manchester University gigs were always special, and we all got a buzz out of playing there. One time, the character Curly Watts from the long-running British TV soap opera, *Coronation Street,* was booked on the same bill as us with his band Kevin Kennedy and a Bunch of Thieves. He was stood chatting with his manager in the main hall, when I approached him and jokingly grabbed him by the bollocks. We called it the Lymington Greeting, and if you did it now, you'd probably be locked up. Kevin sort of smiled at me, looking a shade embarrassed, before making his excuses and walking off with his manager.

On another occasion in Manchester, I think it was at a spring ball, The Cropdusters were booked to play on the same bill as Rik Mayall, star of the early 80s TV comedy show, *The Young Ones*, who was headlining the event. Rik had plied his trade at the university a few years before, and the promoter was over the moon that he'd been able to persuade him to return and perform there. He knew he'd managed to pull off a real coup, and like everybody else, couldn't wait to see him up onstage. The band's dressing room was right next door to Rik's, and after we'd played our set, we went out front in anticipation of watching what he was going to do.

The hall was rammed that night, and as soon as Rik took to the stage, he began getting heckled by a few drunken guys in the audience. These blokes just wouldn't shut up, and you could sense the frustration Rik was feeling as he tried in vain to carry on. After about fifteen minutes, he'd had enough and stormed off the stage. His manager was waiting for him and immediately shepherded him into a car parked outside. They then drove off.

The promoter jumped up onstage and grabbed hold of the microphone, then burst into tears. Admonishing the mindless few idiots in the crowd, he told them they were ruining the night for everybody else and should be ashamed of themselves. Some of the Dusters returned backstage and went to have a nose around Rik Mayall's dressing room. While we were in there, we devoured all of his rider: vast amounts of bottles of untouched beer, and platefuls of fresh sandwiches; cheese and tomato, egg and cress, tuna and mayonnaise, ham and mustard, salmon and cucumber, enidras and otamot etsap. You name it, we ate them. Those were the days.

In January 1989, we prepared to go on our first European tour, three weeks playing in Germany and Austria. The band was well rehearsed, and we were really looking forward to the gigs over there. Rod Hamilton, who'd recorded the *Hard Times* EP in '86, came with us as our sound engineer, and *Rocket Pod* was our road manager. We'd hired a van for the tour, and our mate Dave Bindon, was the driver. I remember we had such a laugh in Germany. It's a great country, and the people we met were friendly and hospitable towards us. The tour dates were as follows:

16TH NOVEMBER KEMPTEN, SONNECK

17TH NOVEMBER WURZBURG, W71

18TH NOVEMBER FREIBURG, CRASH CLUB

21ST NOVEMBER GAMMELSDORF, CIRCUS

22ND NOVEMBER COLOGNE, ROSE CLUB

23RD NOVEMBER BIELEFELD, CAFÉ EUROPE

25TH NOVEMBER OLDENBURG, KULTURCENTRUM

28TH NOVEMBER FRANKFURT, NEGATIV

29TH NOVEMBER WUPPERTAL, DIE BOERSE

30TH NOVEMBER BERLIN, PIKE

1ST DECEMBER BERLIN, K.O.B

2ND DECEMBER HAMBURG, GROSSE FREIHEIT

We had to catch a ferry over from Dover to the French port of Calais before driving across France and over the border into Germany. I was drinking the German herbal spirit Underberg and had even bought a twenty-bottle Underberg 'gun belt,' which I wore across my chest like some crazed modern-day Mexican bandit. I was ploughing through the little 24cl bottles when Marcus dared me to drink a half a pint of Jameson's whiskey neat, from a litre bottle he was holding in his hand, in one go. Stupidly, I accepted the challenge and poured the whiskey straight down my throat. Unsurprisingly, the effects took hold immediately, and before long, I was lying on the back seat of the van unconscious.

When I finally came round, we were pulling up to the Station Bar in Cologne, Germany. It was around 3 am, and incredibly, we all went inside the bar and started hitting Asbach brandies and tequilas. At some point I must have passed out, because when I awoke from my drunken stupor, I realised the band had left the bar, and we were now back in the van. There were bodies lying prone everywhere, one on top of another, and I really needed to take a piss.

Crawling out from under someone's boots that were stuck in my face, I reached over to slide open the side door. I assumed the van was parked up outside the Station Bar, so everyone could get some much-needed sleep before the first gig of the tour that night. I was so desperate for a piss that I decided to jump out of the van, and I'd already unzipped my jeans and began urinating as I dangled one foot out of the door. This ultimately saved my life. As I was about to leap outside, Cob suddenly emerged from his drunken haze, grabbed my arm and screamed 'Shaun, get back in the van!' We were on the autobahn, doing more than 80mph, and the spray from my piss had blown back into Cob's face, instantly alerting him to the danger. I'd been one step away from certain death.

Another time, Cob dragged me away from under the wheels of an oncoming tram at the last minute, in Amsterdam. God bless that man. Once, the band were in the van, tearing along the autobahn in Germany, and everyone had fallen asleep, including Rod, the driver. Cob woke up and looked into the rear-view mirror and noticed Rod's eyes were closed. He shouted 'Rod, wind your window down. Get some air in here, you're falling asleep!' Rod immediately pulled himself together, and we all lived to fight another day.

We used to love winding up Dave Bindon. There was always an issue with the driver's door window; Bunders, as we sometimes called him, wanted it open because the fresh air kept him awake, but it was freezing in the back of the van, where the rest of us were seated. That window went up and down like a yo-yo for the whole three weeks we were on the road.

One day, we stopped at a service station to buy fuel, and Dave went inside to pay for it. While he was doing this, Podders unwrapped a load of condoms and stretched them tightly over the van's gearstick. After getting back in the van, Dave switched on the engine and put his hand on the gearstick. When he'd realised what we'd done, he shook his head in despair and gave us all the silent treatment for the next few hours.

At the time, Dave Bindon was renting a room above Long's Wine Bar in Lymington. The landlord there in those days was a Brummie guy called Richard Savin. One afternoon, he was in the room next to Dave's, shagging this random woman he'd just pulled, when the ceiling collapsed, and the pair of them came crashing down in a cloud of dust into the bar on top of people drinking in there, still going hell for leather at it on the bed. Fucking madness, it was.

Dave Bindon once told us a story about when he was a trainee submariner in the British Royal Navy, based in Portsmouth in the early 70s. At the time, the Navy were conducting top secret submersible manoeuvres throughout the world's oceans, and a crucial part of Dave's training involved spending six months underwater in a submarine.

The whole purpose of the exercise was to ensure the trainees were suitably acclimatised to a life where men spent months at a time squeezed into tight spaces, confined in extreme close proximity to each other. They needed to convince their superiors that they were qualified to carry out their assigned duties to the best of their ability in a professional manner, under significantly difficult circumstances.

The trainee submariners were also required to conduct themselves appropriately, in keeping with the traditions of the Royal Navy.

One morning, Dave and his fellow trainees were summoned to a meeting with their chief officer. They were informed that they were about to embark on a long training exercise out at sea, the location of which was kept strictly confidential. None of the trainees were allowed to know where they were going to.

Dave told us he spent a whole six months on submarine manoeuvres. He assumed he was out somewhere in the Pacific Ocean, thousands of miles away from home. When the submarine resurfaced, he realised he'd been going round and round Portsmouth Harbour underwater for the past six months. The band used to jokingly refer to Dave as Tugboat Willie – Schlepperboot Wilhelm, in the German language. 'Arms Across the Sea,' was his frequently mentioned motto.

On a later Dusters tour, I think somewhere in Belgium, the band and crew were sat together round a dinner table at a restaurant waiting for our food to be served. There were little pieces of paper on the table with each of our names written on them, indicating where we should sit. Someone, probably the gig promoter, had spelt Dave Bindon's surname wrong. Instead of Bindon, he'd written Binoon. Cob looked over at Dave and came out with something that cracked all of us up: 'The Dark Side of Binoon,' which was an obvious take on the early 70s Pink Floyd album *The Dark Side of the Moon*.

Dave Bindon had a real thing about the Met Office shipping forecast. It was an unhealthy fascination, to say the least. The programme, which had been broadcast on BBC Radio since the 1950s, used to send him into orbit. During the 70s, he couldn't wait for Sunday evenings to come round and became hopelessly aroused at the sound of the female continuity announcer's voice. The woman in question was called Jane Steel, and she really did a job on him. There were thirty-one sea areas covered in the forecast, and she'd slowly and methodically read them off in order: beginning with Viking and ending with Southeast Iceland. When she reached number five in the list, Cromarty, Bindon would start getting turned on. Jane would then describe the weather conditions in Forth, Tyne, Dogger, Fisher and German Bight. Apparently, it was the way she pronounced the words 'German Bight' that sent him into raptures, and eventual climax.

That first Cropdusters tour in Europe was an absolute blast. The band had gone down well at all the gigs we played, and it was great travelling around a foreign country, doing what we loved doing the most. The audiences had been appreciative of us, and we were treated with respect by the promoters, some of whom even put us up for the night in their homes. The final date on the tour was at the U4 club in Vienna, Austria. The band didn't come onstage until four o'clock in the morning, and it turned out to be an epic gig.

In March, the band recorded a gig at the Mean Fiddler, six songs of which subsequently appeared on an album released by Link Records titled *If the Sober Go to Heaven*. It was a one-off deal. The Dusters had grown increasingly disillusioned by the distinct lack of promotional support from DDT Records, and it was time for us to move on. The album also features all the tracks off the first two singles, and a black and white photo of a cool looking Maurice Cooper on the front cover. The picture was taken by Mark Uniacke, an extremely talented photographer and a good mate of ours, who is now sadly deceased. Mark was ably assisted by his glamorous girlfriend at the time, Holly Newman. That man Maurie managed to get his name up in lights once again.

Next on the agenda was the biggest gig The Cropdusters ever played, headlining the Mean Fiddler tent at Reading Festival on August Bank Holiday weekend. What a mind-blowing experience that was. The Pogues were on the main stage at the same time we were playing on the Mean Fiddler stage. Apart from The Pogues, the headlining acts on the main stage that weekend were New Order and The Mission.

I'll never forget that night for as long as I live. I was as nervous as fuck beforehand and tried to calm myself down by drinking a load of beer and a couple of shorts backstage. The adrenaline was off the scale, and when it was time for us to go on, I threw up into a container at the side of the stage. That got me fully focused, and we ended up playing to nearly 5000 people in the tent that night. The gig turned into one gigantic, almighty hoedown and the band were on fire. Afterwards, we were buzzing so much, it was incredible. People later told me that punters were leaving the main stage area midway through the Pogues' set to come over and watch the Dusters show.

One thing that often used to frustrate some of us in the band was the lack of reviews of our gigs in the national music press. We were especially pissed off after there was not even a mention of our storming performance at the 1989 Reading Festival. Don't get me wrong, the local press were extremely supportive of The Cropdusters during our existence. Journalists at newspapers such as the *Southampton Daily Echo, the Bournemouth Echo, the Salisbury Journal* and even the *Lymington Times* couldn't have been more helpful and went out of their way to promote the band.

I firmly believe some of these music journalists can't even be bothered to turn up to gigs half the time, and when they do, they write reviews based on what mood they happen to be in at the time. The NME did cover a Dusters gig at the Clarendon Hotel in London, in '87, and it was a great review, to be fair. In the write up, I recall they mentioned the pop-eyed singer, which was quite amusing. Melody Maker also wrote a feature on the band, in '89, and the photo they used was quite a good one of us standing in Hackney graveyard. This national exposure was greatly welcome, but it was few and far between.

Some of our record releases also received favourable reviews in the national music papers, most notably, the *Just Poppin' Out to Fight a War* 12" single. I suppose, ultimately, it's simply one person's opinion. Why should a journalist know more about music than anyone else does? In answer to that question, some of them would probably say they've studied music at university or whatever, and therefore they know what they're talking about. Personally, I think that's a load of bollocks. In the end, it all comes down to personal taste, I suppose. The trouble is, unfortunately, many of these so-called music journos have the power to make or destroy bands. It's called the power of the pen. It can be maddening as hell at times, but there you go.

Another thing that used to piss the band off at the time – well, Mike and me, anyway – were the crap PA systems set up in some of the places we played in. I'm not a technical person by any means, but my heart used to drop when I walked into a venue and the first thing I noticed were these obviously inadequate speakers set up in front of the stage. I knew there and then that I was up against it, and I was going to have my work cut out struggling to get heard above cranked up guitars and drums. It could be really demoralising, and shitty PA systems took a terrible toll on my voice, especially during the early days of the Dusters.

A long time later, around 2011, I was experiencing quite severe problems with my throat, and thought I might have polyps that needed to be removed. I visited a specialist at Christchurch Hospital, and he told me it was all down to years of singing through shite PAs. Luckily, my diagnosis wasn't serious, but it just goes to show. Nowadays, PA systems are a lot more advanced, and the onstage monitors are of such good quality that singers can hear themselves properly, even in the smallest of music venues.

In September, the *If the Sober Go to Heaven* album was released, and the band went on a short UK tour to promote it, then travelled to Holland for a few dates. The Dusters played their first ever gig in Holland, at the legendary Melkweg, in Amsterdam. The Levellers supported us on that occasion, and it was a brilliant night all round. We loved playing at the Melkweg; it's such an iconic venue, and the band returned there several times over the coming years. A Dutch guy call Gerrit was the club's resident lighting engineer, and we became firm friends with him.

At some point in 1989, my parents moved to Beaumaris, a suburb in Melbourne, Australia. Dad had been offered a position at the Exxon oil refinery in Altona, and they lived out there for the next three years. While they were in Australia, they rented out their house in Lymington to a Canadian family. The father had a placement at Fawley refinery. My brother was under eighteen, so he was a dependant and could fly to Melbourne as many times as he wanted, all paid for by Exxon. I think he visited my parents around five times while they were living out there. My sister spent

Christmas '89 in Beaumaris. I flew to over to Australia in May 1990, to stay with my folks for a few weeks.

The Cropdusters were due to go on tour again in December, playing shows in Holland and Germany. A few days before the tour started, our drummer Bill dropped a bombshell. He turned up at Cob's house in the evening and announced he wasn't going on tour abroad with us. He said his girlfriend had arranged for them both to fly to the USA to stay with her father out there, and that he was paying for the flights. We were gobsmacked.

After much heated discussion, we eventually managed to persuade Bill to come on the tour. Or so we thought. A day or so later, he phoned Marcus from Heathrow Airport and told him he couldn't resist the opportunity of an all-expenses paid holiday in the States. It was simply unbelievable. We were just about to travel to Germany and Austria for three weeks, to play a series of dates, when our drummer drops us in the shit, big time.

Thankfully, Marcus's younger brother Krish, who played mandolin in the Shrewsbury based bluegrass band Kentucky Ridge Runners, could also play the drums. He immediately stepped in to the void and saved the day, just in the nick of time. Although it was a gut-wrenching decision to have to make, we felt we were left with little choice but to sack Bill from the band forthwith. Krish now became our permanent drummer.

Krish didn't let anyone down on the tour. He was a big fan of the band anyway and slotted in perfectly. We kicked ass in Holland, then headed on to Germany. The Soviet Union was slowly beginning to disintegrate, and the month before, the Berlin Wall had come down. It was a monumental period in history and The Cropdusters were about to arrive slap bang in the heart of it.

Driving through the Berlin corridor, we pulled into a service station for a break. On the way back out, we bought a bottle of ethyl rectified alcohol. This was seriously strong moonshine, upwards of 95 percent proof. It was so powerful, the band used it to fire up their Zippo lighters. When you drank the stuff, you'd feel a sudden burning sensation, followed by a rush of blood to the head. After that, a warm glow would wash over you. We'd have a swig out of the bottle before going onstage, and it would get you right in the mood for the gig. It was crazy shit. We even brought some back to the UK with us after the tour had finished.

Another souvenir we returned home with, were pieces of the Berlin Wall, small chunks of concrete that we'd chiselled out during our stay in the city. They made for perfect Christmas presents to give to all the family. We played two shows in Berlin, both at the KOB Club on Potsdamer Strasse. The KOB was a rocking venue, and we slept upstairs in bunk beds in a small self-contained flat while we were there.

The day before New Year's Eve 1989, Mike and I went for a drink in the Sportsman's Arms in Pennington. I was still living at Sharon and Cob's, and before we left the house, we put a litre bottle of Blue Smirnoff vodka on hold in the freezer. After a few pints of lager in the pub, we returned to the house and started getting stuck into the vodka. We were both well on our way, and at around 6pm, we staggered off out to the White Hart pub, not that far away. We must have been smashed because someone later told me they'd seen the pair of us rolling about helplessly on the mini roundabout outside the White Hart. Mike and I somehow managed to pull ourselves together for a moment and walked unsteadily into the pub and went and sat down on stools at the bar. I could barely function and toppled straight off my stool onto the floor. John Mayman, the landlord, and a lovely chap, saw what was happening, and said to us 'Oh no! No, no, no. I don't think so. Come on boys, I'll take you home.' We collapsed into the back of John's van in the pub car park, and he drove us back the short distance to Cob's place in Bay's Road.

I'm not sure what happened to Mike that evening, but after John had dropped us off, I somehow ended up in the wrong house. To make matters worse, in a futile effort to stand up straight, I'd grabbed hold of a garden trellis on the outside wall and ripped it clean off and was now covered head to toe in honeysuckle. I opened the front door and stumbled into the living room. To my horror, a man I knew called Steve Topp was in there, sitting down on an armchair watching television with his family. It was his fucking house for god's sake, and there I was stood right in front of him, an uninvited guest.

Even though I was in a right mess, I somehow managed to realise my mistake. He exclaimed 'What the fuck?!' The poor man must have thought he'd been invaded by a military sniper in a 3D ghillie suit. Mumbling an apology to him for being so stupid, and promising that I'd never pull off a stunt like this ever again, I walked outside, looking for Cob's house, the broken trellis still wrapped round my head, draped in clinging foliage and the roots trailing along the ground behind me. When I was safely inside, Cob informed me that it would probably be a good idea if I found somewhere else to live. The whole sorry but infamous episode found its way into local folklore and subsequently became known to us all as Toppy's Trellis Trauma.

In early 1990, I moved to a bedsit in a house in Woolston, Southampton. My mate Flash was renting a room there, and I was in the one next door to him. At the time there were some strange characters living in that house, for sure. I recall a bloke named Roy who rented one of the rooms upstairs. Roy was probably a bit older than me, short, and a bit podgy. He had a dark, shaggy perm and a thick moustache, and he reminded me of the Scousers characters in the Harry Enfield comedy TV programme that was popular at the time. He was a friendly enough chap, although he had cloth ears and could be a bit of a busybody.

One Saturday morning, while I was toasting bread in the communal kitchen, Roy walked through the door. He looked at the toaster and turned to me and said 'Toast, eh?' It could hardly be anything else, for fuck's sake; toast is toast. I was hardly ever at the house in Woolston, as I was either away doing stuff with the band or drinking with my mates back in Lymington. Our tour manager, and sound engineer at the time; a good mate called Sean Cranny from nearby Blackfield, nicknamed Rampton, would sometimes stay in my room while I wasn't there.

On St. Patrick's night, in March 1990, the Dusters headlined a hugely successful concert at Shoreditch Town Hall in East London, ably supported by the bands Sons of the Desert and Macavity's Cat. The event was promoted by Gary Butterworth from Link Records, and it was a sell-out, with 1300 people in attendance. It was a glorious night and one of our best gigs ever.

In April, the band headed back to Holland and Germany for another tour. That Easter, we played two consecutive gigs at the Eastpoint Centre, in Thornhill, Southampton. Flash promoted the shows, and both nights sold out.

I'd arranged to fly to Australia in May, to visit my parents in Melbourne for a few weeks. The night before I was due to travel, the band returned to the Zap Club in Brighton, scene of the infamous spray can fiasco two years earlier. This time, I managed to behave myself and avoided getting arrested. We played a blinding gig, and afterwards, we went to an all-night party in the town. Around breakfast time, we left the party and Mike and Krish accompanied me to Gatwick Airport to wave me off. I had with me one of those old-fashioned, tattered white luggage cases, and Rampton had scrawled across it, in black marker pen, the words 'Melbourne or bust!' I'd planned to stay in Australia for three and a half weeks; I would have gone for longer, but the Dusters had a big show scheduled at Southampton Guildhall at the end of the month, and I needed to get my ass back for it.

I was flying with British Airways, and it was a long flight; 27 hours I think, including a quick stopover in Bangkok to refuel. In those days, you could smoke on the plane and order as much free alcohol as you pleased. It was completely different to the way it is now. To occupy my time, I set about drinking miniature bottles of vodka – lots of them. In the end, the stewardess got so fed up with serving me one bottle at a time that she tipped a dozen or so of them straight into my lap. When the plane finally landed at Melbourne International Airport, in the early hours of the morning, I could hardly stand up.

After clearing immigration, feeling the worse for wear, I walked through to the arrivals hall, where my parents were waiting to meet me. I hadn't seen them in over a year and was looking forward to catching up on their time spent out here, so far. After the jet lag had worn off, I set about discovering the delights of Melbourne. The city is known as Australia's cultural capital, and is famous for its music, theatre, art scenes and festivals. Melbourne has been called 'The live music capital of the world,' and apparently, it has more music venues per capita than any other city in the world.

I spent quite a lot of time writing new songs for the band during my stay in Beaumaris. I also spent long periods of the day drinking beer and eating decent food. The steaks you could buy in Australia in those days were delicious, and I put on a stone and a half in weight while I was out there. Beaumaris is the residential area the TV soap opera, Neighbours, is based upon. I bought a pair of boots in Melbourne city centre, from a place where some of the cast of Neighbours shopped regularly.

Dad used to play squash at a local sports centre sometimes after he'd finished his day at the oil refinery, and one evening he returned to the house with his leg in plaster. He'd snapped his Achilles tendon and was in a lot of pain. It was a nasty injury. During the remainder of my stay in Beaumaris, he was laid up on the sofa with his leg outstretched on a table, and unable to go to work.

My most abiding memory of my time over there was the day my father took me to watch an Aussie rules football match at the Melbourne County Cricket Ground, between St. Kilda and Collingwood. It was the same day Manchester United played Crystal Palace in the FA Cup Final at Wembley. It was my last full day in Australia, and one of my parent's friends, who lived a few doors away, promised me he'd take me to a party that night.

We caught the train to the ground and arrived in plenty of time for the game. I thought I'd start drinking early so I was in the right mood for the party later. While the match was going on, I stood next to Dad on the terraces, necking cans of Foster's lager. I remember, at half time we ordered some Penny Pies for our lunch. When the game finished, I was already well on my way.

As soon as we arrived back in Beaumaris I started on the wine. Around midway through the evening, the next-door neighbour showed up and we drove to a hotel bar, where he introduced me to some friends of his. He said it was way too early to hit the party, so he took me to another couple of bars. Around midnight, he drove us to the party, which was happening in someone's garage.

It was great fun meeting all these new people, and there was alcohol everywhere you looked. I recall swigging out of a bottle of Jim Beam before the room began to spin. The next thing I remember was being slumped over the neighbour's shoulders as he was knocking on my parent's front door. It must have been three o'clock in the morning as Dad opened the door to let us in. We'd woken him up and he wasn't impressed at all by the state I was in. I crawled into bed and went out like a light.

My departure flight from Melbourne was booked for later that afternoon, and as I resurfaced from my drunken slumber, I felt worse than awful. I put on a video recording of the previous day's English Cup final, but couldn't focus on the match properly, as I kept having to run to the bathroom to throw up. I was dreading the flight home. After we'd driven to the airport, feeling like shit, I said goodbye to my parents and prepared myself for the return journey back to England.

Before I left for Australia, I'd arranged with Flash to meet me at Gatwick Airport and drive me home to Southampton. As I was waiting around in the arrivals hall, jet lagged and a little agitated, it didn't take me long to realise he wasn't there. I called his phone numerous times, but he didn't answer. I assumed he'd had a heavy session the previous night and was still in bed sleeping it off. I must have been hanging about the airport for at least six hours before I eventually got hold of him. Flash finally turned up, and we drove back to our place in Woolston, where we polished off a crate of Foster's lager that I'd bought at the airport in Melbourne.

There were plenty of Cropdusters gigs throughout the summer of 1990. One absolute cracker was the Neurorock Festival in Limburg, Belgium. Another memorable show was at the Powerhaus in Islington, London. The Powerhaus was a great venue to play in, and we always packed the place out. At one time, the Dusters held the record for bar takings there.

In September we played a gig that's gone down in local folklore. We used to rehearse in an old cow pen at a place called Bampton's Farm, just over the water from Lymington, near the Wightlink ferry terminal. An old friend of Cob's, a farmer named Brian Goodall, ran the show at Bampton's. His father Alan owned the land and Brian loved what the Dusters were doing. He was always full of encouragement and asked us to play a show in one of the family's fields.

When the band first started out, in 1986, Brian organised an outdoor event in one of the fields, and The Cropdusters headlined it. It was a mental, hedonistic gig, and the party went on all night long. He approached us and asked if we'd be interested in doing the same sort of thing again. We thought it was a great idea, and straightaway, got the word around town.

We didn't even need to put up posters for the show, and it certainly wasn't advertised in the local press. It was all done through word of mouth, but nearly 1500 people turned up to watch us that night, such was the band's appeal at the time. I love Cajun music, and we had the awesome Flatville Aces opening for us. Somewhere in a field in Hampshire, on a balmy Indian summer night, the sound of the Louisiana swamps could be heard permeating the air for miles around. Accordion and fiddle blazing, the Flatvilles lived up to their name. They were indeed ace.

Rampton was engineering our sound that night, and he made sure the band were sonically spot on. The whole event was epic, and folk still talk about it today. That Dusters show was truly one monster of a hoedown, with hundreds of people gathered in front of the tractor trailer stage while we were playing: dancing their asses off and going crazy. It seemed that everyone and everybody was there on that night.

It was one of those gatherings you're never likely to forget, and justification for all our hard-earned efforts in entertaining the troops.

In October, Mike phoned me with some devastating news. Graham 'Bill' Haley, the original drummer for The Cropdusters, had passed away. He had been the baby of the band and was only twenty-five years old when he took his own life. Bill had been diagnosed with Crohn's disease several years previously and had begun suffering from the effects of depression. Although Bill wasn't in the band anymore, we were all gutted. He'd been there at the very beginning and was a huge part of the evolution of the Dusters. He was also an extremely talented drummer.

Around this time, I was walking to the High Street, and as I passed the park behind the town hall, I bumped into my old friend Michaela, who had just had a new baby daughter called Stephanie, born on the 14th November 1990. Her big sister Kylie was playing on the bouncy toys in the park, and we chatted about the sadness surrounding Bill's untimely death. Little did I know then that these gorgeous girls would one day become my beautiful stepdaughters!

At the end of the year, the band embarked on another tour of the UK. The dates we played on that tour were:

1990

7TH DECEMBER BATH COLLEGE OF HIGHER EDUCATION

12TH DECEMBER MANCHESTER UNIVERSITY

14TH DECEMBER WRITTEL COLLEGE, CHELMSFORD

17TH DECEMBER BOURNEMOUTH ACADEMY

23RD DECEMBER EASTPOINT CENTRE, SOUTHAMPTON

24TH DECEMBER MEAN FIDDLER, LONDON

1991

11TH JANUARY THE VENUE, NEW CROSS, LONDON

16TH JANUARY SIMPLON, GRONINGEN, HOLLAND

17TH JANUARY TIVOLI, UTRETCH, HOLLAND

18TH JANUARY GIGANT, APELDOORN, HOLLAND

19TH JANUARY UNITAS, WAGENINGEN, HOLLAND

20TH JANUARY Venue tbc, LOTTUM, HOLLAND

21ST JANUARY Venue tbc, BELGIUM

22ND JANUARY ROTOWN, ROTTERDAM, HOLLAND

23RD JANUARY MELKWEG, AMSTERDAM, HOLLAND

24TH JANUARY Venue tbc, ENSCHEDE, HOLLAND

25TH JANUARY GROSSE FREIHEIT, HAMBURG, GERMANY

26TH JANUARY DE KOOG, NOORD SCARWOUDE, HOLLAND

27TH JANUARY TROLL, HOORN, HOLLAND

The Dusters played their second Reading Festival on August Bank Holiday,

1991, once again in the Mean Fiddler tent. We didn't headline the stage that year; the Blue Aeroplanes did. We were third on the bill and went on just before the brilliant Manchester band New Fast Automatic Daffodils. The headliners on the main stage that weekend were Iggy Pop, James and the Sisters of Mercy. Backstage, in the beer tent, was weird. At one point, the only people in there were members of the Sisters of Mercy and folk from the Old English pub, who were on our guest list. We played a great gig, and just like in '89, we blew the house down.

In 1991, the band travelled over to Belgium to play at a big music festival in Sint-Niklaas. It was an outdoor event situated in the centre of the town square, and the whole place was sealed off. There must have been over 10,000 people in attendance, when we came onstage. Another memorable gig the Dusters played at in Belgium was a massive music festival on the coast.

We'd had a gig the night before, at the Melkweg in Amsterdam, and had left the club in the early hours of the morning. It had been a heavy night, and when we took to the stage, at 11 am, I was feeling a bit shot away. I remember the stage, which was huge, faced out onto the beach, and in the distance was the sea. The band was first on the bill that day, and I remember people in the audience bringing beach towels along with them, and large stones to stop the towels from blowing away in the wind.

Van Morrison was headlining the festival that year, and I recall Mike trying to gee up the crowd and get them moving. He grabbed hold of his microphone, and yelled 'Come on you lot, get yourselves down to the front and start dancing! All you've got to look forward to later is that miserable fucker Van Morrison!' How to win friends and influence people, eh? While we were onstage, just going into Strange Olde Song of the Seas, I threw up in Podders' pint of lager. The Melkweg gig the previous night was obviously catching up with me.

Backstage, after we'd finished our set, we sat down at an outside table and started on a marathon drinking session in the sunshine. Van Morrison was standing with his minders by his limousine, which was parked about fifty yards away, and he couldn't keep his eyes off us. He didn't say anything, but he kept on staring at us for ages, with a grumpy expression plastered all over his face.

Around this time, I attended my first Flowered Up gig, at Portsmouth Guildhall, and they blew me away. Flowered Up were an alternative indie/dance band from Camden, north London, and they were brilliant live. Over the next two years, I saw them play many times, at places such as The Venue in New Cross, London, Bournemouth Academy, and the Eastpoint Centre in Southampton. I remember seeing them at a big festival in London's Finsbury Park. I loved Flowered Up back in those days, and their album *A Life with Brian* was played constantly on the stereo in The Cropdusters' van.

In late '91, the Dusters began working on their next project, recording tracks for the album *Homemade Agent Orange*. We'd booked a recording studio in Denmead, Hampshire, and I remember the band commuting there from Lymington for days on end. In December, we appeared on the Japanese talent show *Bandbreakers*. The show was filmed at the BBC studios in London, and we performed *Done for You*, a track off the forthcoming album. Blur and James were the stars of the show that day, and both bands played a couple of songs. I remember the ex-*Sisters of Mercy* bassist, Ben Gunn, was the make-up artist for all the acts there on that occasion.

By early 1992, we'd completed our work on the *Homegrown Agent Orange* album. It was due to be released on the Dutch label Top Hole Records, based in Amsterdam, and to promote it, World Service Agency organised a massive five-week European tour for the band. The tour took in six separate countries: Holland, Belgium, Germany, Sweden, Denmark and Norway.

When we arrived in Amsterdam, we were chuffed to discover the album had reached number three in the Dutch independent album chart. It was a buzz knowing the band had made an impact in a foreign country. I think the best Cropdusters show we played in Holland, and indeed on the whole tour, was at the famous Paradiso music venue in Amsterdam. Even people from Lymington flew over for that one.

On the Dutch leg of the tour, the band played a gig at a venue in Arnhem. Touring at this rate was hard work, and singing night after night put a huge strain on my voice. In the sound check that afternoon, I knew my throat had had it. I could hardly speak. We were due onstage in a few hours, and I was getting really stressed out with the situation. The promoter realised what was happening and told me he knew someone who could help me, a local doctor. He told me he'd drive me to the doctor's house, where I could get a hydrocortisone and adrenaline injection, for a small fee. We arrived at the doctor's house and knocked on the door. The doctor opened the door and beckoned me inside. He told me to take my trousers and pants down and wait in the hallway, while he went off to fetch a syringeful of hydrocortisone and adrenaline. When he came back, he asked me to bend over forwards, then plunged the syringe into my right buttock. I paid him the money and thanked him, and we drove back to the venue.

Within less than hour, my voice had returned to normal. It's amazing how quickly hydrocortisone takes effect, and I was happy I could now do the gig without having to worry about fucking up my voice any further. Apparently, the drug works by coating the white cells on the back of the throat. It's a temporary, unnatural cure, but it worked well for me that night.

After one gig in Holland, Rod drove his car through the night to Berlin, with Mike and me sitting in the back. The two of us had dropped an ecstasy tablet, and it was on this trip, that Mike introduced me to an amazing band called Thule. He'd managed to get hold of their CD album, *321* (Normal 2), from somewhere, and we played it repeatedly on Rod's car stereo, on the way to Berlin. That album remains one of my personal all-time classics until this day. To both of us, that night will forever be known as The Incredible Journey. The lead singer of Thule was a New Zealander called Martin Byrne, and we became firm friends. Martin even had a stint playing in the Dusters, as one of our guitarists.

Scandinavia was a new experience for all of us. The first gig we did in Sweden was at a youth club, and our accommodation that night was in a building in some sort of scouting camp. It was in the middle of nowhere. After we'd sound checked, the promoter took us to his parents' house for dinner. Looking back, it was bizarre. After the gig, the band headed back to the scout camp. In the grounds of the camp was a large lake, and in the centre of it, there was a small island, shaded by a clump of several trees.

When Marcus ventured outside to smoke a cigarette early the next morning, he could just make out the silhouette of his brother Krish, through the mist rising from the water, in a boat on the lake. Krish was rowing back from the island, where he'd been casually masturbating without a single care in the world. *Anytime, anyplace, anywhere*, was Krish's motto. The whole incident was hilarious, and we christened that small piece of isolated land Wank Island. It was on this tour that Mike tried to convince us all that Krish was leaving the band to play with the Belgian/ Dutch dance music act, 2 Unlimited. Outlandish as it sounds, I'm sure a few of us genuinely believed him.

The second Swedish show the Dusters played was at an arts centre in a large city. I remember the audience there were very downbeat and stand-offish. They just wouldn't enter into the spirit of it, and didn't get us at all. The third and final gig in Sweden was the total opposite. It was in a nightclub, and the crowd in there that night mainly consisted of hordes of loud, drunk, grimacing bikers. They reminded me of the Varangians, Swedish Vikings from the 9th century. The place was absolutely jam packed, and when the band came onstage, around midnight, the Varangians went completely and utterly berserk.

At this point in the book, I'd like to add another Cropdusters tour memory from Marcus.

A quick coffee!

We were waiting in the ubiquitous queue for boarding the Ferry for (France?) and the usual 'in the queue' tedium had set in. It's pretty much a brain-disengaged period where if you try to alleviate the boredom by actually thinking you end up in a downward spiral!

Anyway, the moments can be broken up by the occasional events and activities of other people in the queues around you. Bearing in mind we were in a 47-seater coach, we also had a grandstand view of the surrounding events and, just ahead of us and in the row to the left of us, there were a couple of guys 'standing' by their car who were quite obviously absolutely arseholed.

Now, you can be refused boarding onto the Ferry if you are deemed to be too inebriated or 'out-of-control'. These guys were seemingly aware of this potential problem, or it had just occurred to them. Their solution to this potential problem transpired to be to rip open a packet of ground coffee (badly, so it was going everywhere), throw their heads back and pour a huge amount into their mouths and then, wait for it...wash it down with an inept swig from a MASSIVE bottle of vodka!

Thinking about it, the theory was sound (in a child-like fashion). The practice, on the other hand, was pure gold from a spectator's point of view! The guy's mouth was SO full of dry, pure coffee that he couldn't actually fit a lot of vodka into it and, after a huge attempt at a swig, he then coughed and spluttered massive amounts of the unholy mixture all over himself, his (designer sporty) clothes and the floor around him, his eyes streaming with water and turning bright red. The apparition of this chap when he 'stood up' was a thing I can still picture if and when I'm reminded of it, as if it were happening in front of me right now (AND they got onboard as well, continuing their consumption of vast amounts of said vodka)!

So... thanks for reminding me, Shaun!
Marcus Stott

Our one gig in Denmark on the tour was at Freetown, Christiania, a commune in Copenhagen, on the island of Amager. It's famous for Pusher Street, and the open trade in cannabis. As soon as we arrived there, in the afternoon, Krish and I wandered off to check the place out. We located the band's dressing room and were introduced to the venue's promoter. He immediately asked us if we'd like to smoke a bong with him, and of course, we said we'd love to. He loaded the bong with hashish and fired it up. That thing knocked our socks off, and I remember lying prostate on the dressing room floor, totally stoned.

Before the show that night, the band were treated to a wonderful meal in the commune's restaurant. Everyone on that island smoked dope. Even the waiter had a large joint hanging from his mouth as he approached our table to serve us our meals. What a place. It was unreal. The last country we played in on the tour was Norway. The Cropdusters played three gigs in the country: Oslo, Bergen and Trondheim. The Bergen show was by far the best out of the three.

One memorable event from 1992 was when we were booked to play at the Lowlands Festival at Biddinghuizen in Holland, two miles east of Amsterdam. Lowlands is a massive three-day music and arts festival, and I was told there was a crowd of 90,000 people there on each day of the event. Regardless of how many of them watched the Dusters play, that was surely the most people the band ever performed to.

I remember a gig at the Rock City in Nottingham. It was an all-nighter, featuring the American death rock/gothic rock band Christian Death, Crazyhead, another band, and us. The frontman of Christian Death was a guy called Valor Kand, a thoroughly dislikeable individual by all accounts. I remember when he turned up at the venue, in the late afternoon, I said hi to him and he totally blanked me. I've never in my life seen a band take so long to sound check. Kand was up onstage and acting like a dictator to the rest of his band. They must have sound checked for nearly three hours, leaving hardly any time for the other acts to prepare themselves.

Eventually, His Lordship decided he was satisfied with everything, and Christian Death finished sound checking. Kand went to his dressing room backstage and lay down and fell asleep on top of a bass cabinet flight case. I wasn't there, but Marcus later told me that he and Mike had walked into his dressing room, and while he was still asleep, they began hurling insults at him. Kand woke up, and before he had the chance to say anything, Marcus thumped him squarely on the jaw, knocking him clean out cold. At that exact moment, the lights went out in the venue; there was a power cut. I think that's an ace 'what happens on tour' story.

At Christmas '92, the band travelled over on the ferry from Dover to Calais in France, before driving down to Paris for a gig at an auditorium in the city. The day after the gig was Christmas Eve, and I remember when we arrived back in Calais, we went into a hypermarket there and stocked up as many crates of beer and bottles of wine as we could fit into the van. Not all the band members were in the van; Rod was the sound engineer for the Paris show and had taken his car over to France. I'm not sure, but I think Mike was in Rod's car, and possibly Roger and Krish.

The two vehicles drove to the Calais ferry terminal in convoy, with Rod's car ahead of us, in the van. An old mate of ours, Stuart Gates, was the designated van driver on this trip. We were in the queue, waiting to board the ferry, when some customs officers wearing silly hats approached the van and pulled us over. They told us to get out, and to go and stand over by a building nearby while they conducted a search of the van. I recall looking towards the ferry and seeing Rod driving onto the car deck. I thought, bollocks, we're never going to make this crossing. Shortly afterwards, the ferry departed and set sail for Dover without us.

The customs officers were busy searching the van when one of them found a bag containing Marcus's needles and syringes, and the insulin he needed for his diabetes. They immediately became suspicious of us, and it was obvious they thought we were smuggling drugs. One of the officers told us to line up alongside the wall inside the building, with our noses pressed up against it.

A little while later, the customs blokes decided to conduct a body search. When it came to my turn, one of the officers gestured for me to turn out my pockets. I did as I was asked and was gobsmacked to find I'd pulled out a small lump of hash. I honestly didn't know it was in my pocket. The customs man glared at me and said there was a good possibility we'd all be spending Christmas in a Calais prison cell. We stood up against the wall for what felt like hours, before one of the officers, looking disgusted, told us we were free to leave. Turning to me, he said 'Go home, English drug smuggler.' I replied, 'And Merry Christmas to you too, Napoleon.'

It was late in the day before we finally boarded a ferry. I remember thinking the others were probably back home in Lymington by now, enjoying the festivities. At least we had a van full of alcohol, which we could drink on the ferry crossing back to England, so it wasn't the end of the world. Between us, we managed to polish off a couple of crates of beer and a few bottles of wine on the journey. It was nearly midnight on Christmas Eve when we finally made it home.

There was always loads of stuff going on whenever the Cropdusters were away on tour. Whether it was our driver, Dave Bindon, getting poked in the eye by a Turkish man at 4 am in Berlin after he'd kicked the bloke's pushbike over, or accidentally setting fire to our dressing room at Bradford University. On the Banjo Hill tour, in 1998, we were on the coach one morning, driving through Edinburgh, on the way to a gig in Glasgow where we were booked to play that night. Walking along the pavement, we spotted Joe Kingman, a member of Edinburgh-based indie folk/country/cajun band We Free Kings, minding his own business. We pulled into a lay by on the side of the road, and grabbing Joe's attention, we beckoned him to come over to us. As soon as he put one foot in the door of the coach, we dragged him inside and told him he was coming to Glasgow with us; there were no bones about it. We kidnapped him, essentially. Poor Joe had only popped out to the shops to buy a pint of milk. He really didn't mind though, and we all ended up having a great time together in Glasgow.

After playing a gig in Amsterdam one night, the band all headed off to the red-light district to carry on partying. We were in a bar, and I recall a bunch of Turkish guys brazenly snorting cocaine in front of everybody in there. I was in possession of a bag of rocket-propelled Dutch amphetamine that night and wondered what I was going to do with it. Thinking it was okay to pretty much do as we liked in the bar, I went into the WC and racked out a load of lines on the toilet roll dispenser. I had let the others know what I was up to, so they formed a queue outside the toilet, and one by one, went inside and snorted a line. The bar manager flipped out when he saw what was happening. He dashed across the room with a damp cloth and wiped the remaining powder off the dispenser. For some reason, he didn't chuck us out, merely warning us not to do it again.

My abiding memory of that night was Podders falling face-first off a barstool onto the floor. Outside, later, Marcus was rebuking him for his perceived bad behaviour. He was pulling him up the street by his ear, saying 'Come on lad, it's time you went to bed!' I remember Podders replying, 'Get off me, who do you think you are, my fucking dad?'

Another time in Amsterdam, after a gig at the Melkweg, the band were in a hotel room smoking this eighteen-inch long joint of weed. The Dutch bloke who'd given us the joint had ominously inscribed on it, 'This machine kills Cropdusters!' He wasn't kidding. Before long, we were all virtually unconscious. One night, while we were partying in a hotel room in Europe, Marcus fell asleep and was sprawled out on the floor. When he came round a little while later, he was greeted by the unnerving sight of Rampton hovering above him, holding one of his syringes in his hand. He thought Marcus had slipped into a diabetic coma and was preparing to inject him with a jab of insulin. Just as Rampton was about to plunge the needle into him, Marcus came round and bellowed at him, 'What the fuck do you think you're doing? I don't need it now, I just passed out coz I was hammered! Give me that syringe, now, you idiot!' It was fortunate Marcus woke up when he did.

One time, at some ungodly hour of the morning, a drunken Roger scaled the roof of a service station, lunging about like Spiderman, while the rest of the band looked on in hysterics, singing 'Roger Ramjet, he's our man, he's our man, he's our man. Roger Ramjet, he's our man, good old Roger!' I remember once in Holland we'd gone into a coffee shop and asked the guy behind the counter to sell us a large bag of the strongest weed he had to offer. After smoking a joint of it, Krish was found keeled over in a shop doorway, his face a deathly shade of green.

We left Holland early that morning and drove in Rod's car to Belgium for another gig that night. We were smoking spliffs in the back of the car, and you could barely see out of the windows, the smoke was so thick. After we'd checked into the hotel in Belgium, we realised Cob had disappeared. We later found him huddled on top of the wardrobe in his room. It wasn't even midday.

One night in Amsterdam, Krish and I decided we didn't fancy going back to our hotel as it was far too early, and we were in the mood to party all night. We scored some ecstasy pills off an ex pat Brit in the Melkweg who was living in a squat in the city. We went back to the squat with him and stayed there for a few hours, getting royally hammered.

When the Cropdusters were on tour, Krish always shared a hotel room with Roger. Cob and Marcus hooked up together, and Mike and I did the same. Krish and I arrived back at our hotel around five o'clock in the morning and weren't ready to crash yet. I suggested we keep the party going in his room. The problem was, Roger was sound asleep in there. The beds in the hotel rooms were on wheels, and silently taking the brakes off, we pushed Roger and his bed outside into the corridor. Roger immediately woke up, spluttering 'What's going on? What the fuck do you think you're doing?!' and that was game over.

We saw some real strange sights while travelling around Europe on tour. One day, we pulled into a service station in Holland to see a row of pushbikes parked outside in the car park with Harley-Davidson motorcycle fairings fitted to them. Their young owners were standing around chatting nearby, grinning like village idiots and holding crash helmets in their hands. We were smoking weed in the van at the time we came across them and couldn't stop laughing for hours afterwards.

Service stations abroad often provided the band with serious amusement. On one occasion on tour in Holland, we stopped off to refuel the van and get something to eat. A few of us had been smoking grass, and while we were sitting at a table in the restaurant part of the services, Marcus slowly started shaking his head in disbelief, and snickered, 'My God, look at that man. What on earth does he think he looks like?'

Intrigued, I glanced over to the serving counter and saw this extremely peculiar looking middle-aged chap standing there in the queue. He had an obvious dark wig perched precariously on his head, which appeared like it might slip off at any moment, thick-rimmed spectacles, and was wearing a green turtleneck jumper and horrible brown flared trousers. He was a dead ringer for the Tom Patterson character in the 70s TV sitcom *The Fall and Rise of Reginald Perrin*. The only thing not evident was a smoking pipe. It was hilarious. We were literally sobbing with laughter for ages afterwards, but eventually it reached the point where it simply became too painful to laugh anymore. Oh, the little things in life, eh?

Regarding dead ringers, several of the Dusters were drinking in an

Amsterdam bar one night when Marcus turned to me and said, 'Fucking hell, that Dutch bloke sat over there looks just like Steve McMahon! It's him innit?' Steve McMahon was a footballer who played for Liverpool in the late 1980s, and looking at the bloke in the bar reinforced my belief that everyone's got a doppelganger somewhere. Perish the thought.

Within The Cropdusters' immediate circle, it was often remarked how various band members and crew bore an uncanny likeness to well-known people, such as heads of state, Royal Family members, religious figures, politicians, movie actors, television personalities, musicians etc. The band's roadie, Podders, was regularly told that he looked like a young Bernard Cribbins, the late, great British actor. Mike Case was compared to Soviet president Mikhail Gorbachev, especially after he'd put on a lot of weight through drinking copious amounts of Guiness. Marcus Stott had a touch of Jeff Stewart, PC Reg Hollis in the TV series *The Bill*, about him. Cob Cook could easily be mistaken for the Baldrick character in the television comedy *Blackadder*, played by Tony Robinson. Jonathan Webb, who was briefly the band's guitarist towards the end of our existence, always reminded me of actor Bill Pertwee, ARP Warden Hodges in the TV sitcom *Dad's Army*. Spike O'Sullivan, who also roadied for the Dusters, resembled, to my mind anyway, a hybrid of the British actor Todd Carty and Kristian Schmid, who played Todd Landers in the Australian soap opera *Neighbours*. Spike responded to my observation by claiming I looked unnervingly like Wilfred Brambell, who was most famous for playing the grubby rag-and-bone man Albert Steptoe in the long-running BBC sitcom *Steptoe and Son*.

The Dusters used to have great fun messing about with guest lists at the venues we played. In addition to real people, we'd write down ridiculous names, such as Ali Baba + 40, Yul Brynner + 6, One little pig + 2, Cruella Deville + 101, D'Artagnan + 3, John Buchan + 39, Enid Blyton + 5, One wise monkey + 2, Blake + 7, Moses + 10, Lee Marvin + 11, One Billy Goat Gruff + 2, Henry VIII + 6, Frankie Valli + 3, One blind mouse + 2. And so on.

While out on the road on tour, we'd pose each other questions like 'Who's the spottiest in Derek and the Dominoes?' and 'Who's the most claustrophobic in Crowded House?' That kind of thing. At times, I thought I was going out of my mind with the craziness of it all, but it relieved the pressure and was funny as hell.

While we were away touring, we'd all endeavour to keep ourselves and each other entertained. Cob used to come out with some real fantastical stuff. He'd say things like 'If a fly dies, you can bring it back to life by pouring salt on it,' and 'You can buy miniature horses, the size of pygmy shrews, through mail order. You can train them to gallop about on a coffee table and jump over pieces of Lego. They only live for twenty-four hours, though.' Or: 'I bet you didn't know there's an actual Oompa Loompa living in Lymington. He's got a cottage down on the quay. You don't see him about much, as he likes to keep himself to himself. Honest. It's true!' Or: 'There's a highly infectious disease called HOD. You catch it through working on building sites, and I knew a couple of labourers who were diagnosed HOD positive. When the foreman found out, they were both told to leave the site with immediate effect.'

I think Cob sincerely believed in what he was saying, and I'm sure the rest of the band all thought the same. We used to call his outlandish anecdotes Cobisms. Seriously though, Cob was a very talented man. Aside from being a wizard of a fiddle player and master craftsman; when he was at art college in the early 1970s, he won a nationwide competition to design a logo for the Anadin painkiller brand. In physical education lessons at Priestlands secondary school, he was a remarkable discus thrower and represented Hampshire in the sport.

On one occasion, at which I wasn't present, Cob went into the Safeway supermarket in Lymington with Mike and Marcus to buy stuff for a morning breakfast fry-up. They were standing at the deli counter when Cob suddenly exclaimed 'Look, they've got Rindles bacon here! It's the best bacon in the world, I'm telling ya!' He'd missed the last letter in the word 'rindless' and just made it up on the spot. That was a classic Cobism.

Sometimes, in the band, it felt like we were talking a different language to everyone else. We christened this unorthodox method of communicating Bibble, and the supreme power and figurehead of all this hokeypokey was the almighty Bibble Bison. Marcus, a talented graphic designer, came up with a drawing of the Bibble Bison, and the artwork appears on a couple of The Cropdusters T-shirts and various other paraphernalia. Talking of T-shirts, there are countless different Dusters T-shirts floating about the planet, ninety-nine per cent of which were designed by Marcus.

Cob's wife Sharon was responsible for the band's mailing list. She went under the pseudonym Viola Frogmorton, and people could order merchandise and keep up to date with gigs, tours and other relevant news by contacting her directly. This was all long before the advent of mobile phones, the internet and social media. In those days anyone wanting information on the band had to make a phone call from a landline or send a letter.

Bands' dressing rooms, worldwide, are covered in graffiti. At each venue The Cropdusters played, we'd bring our own unique brand of humour into the equation. Marcus always carried a black marker pen in his pocket and would usually be the first member of the band to write on the walls. I remember him spraying the words 'Gold Against the Soul' on the dressing room wall at the Melkweg, in gold paint. The Manic Street Preachers obviously saw it, because they released an album with the same title soon afterwards. One night in Belgium, Marcus even sprayed 'Gold Against the Soul' on the road outside the venue we were playing at, in gigantic gold letters.

When the Dusters were on tour, we'd often cover dressing room walls in nonsensical graffiti. 'Colin Occupants of Interplanetary Craft', 'Imran Can you Dig it?' by Pop Will Run Itself Out, 'Cleanliness is Next to Godfreyness' and 'I Can See Mike Brierley Now the Rain Has Gone' were just a few of our unhinged scribblings that spring to mind. We'd draw absurd cartoonish depictions of our fellow band members on the walls, amongst other things. A picture of a half hammerhead shark-half washing machine was just one of many preposterous creations we plastered over various dressing room walls.

At one venue we played abroad, I think somewhere in Holland, I drew a picture on the wall of Wattie Buchan from The Exploited, in thick black marker pen. For some reason, I decided to change the drawing of

Wattie into a part stereotypical Hawaiian man. I gave him a curly black Mohican hairstyle, floral lei, Hawaiian shirt and traditional grass skirt. I added tattoos, ear and nose rings, chains, a studded belt and jackboots, and christened my artistic creation 'Wa Ti Bu Chan, The Heathen from Honolulu'.

A lot of time on tour is spent idling away in hotel rooms, recovering from the night before and catching up on some sleep. In the rooms Krish shared with Roger, the American cable television channel MTV seemed to be on permanently in the background. The MTV format mostly comprised videos of bloated, corporate, formulated stadium rock music. I remember in 1992 one particularly grating song dominating the channel, receiving constant airtime: *Sexy M.F.* by Prince & the New Power Generation.

One morning, the band were in the van, driving through the back streets of Amsterdam, looking for somewhere to park. We eventually found a car park, but some miserable dustmen barred our way and wouldn't let us through. They were wearing brightly coloured boiler suits, and collectively, they reminded me of a bouquet of sorrowful artificial sunflowers. Remembering the lyrics to the Prince song, we all began chanting 'Man in the yellow overalls, you sexy motherfucker!' The looks on those blokes' faces were a mixture of bemusement and hostility.

On another occasion, the band had just completed a gruelling tour of Germany and had driven across France to Calais for the ferry trip home. We got into a vodka drinking session in the ferry's bar area, and it wasn't long before I passed out. When I woke up, I was sprawled across some seats, humping them. There was an entertainment show happening directly in front of me, and I'll never forget this woman singing, 'You say potato, I say potahto, let's call the whole thing off.' I remember thinking, what the fuck's going on? Where am I?!' I turned around, looking for the rest of the band, and there were hundreds of strangers stood there staring at me. God knows what I'd been doing or saying while I was out for the count.

Once, on yet another ferry crossing from Dover to Calais, most of the band had got roaring drunk in the bar area. Heaven knows what we were drinking, but after several hours, Mike and I decided to wander off and find somewhere comfortable to get our heads down for the remainder of the night. I'm not sure what was going through our heads, but we somehow ended up in one of the staff employees' private cabins, which happened to be unoccupied at the time. Intruders, that's what we were, with no right to be there.

Stretching ourselves out on a pair of bunk beds, we were soon sound asleep. Our good fortune didn't last long, however. We were abruptly woken up by a startled and clearly unhappy stewardess, exclaiming, 'What the hell are you doing in my cabin? Right, get out now, before I call the authorities! There are cabins on board this ferry that you pay for. Why don't you go and book one of them? Either that or bugger off back to the bar area and doss out there for free! I'm tired after working a long shift and need my bed! Please get out, now!' Feeling a bit embarrassed with ourselves, Mike and I mumbled an apology to the stewardess, left the cabin, and returned to the uncomfortable seats in the bar area.

We were in a hotel one night in Aachen, a German city on the Dutch border. It was 1993, and earlier, we'd played a gig in one of the music venues there. After the show, a couple of us were taken to this house to score some gunpowder, so we could stay up all night. I recall entering this room in a flat, and there was a couple sat there in an armchair, the speed dealer and his girlfriend. It was funny because they were dead ringers for Sid Vicious and Nancy Spungen. We paid for the goods and walked back to our hotel. The band had all chipped in and bought a crate of lager for the long night ahead.

I think the party was going on in the room which was Mike's and mine. The music was banging, and everyone was flying and having a good time. After a while, there was a knock at the door. We opened it to find the hotel manager, a woman, jabbering something incomprehensible at us. She couldn't speak any English, but it was obvious she wasn't happy. Anyway, we pretty much ignored her, closed the door, and carried on with what we were doing. It wasn't long before there was more knocking at the door, louder this time. Again, we opened it, and the hotel manager started howling, and waving her arms about in unintelligible protest. She appeared to be some kind of neurotic. Once more, we closed the door on her and continued with our party.

Ten minutes later, we heard loud voices shouting at us to open the door, or they'd smash it in. Upon doing so, a group of armed German police stormed into our room. Pointing their guns at us, they ordered us to leave the hotel immediately. These guys were deadly serious and meant business. They would have had no hesitation in blowing us all to kingdom come, if need be. It must have been around 4 am by now, and I can remember sitting outside on the hotel steps with a bitch of a comedown, feeling right pissed off.

Once, we were standing on the ferry's car deck after pulling in at Dover, having completed yet another successful tour around Europe. I'd got well and truly hammered on the ferry crossing, and even though I didn't have a driver's licence at the time, I attempted to manoeuvre the band's van off the ferry and onto dry land, when it was time for us to leave the car deck. It all went pear shaped, and Dave Bindon asked me what the fuck I thought I was doing and advised me to walk on ahead. Then he jumped into the driver's seat himself and drove into the ferry terminal.

As I staggered across the ferry ramp, I came across an inebriated Mike Case, a carton of steaming hot coffee in his hand. For some reason, he poured some of it into my ear, perforating the eardrum. I never held a grudge against him for doing that to me; it was part and parcel of who we were. He's one of my oldest mates, and we'd just shared an unforgettable time on the road together. Who knows? If the boot was on the other foot, I could easily have done the same thing to him. What a carry on, if indeed a painful one.

I could tell you so many rock 'n' roll tales of The Cropdusters' exploits while on tour, I'm sure they'd keep you enthralled for hours on end. For instance, I remember returning to the hotel one night, after a gig somewhere abroad, to find Mike on all fours, crawling around the lobby in circles with his trousers around his ankles, loudly barking his head off. He was so pissed, he honestly thought he was a dog. It was good natured riotous behaviour, in keeping with the spirit of it all, and highly amusing, to say the least.

In early 1993, Krish announced he was leaving the band. He told us he wanted to get into the filmmaking industry, as it had always been a passion of his. Whether this was the real reason he left the Dusters, only he would know. Playing in a touring band isn't exactly good for your health; rock 'n' roll is dangerous. Maybe all the drinking and whatever had made him reflect on his future. Marcus reverted from the banjo, and occasional second guitar, to playing the drums. He had been a drummer originally anyway, and this now gave us the scope to experiment with heavier, tribal, Killing Joke style drum patterns.

Not long afterwards, Roger dropped a real bombshell on us. He announced he'd had enough of all the touring and was leaving the Dusters. I knew Roger had discussed quitting the band with Cob at a gig at the Melkweg previously. He'd told him he thought he was turning into an alcoholic with the amount of time he was spending idling away the time in music venues. Cob sympathised with him entirely, and said it was getting to the point where he was going to have to leave the band himself, for the same reason. As it turned out, Cob was right there until the bitter end, when the band finally split up in 1994.

An old friend of ours called Jonathan Webb, who lived locally, replaced Roger as the band's guitarist, but it was never the same, to be honest. I was gutted to lose Roger. Not only was he one of my oldest mates, but he was an original Cropduster, who'd been instrumental in the band's songwriting process and was a vital component. He also had a great sense of humour. The departure of Roger and Krish changed the overall dynamic in the Dusters, without doubt, but what could the rest of us do at the time? Ultimately, we could only respect their decisions.

The Cropdusters were determined to soldier on regardless. In September, the new line-up went on tour across the UK, complete with Max, our new roadie, and Richard 'Grizzly' Holt, our new sound engineer from the town of Reading, in Berkshire. 'Grizzlysound' was the buzzword now. Grizzly could be an intimidating man with a penchant for gratuitous violence, who had it in his make-up to terrify the living shit out of people he came across. Bald, squat, and with a badass rock 'n' roll attitude, he was someone not to be messed with, that's for sure.

One evening, on that tour in '93, I was hanging out in the dressing room at The Crazyhouse in Liverpool before the Dusters were due to sound check. I grabbed a pen and a piece of paper from somewhere and started drawing a caricature of Grizzly. I thought I hadn't done a bad job in capturing his likeness, and for the coup de grace, I added a pair of Pom-Pom ballet slippers. I showed the drawing to Podders, and he pissed himself laughing. At that very moment, Grizzly walked into the dressing room and asked us both what we found so funny. Composing himself for a moment, Podders managed to divert Grizzly's attention while I hurriedly screwed up the paper and stashed it in my pocket. If Grizzly had seen the picture I drew of him, he'd have probably battered the crap out of me.

The band had recently changed booking agencies. We were no longer with World Service and had signed up to Value Added Talent Agency. These were the dates on what would prove to be the last ever Cropdusters tour:

11TH SEPTEMBER GLOUCESTER GUILDHALL

16TH SEPTEMBER BATH, HUB CLUB

17TH SEPTEMBER THE VENUE, NEW CROSS, LONDON

18TH SEPTEMBER THE FORUM, TUNBRIDGE WELLS

22ND SEPTEMBER THE BOAT RACE, CAMBRIDGE

24TH SEPTEMBER THE SQUARE, HARLOW

25TH SEPTEMBER THE CASTLE, BRENTWOOD

26TH SEPTEMBER WEDGEWOOD ROOMS, PORTSMOUTH

2ND OCTOBER NEW ADELPHI, HULL

3RD OCTOBER WHEREHOUSE, DERBY

4TH OCTOBER PRINCESS CHARLOTTE, LEICESTER

6TH OCTOBER THE PLAZA, WOKINGHAM

8TH OCTOBER MARKET TAVERN, KIDDERMINSTER

9TH OCTOBER THE VENUE, OXFORD

13TH OCTOBER HIPPODROME, COLCHESTER

14TH OCTOBER ARMY & NAVY, CHELMSFORD

15TH OCTOBER THE GARAGE, HIGHBURY, LONDON

16TH OCTOBER THE ANGEL, BEDFORD

20TH OCTOBER PIRATE INN, FALMOUTH

21ST OCTOBER TJ'S, NEWPORT

22ND OCTOBER SALISBURY ART'S CENTRE

1ST NOVEMBER FLEECE & FIRKIN, BRISTOL

I remember that year the Dusters played at a club in Berlin, in what was the old East Germany. The Berlin Wall hadn't long come down, and the east of the city was littered with broken down vehicles, and the streetlights didn't work. Discarded newspaper pages choked the gutters, and it was eerie experience being there. I couldn't help wondering what life had been like for the people living on the other side of the wall. East Germany was a communist state, and its secret police, the Stasi, was the largest security apparatus in the world at the time.

At some time during the autumn, the band flew out to play a show at a music festival in a town square in Zürich, Switzerland. It was the most The Cropdusters ever got paid for doing a gig; somewhere in the region of two grand, I think it was. It was never really about the money with us, although that certainly helped; it was more to do with the enjoyment of playing live music to the masses and watching them get off on it.

Christmas '93 was one I'll never forget. The Dusters headed over to Holland for a series of gigs, the high point of which was a blistering Christmas Day show at the Melkweg, in Amsterdam. Jonathan, our new guitarist, got so hammered he fell into the moat outside the venue. The next day, Boxing Day, the band played two shows in different places before travelling home. One of the gigs was in Groningen; I don't recall where the other one was.

1994 was the year in which the Dusters disbanded. I think it was around June when we finally decided to call it a day. Looking back, it wasn't the same anymore, without Roger and Krish. We'd had an incredible experience doing what we loved doing the most. The band originally formed in a small town on the Hampshire coast, a place that many people couldn't even point out on a map, and in no time at all, we'd elevated ourselves to a position most of our contemporaries could only dream of. The Cropdusters played close to around a thousand gigs during our initial eight-year existence. We travelled to many different countries and met loads of wonderful people. I guess we were more fortunate than most, in that respect. I believe that ultimately, the legacy of the Dusters lies in its music; the fun we had in making it, and the joy the music brought to others. As a footnote, I'd like to add a list of everyone who was directly involved with The Cropdusters during those crazy eight years:

Shaun Morris, Vocals.
Roger Figgures, Guitar.
Mike Cass, Bass.
Cob Cook, Fiddle, Mandolin, Acoustic Guitar.
Graham 'Bill' Haley, Drums.
Marcus Stott, Banjo/Whistle/Harmonica/Guitar/Drums.
Krish Stott, Drums/Mandolin.
Nigel Hasler, World Service Agency.
Jonathan Webb, Guitar.
Martin Byrne, Guitar.
Scott Tobin, Drums.
Yanny, Mandolin/Saxophone.
Rod Hamilton, Sound Engineer/Driver.
Rampton, Sound Engineer/Band Manager.
Rik 'Podders' Smith, Road Manager/Driver.
Davey Cooper, Sound Engineer.
Dave 'Bunders' Bindon, Driver.
Mark Wellman, Roadie/Driver.
Gerrit Hoek, Lighting Engineer.
Toby Burden, Tour Manager
Mark Widdowson, Roadie/Driver
Nigel Gilroy, Recording Studio Engineer.
Gary Butterfield, Link Records.

Richard 'Grizzly' Holt, Sound Engineer

Ashley, Band Manager.

Alan, Sound Engineer.

Stuart Gates/Driver.

Mark 'Toad' Pellow, Roadie.

Rik Cook, Band Manager.

CHAPTER 6

THE WILDERNESS YEARS

The last six months of 1994, and the whole of 1995, were a strange time for me. The Cropdusters were no more, and I missed the gigs and the tours and everything else that came with them. I was feeling lost and often wondered if we'd made the right decision in splitting up the band. I remember thinking, what if we'd carried on? Would people still be into our music and flock to our shows? After Krish and Roger had left the band, in '93, the Dusters overall sound had inevitably changed. It was no more built around elements of American bluegrass/hillbilly and traditional Irish music. We'd gone back to our punk roots and were a lot more electrified.

What if we'd taken a step back and returned to our original, stripped-down hoedown manifesto? At one gig at Bournemouth Academy, The Cropdusters had outsold Motorhead, for fuck's sake. There were many 'ifs' floating about in my mind at the time. In retrospect, I believe we made the correct decision in calling it a day. Times move on, and to evolve as a band, you need to keep pace with the changes that are happening around you.

When the Dusters had started out, in '86, there was a clamour for bands like The Pogues, The Men They Couldn't Hang and us. By 1988, the underground acid house scene was springing up in the clubs in the UK, and the following year, the alternative dance genre, labelled Baggy, was taking a grip of the nation's musical consciousness. Rave parties were happening everywhere, often illegally, which made them even more attractive to young people, who were fed up with the rat race.

Baggy was primarily a scene centred in Manchester, or Madchester, as it was known, and leading the charge were bands such as the Happy Mondays and the Stone Roses. Flowered Up were London's answer to the Madchester scene, and the capital's music press were keen to promote them as such, giving them as much exposure as possible. I remember Flowered Up were featured on the front cover of the NME before they'd even had a record out. They were a talented band, and it was distressing to hear about the death, at forty-one, of their charismatic frontman Liam Maher from a heroin overdose in 2009. Liam's younger brother, Joe, Flowered Up's guitarist, died from complications of long-term ill-health in 2012.

In the early to mid-1990s, I was listening to a lot of dance music, mainly techno. I remember going to all-night raves with my mates at a castle near Yarmouth on the Isle of Wight, and house parties in Bristol and Bath. One of the guys hosting some of these parties was an old fan of The Cropdusters called Tony Duvall. Back in the late 70s, Tony had been the manager of Winchester punk band The Mental, and I used to bump into him sometimes at gigs in Southampton and the surrounding area.

In 1987, The Dusters and The Men They Couldn't Hang played at a huge party at Tony's father's house in the south-west of England. In '94, we performed at Tony's wedding in a village hall, also in the West Country. The first house party I went to in Bath was in another house that Tony's father owned. I'm not sure where he'd disappeared to because he was nowhere to be seen, and the place was totally deserted and had no electricity. Rumour had it that he was a bit of a rogue and he'd done a runner to the Costa del Sol in Spain due to tax evasion.

I'd travelled to Bath with some of my mates, including Ed English. After meeting up with Tony in a pub there, we all headed off to his dad's house for the party. One of Tony's friends was an electrician, and after we'd forcibly gained entry to the property, he sorted the power out without any problem. The DJ that night, whose name I can't recall, played some real banging tunes, and I remember all the people who were there having a smashing time of it.

Closer to home, my old friend Cathy McColl, the punkette from Priestlands school, used to host some serious parties at her house in Middle

Road, Lymington. These debaucherous affairs would sometimes go on for days and nights on end and were tremendous fun. Cathy had long since moved on from the days of spiking her hair up and dying it bright colours and wearing her punk rock clothing. She was a fully-fledged biker chick by now. However, once the whole punk attitude's inside you, it never, ever goes away.

The regular party goers at Cathy's place during those days included some good mates of mine I'd known for years. Apart from Cathy's boyfriend at the time, Dave Smith, who was an extremely funny guy from Southampton, there were the usual suspects, including Steve Carpenter and Stuart Gates. One of Cathy's best mates, Maria Littlefair, known as Min, was a frequent attendee at these unforgettable social gatherings.

On the Easter weekend of 1994, Mike, I and a mate of ours called James Olive- Jones, who was nicknamed Ponce by Dave Dutton, travelled over by car ferry to the port of Calais, France, scene of the Dusters' Christmas Eve misfortune a couple of years previously. Upon reaching Holland, we drove to Amsterdam to see the electronic group Underworld play at the Paradiso. Ponce loved parties, and there's a classic story about him on his last day at Priestlands school. He's three years younger than me and was in the same year as my wife Michaela.

Earlier in the day, Ponce had drunk a whole bottle of vodka and was absolutely battered. Bopper Haynes was addressing the pupils in the sports hall, thanking them for their efforts and wishing them well for the future. Ponce was so out of it he had to be held up by his schoolmates. Bopper was walking up and down the hall, singling out individual boys and girls, and congratulating them for their achievements. At one point, Bopper was standing only a few feet away from Ponce, but he never sussed out what was going on.

The three of us stayed at the home of some Dutch friends, Stephan and Petra, who lived in the city, and we had a wonderful time out there. The Underworld gig was a cracker. I recall they didn't come onstage until 4 am, and when they did, the whole of The Paradiso erupted. It was a fabulous night. The only downer was we'd pretty much spent all our money in

Amsterdam, so on the ferry journey home, we could barely afford anything to eat or drink.

As an early birthday present, in November '95, my brother Richard invited me up to his house in Fulham for the weekend. He had it all planned out to a tee. Rich had bought tickets to watch Arsenal against Manchester United at Highbury on the Saturday afternoon. Accompanying us that day was a good friend of my brother's called Magnus. After the match, which Arsenal won 1-0, the three of us headed off to the West End for a drink around the pubs there. It was my first introduction to vodka and Red Bull, and I recall we got through jugful's of the stuff.

Next on the agenda was an Oasis gig, the following night, at Earl's Court. I quite liked Oasis at the time but can't bear listening to the sound of their music nowadays; it really grates on me, for some reason. I think of them as the third greatest Beatles tribute band of all time. I went to the show with Rich and several of his friends, including Magnus, David 'The Enemy' Frend, whose parents ran the Monkey House pub in Lymington for a while, and David 'Two Methods' Smith. The gig was a sell-out, with 22,000 people in the audience, and it was a damned good night all round. What a weekend that was. I'd been totally spoilt by my brother and couldn't thank him enough for his hospitality.

For most of 1995, I was living in a bedsit in a new extension of a house on Southampton Road in Lymington. Me and my mates used to have a right laugh in that bedsit, getting up to all sorts of mischief, and there was always something crazy happening round there. I guess we were all just totally irresponsible in those days; some of us still are. I'd originally moved into the house in 1991 with my then girlfriend Caroline and rented another room there for four years.

When we split up and she moved away to Bristol, I hauled across the landing into the bedsit.

I'd accumulated a massive collection of CDs and cassettes over time, literally thousands of them, and I stacked them all up against the wall in my room. Eventually, I acquired a large metal cassette rack from the owners of a place in Lymington called Forest Records, which was closing its doors for good. I would spend hours on end putting together my own compilation tapes and painstakingly writing out the track listings for each of them. I gave the tapes unconventional titles such as *Edward the Compressor, Vine Weevil: Mortal Enemy of the Bizzy Lizzy, Wife Swapping by J.R. Hartley, Naked Twister with Your Grandparents, Bringing in the Oaves, Nato on My Shoulders, Den Watts, Bertie Volts and Sherlock Ohms,* and *For Colin's Ears Only*. I played the CDs and cassettes through a mean little ghetto blaster I'd bought in a shop in Bournemouth in the early 90s.

I remember Reg Case was renting a separate room in the house at the time, and one night, after a session in the local pubs, the pair of us went back to the bedsit with another couple of blokes, one of whom was a mate called Adam Smith. We were armed to the teeth with a big box of fireworks, and there was the distinct feeling of mischief in the air. Lymington police station was directly opposite the house, and I recall us leaning out of the window, firing rockets at the building. Later, after Reg had crashed out in his room, he suddenly awoke to hear someone saying, 'I know, let's chuck a load of bangers under Reg's bed, and see what happens!'

Those were the days. With respect to fireworks, when I was a kid growing up in the 60s and 70s, people would have giant bonfire parties in their back gardens to celebrate Guy Fawkes night on November 5th. We'd get to within touching distance of the flames and run around with lighted sparklers, setting off bangers, Roman candles and Catherine wheels. I can't ever remember a single person being injured by a firework back then. It wasn't like it is now, with all the health and safety rules and regulations in place. Nowadays, Bonfire Night is celebrated with large, organised corporate events in sports fields, and ironically, it's at these displays that most of the accidents occur. It's a prime example of how much this country has changed since I was a child.

The woke agenda certain people adhere to borders on the ridiculous. For example, each year on Bonfire Night, you read comments on social media such as 'Oh, what's that horrible loud noise I can hear, coming from down the road?! My precious little woof woof Snuffles is frightened stiff and won't go outside!' 'Oh my God, these people are just so selfish. It sounds like World War 3's just started out there!' Fuck the stupid small-minded idiots, and the woke horse they rode in on. Our dog Tank couldn't give a monkey's left testicle about it.

Whatever happened to the fun and excitement our generation enjoyed when we were young? There are so many misinformed, clueless idiots about that just don't get it. I suppose it's a sad indictment of the society we currently live in. There's none of the oomph, fuck you attitude we all had when growing up. We had Slade, we had The Sweet, we had David Bowie, T-Rex and Roxy Music. We had the Sex Pistols, The Clash, The Damned and The Adverts. These were artists that shaped my life, for God's sake; bands forever ingrained in the psyche.

One time round my bedsit, me and a few mates had been up all night partying when we decided to walk down to Long's Wine Bar, in the High Street, for a pint. It was eight o'clock on a Saturday morning, but in those days, you could get a drink in Long's at any time during the day or night, if you knew the right people. I was with Flash and a good friend called Ed English, who was the younger brother of Urk, my old schoolmate.

After a few drinks, we left the bar and headed across the street to Grove Gardens. We were sitting in the pavilion when for some inane reason, I felt compelled to strip off my clothes. I then ran, fully naked, down to the bottom of the gardens. There happened to be a group of old ladies shuffling up the path, which ran parallel to The Grove, heading to the market in the High Street, to do their morning shopping. Upon seeing them, I let out a loud whoop and started waving my arms about maniacally.

The women stopped in their tracks, and I was horrified to see my mother standing there in the middle of the group. She called out to me 'Shaun, Shaun, is that you?' I could have died of embarrassment at that moment. Regaining my composure, I jogged back up to the pavilion and quickly put my clothes back on, thinking *what the hell have I just done? What the fuck is wrong with me?* That was definitely not my finest moment, by any stretch of the imagination.

Returning to the High Street, I snapped off a stem of pampas grass from in front of a shop nearby, and upon seeing a traffic warden standing outside

Sperrings newsagent, I ran up to him and started tickling him around the body with it. Aghast, he ran off down the street, with me in hot pursuit. Afterwards, I went straight into the Angel Tap bar and proceeded to get drunk. The whole thing was utter madness, when I think about it now.

The landlady of the house where I rented the bedsit, was a kind-hearted, effervescent woman called Ali. One of her young daughters, Tiffany, had a room across the hallway, and her other daughter, Chandy, lived downstairs with her boyfriend. The girls were both lovely. I got on well with Ali, and she was extremely tolerant of my loud music and sometimes mischievous behaviour. She'd warned me on several occasions to tone it down, and I guess it was only a matter of time before she reached the end of her tether. The straw that broke the camel's back was when my old mate, Dean Lancaster, climbed up a ladder outside my bedsit, and put his head through the window, shattering a pane of glass. Reg and I received a letter from Ali the following day, informing us she'd had enough of our conduct and instructing us to move out of the house. I think she gave us a week's notice to find somewhere else to live.

Around Christmas '95, I found myself another place to rent in Lymington. It was a bedsit in a house on Gosport Street, and the landlord, Bob Harris, lived on the premises. We called him 'Whispering Bob,' after the presenter of the television music show *The Old Grey Whistle Test*, also Bob Harris. Bob was an affable chap, and after I'd been living there a month or so, he agreed to let Flash move into the recently vacated bedsit next door to mine.

I don't recall how long I lasted at that place, but soon Whispering Bob was on my case. He was growing sick and tired of the loud thumping music I was constantly playing and the incessant comings and goings of our mates at all hours of the day and night. Things finally came to a head after one particularly mental session in my bedsit. Bob was banging on my door, shouting at us to keep the noise down, and no one took a blind bit of notice of him.

The next day, we bumped into each other in the hallway, and an argument ensued. Bob was becoming increasingly flustered, and looking back, I don't blame the man. He made it crystal clear that he wasn't putting up with all this nonsense anymore and told me he was throwing me out of the house, and I needed to find somewhere else to live. He said he wasn't a well man and needed the pressure of living in the same building as me like a hole in the head.

Meanwhile, my mates and I would spend much of our time drinking in Lymington's pubs. Apart from Long's Wine Bar, places we'd frequent during the mid-90s included The Black Cat, which was originally the esteemed Ye Olde English Gentleman, and had undergone a total refurbishment, and Champagne Charlie's, which eventually became the Lymington Tavern. There was the King's Head and the Ship Inn down on the quay, and the King's Arms at the top of town, known to most of us as the Doom and Gloom, due its unfailingly drab and depressing atmosphere.

The King's Arms at the time was a dimly lit establishment with rickety old-fashioned tables and chairs, and walls and ceilings painted in a horrible dull brown colour. I seem to recall the carpets being brown, also. It really was a dismal place, and the awful, tinny sounding music playing through the cheap, crappy stereo speakers behind the bar only added to the miserable experience. Most of the customers in the King's Arms in those days appeared as if they'd been drinking there since the dawn of civilisation; they were that old. They obviously enjoyed going to the establishment, so good for them. It was their lives, and nothing to do with me. Incidentally, the pub's still there today, although it's changed drastically since the mid-90s.

Another pub, The Coach House, right next to Lymington railway station, had recently changed its name to the Bosun's Chair, and we tended to go there on Sunday evenings, when they had bands playing. The Bosun's Chair was originally called the Railway Hotel, and as I wrote earlier, it was where Peeping Toms played their first ever gig, back in 1982.

I was once told a story of how the infamous hellraising English actor Oliver Reed, star of movies such as *The Bulldog Breed, The Curse of the Werewolf, Oliver! Women in Love* and *Gladiator,* came down to Lymington one night with some of his mates and was drinking heavily in the Lymington

Tavern. He ended up getting into an altercation with one of the pub's regulars, a mate of ours called Paco, who was a big man and someone not to be messed with. Apparently, it reached the point where the pair of them were fronting each other out at the bar, their foreheads coming together. I think it was mostly bluster, and I heard it didn't develop any further than that. Ironically, as mentioned earlier, *Oliver Reed Goes to Salt Creek* is the title of one of The Cropdusters' songs. It's an instrumental and appears on the flipside of the 1988 12" single, *Just Poppin' Out to Fight a War*.

There was a house in East Boldre owned by an older mate of mine called Al Hallett. During the mid to late 90s, Marcus lived at the property, along with Al, his daughter, Jane, and his son, Karl. The drinking sessions round there often lasted for days on end and were fucking mental. Al was a gentleman and a perfect host. If you didn't act like a complete tosser and abuse his hospitality and generosity, then he really couldn't give a fuck. The house eventually became affectionally known to locals as the Hallett Arms, due to the inordinate amount of alcohol being consumed there.

I remember some insane impromptu gatherings round that place, after a load of us had returned steaming drunk from local pubs, namely The Turfcutter's Arms and the East End Arms. Whenever I had the pleasure of being a guest at Al's house, I would invariably be met by the same familiar grinning faces, sitting on a sofa in the lounge. There was Geoffrey Kitcher, nicknamed Jake, Dean Parker, known to everyone as Tash, Gary Sherwood, who had the moniker Bungle, Steve Coombes and Paul West, AKA Frogger. The first three of these miscreants I mentioned earlier, while we were working at the chicken factory together in the 1980s.

In the spring of 1996, I started working for a company in North Boarhunt, near Fareham, in Hampshire, called S.I.S Chemicals. S.I.S manufactured chemicals for wholesale and distribution for the swimming pool industry. The managing director was a man called George Lavis, who along with his wife Jane, were very good friends of my parents. Their son Mark, who I'd been at school with, worked there as the assistant manager, as did an old mate of mine called Barry Fitzgerald, or Fitzy, as he was commonly known. Fitzy was a great bloke; he didn't suffer fools gladly and would say it as it is. He was also extremely funny, and it was a pleasure working with him for the couple of years he was there before he left the company for pastures new.

I remember being in a lock-in with Fitzy and a few others at the White Hart pub in Pennington one night in the early 90s. It was well into the early hours when suddenly there was the sound of smashing glass. I looked up to see Fitzy's beaming face peering straight into the bar from outside. He'd put his head through a small window at the side of the pub. The landlord, John Mayman, wasn't bothered about the damage, he was only concerned as to whether Fitzy was okay, but that was the kind of man he was.

One of Fitzy's many legendary party tricks was dropping his bollocks into the bottom of a pint glass. It's amazing to think a bloke's capable of doing that, when you come to think about it. 'Hung Like a Worcestersaurus' was a popular local saying at the time, dreamt up no doubt by one of the members of The Cropdusters on the road in our tour bus. Fitzy was one seriously crazy dude, and I believe it was that craziness that endeared him to almost everybody who met him.

One of the funniest stories Fitzy ever told me concerned the time he travelled by train in midweek from Lymington to Dorchester in Dorset for a guided tour around one of the town's celebrated ale breweries. Accompanying him that day were my old schoolmate Pete Golden and another good friend of mine called Joe. On the train journey to Dorchester, apart from drinking copious amounts of cider, the three of them dropped some tabs of LSD. To cut a long story short, or rather 'to cut a John Dory short,' as we used to say, halfway through the tour of the brewery, Pete somehow managed to lose his footing and fall into a vat of grapes. After rolling about on his back helplessly for a while, completely immersed in grape juice and laughing uncontrollably, he finally pulled himself together and clambered out of the vat.

Fitzy explained to me that when the three of them eventually arrived back in Lymington later that night, they ordered a taxi from the train station to take them home. The taxi driver happened to be a bloke who was in the year above me at school. Pete was meant to be the first one to be dropped off, but he refused to get out of the taxi until the driver called him a beautiful yellow fish. As the minutes ticked by, and the meter kept running, the taxi driver just stared at Pete disbelievingly, before finally uttering in total exasperation, 'Okay, you're a beautiful yellow fish.' Satisfied by his response, Pete proceeded to fall out of the taxi and staggered off back to his house.

My job at S.I.S Chemicals mostly entailed labelling up plastic bottles and filling them with various powder chemicals, such as acid and alkali, from fifty-gallon drums. I'd then pack the bottles into boxes and stack them on pallets. It wasn't a mentally taxing job, by any stretch of the imagination, but it kept me physically fit, and I enjoyed it. People who know me well might find this hard to believe, but I had a forklift truck licence while I was at S.I.S.

My immediate boss was a quietish guy called Colin, who lived miles away, near Wimborne, in Dorset, and existed on a diet of strong coffee and John Player Special cigarettes. I was living in a house in Lymington at the time, and during the first few months of me working at S.I.S, Colin would divert from his journey to North Boarhunt and pick me up in his van each morning. He'd also take me home after finishing work in the afternoon. It was one heck of a round trip for him to have to make, and I couldn't thank him enough for his trouble. Lamentably, Colin died a few years ago.

Fitzy was as mad about music as I was, and each payday, at the end of the month, he'd drive us into nearby Portsmouth where we'd visit HMV Records and buy a load of the latest CDs. Another S.I.S employee was a guy called Tommy, who worked for the company as a lorry driver and lived locally. Tommy was a great bloke and bang into his music as well.

At the time, Fitzy, Tommy and I were the youngest people working there, and the three of us tended to hang out together. Behind the backyard of the S.I.S site, was an internationally renowned nudist camp, called the South Hants Country Club. Sometimes, we'd climb up on wooden pallets and peer over the fence through the trees, in the hope of catching a glimpse of unsuspecting naked women. Unfortunately for us, we never did. Sadly, Fitzy and Tommy are no longer with us, having left this earth far too prematurely. So many of the people I worked with at S.I.S. back in those days aren't alive anymore.

During the summer of 1997, I moved to a house in Gosport with my then partner and her young daughter. It made total sense at the time. Gosport is only seven miles from North Boarhunt, and I used to cycle to work there and back each day. It was boring as hell living in Gosport, to be honest, and although I really liked my job, in July the following year, I left S.I.S and moved back to Lymington.

In September 2000, I began working at a care home in the small village of Hordle, a few miles away from Lymington. The job entailed looking after adults with severe disabilities such as cerebral palsy. The home was run by a lovely couple called Fred and Marcia Hayward, and while there, I worked with their daughter, Mandy, who was my immediate boss. I was employed at the care home for several years and it was an eye-opening experience for me. However, it all ended abruptly one day, several years later in October 2006.

It was a Saturday morning shift, and I decided to take one of the service users, a male in his 40's, out in his wheelchair for a walk around the lanes of Hordle. It wasn't long before we found ourselves standing outside the Three Bells pub in the village. The pub opened at 11 am, and although it was forbidden to drink alcohol on duty unless you had permission from the boss, I thought it wouldn't do any harm to nip in for just one swift beer.

I pushed the wheelchair through the pub's front door, and the service user and I headed towards a table inside. As it was so early, we were the only customers. I ordered a glass of Coke for the guy and a pint of lager for myself. After finishing my drink, instead of doing the sensible thing and heading back to the care home, I bought another pint of lager and a half pint for the service user. The guy really seemed to be enjoying himself, and before I knew it, I was necking down pints of lager, and he was drinking halves. It was approaching 1 pm by now, lunchtime, and the pub was slowly starting to fill up with customers. I ordered us both something to eat and I, not him, I hasten to add, carried on drinking.

It must have been midway through the evening when my phone rang. One of the staff at the care home was trying to get hold of me because it was now the start of her shift, and I was supposed to be there for handover. Stupidly, I ignored the woman's call and bought yet another pint of lager. A short while later, the phone rang again. Once more, I ignored it.

By now, it was pitch black outside, and I was shot to pieces. The next thing I knew was when my team leader, a female, turned up at the pub from out of nowhere and asked me what the hell I thought I was doing. 'Where have you been all day, Shaun? We've been trying to contact you and you're not answering your phone! How long have you been in here? How much have you had to drink, for God's sake?' Slurring my speech, I replied I honestly didn't know, but that the service user had just spent the best time of his life with me in The Three Bells that day.

The team leader looked at me with an expression of absolute frustration and dismay and asked me to follow her out into the pub car park. While another member of the care staff wheeled the service user out of the back door, I blindly followed on behind. The team leader, addressing me, said, 'I'm sorry Shaun, but you're sacked.' At that very moment, babbling incoherently, I collapsed helplessly into her arms, and she had a job holding me upright. As it turned out, I'd ended up spending over £100 in The Three Bells that day. It was typically irresponsible behaviour on my part, and ultimately, it cost me my job.

CHAPTER 7

APOCALYPSE NOW

Towards the end of 1994, I decided I was going backpacking around Vietnam for a month. I just about had enough money left from my grandad's inheritance to achieve this. I'd been fascinated by the Vietnam War for a long time, ever since I'd watched *Apocalypse Now* on the TV in the early 80s. I still believe it to be the greatest movie ever made. Vietnam was the rock 'n' roll war and was happening at the same time as I was growing up in the 60s.

There's a certain mystique about young American soldiers going off to fight in the tropical jungles, mountains, paddy fields and swamps of an alien Asian country thousands of miles away from home. However, most of the Nam veterans I've spoken to over the years will tell you the place was a hellhole during the war, an absolute bitch. I can't even imagine what those people went through back then, soldiers on both sides and civilians alike.

I'd seen most of the other 'Nam films, such as *Platoon, Hamburger Hill, Casualties of War, The Deer Hunter* and *Full Metal Jacket*, and I had also built up quite a large collection of books on the subject. I think some of the best ones are *A Rumor of War, The Tunnels of Cu Chi, If I Die in a Combat Zone, A Viet Cong Memoir, Dispatches, Chickenhawk* and *Tim Page's Nam*.

Tim Page was a cool, fearless daredevil British freelance press photographer who stringed for United Press International (UPI) and Agence France-Presse (AFP). His pictures appeared in numerous publications, including *Life* magazine, and are considered some of the most iconic of the Vietnam War. Page would ride out on a motorbike to the frontline during battles between the Americans and the Vietcong; a place few other reporters would dare venture, as close to the action as possible to get the photos he wanted. He was wounded four times in action, and on one occasion, given the last rites. Tim Page was reputedly the inspiration for the Dennis Hopper journalist character in *Apocalypse Now*. When his book *Nam* was released, Page toured the world to promote it. He was at a book signing session at a shop on London's Tottenham Court Road one day in 1997, and my brother went along there and bought me a personally signed copy as a gift.

I didn't want to travel to Vietnam on my own; I wanted to share the experience with someone else. I wasn't in a relationship at the time, so I didn't have a partner to come away with me. I started asking my mates if they fancied joining me on a trip of a lifetime, but none of them had either the inclination or the funds. Eventually, a friend of mine called Dougal said he was in a good financial position and was up for it. We went down to a travel agent on Lymington High Street and bought two return plane tickets to Saigon, now known as Ho Chi Minh City. We were booked to fly out a month or so later, in January 1995.

When the day arrived to travel to Vietnam, I was so happy it was unbelievable. Dougal's father drove us to Southampton Airport, and we flew from there up to London's Heathrow Airport. The flight took around fifteen hours, and we occupied our time eating and drinking alcohol. I couldn't sleep a wink as I was so excited at the prospect of what lay ahead for us over the coming month.

Dougal had a window seat on the plane, and I'll never forget his words to me: 'Shaun, you need to get a look at this!' I gazed out the window and realised we were flying over Vietnam's Mekong Delta, in the very south of the country. The delta is pancake flat and laced with countless rivers, tributaries and canals. It's one vast expanse of shimmering, emerald-green rice fields. The Mekong Delta is the most populous part of Vietnam, and the rice bowl of the country. You need to be right down there, in amongst it, to fully appreciate the stunning beauty of it all.

We landed in the evening at Tan San Nhut airport in Ho Chi Minh City, and the moment we stepped off the plane, we were hit by this tremendous tropical heat. Even at that time of day in Vietnam, the weather is stiflingly hot, and January is one of the cooler months over there. Aside from the climate, the sights, sounds and smells of the country knock you for six. I'd never experienced anything remotely like it.

After we'd completed the time-consuming visa formalities, we walked out through the airport terminal and hailed a taxi. We'd pre-booked a hotel in Dong Khoi Street in downtown Saigon and asked the driver to take us there.

The taxi journey to the hotel was mind-blowing. It was completely dark by now, and once we reached the streets of Ho Chi Minh City, it became apparent to us that this was one hell of a crazy place. It was vibrant and chaotic, and I knew right away that Dougal and I were about to experience something neither of us would ever forget for the rest of our lives. It really was an assault on the senses. The ceaseless flow of motorcycle traffic and the sight of beggars and amputees everywhere completely took your breath away. Bars on both sides of the roads were lit up with a myriad brightly coloured neon lights, and banging dance music could be heard playing in several of them. The overwhelming aromas of charcoal, burning incense and exotic spices were omnipresent. The pungent redolence of nuoc mam, a tangy Vietnamese dipping sauce made from rotting fish, commonly used in Vietnamese cooking, hung in the air.

The bustling streets were lined with food stalls and cooking fires, their owners selling a great diversity of exotic fare. There were stalls peddling chicken, beef, pork, duck, fish, eels, shrimps, crusty baguettes and pho, which is a famous standard Vietnamese noodle soup. The authenticity of it all was astonishing. It was like being in another world, and I felt like I might as well have been on the moon. I thought the coolie hats many of the locals wore were indeed cool, and the young ladies in their traditional ao dais, long flowing tunics, looked so elegant. As they breezed slowly along the pavements, they carried with them the certain grace that's unique to Oriental women.

We arrived at the hotel, and the taxi driver helped us inside with our backpacks. We went to the reception desk and got the keys to our room. Even though it was nighttime and I hadn't had any sleep, I was far too pumped up to try and get some shuteye. I wanted to get out into the chaos right there and then. I'd read about a place called the Apocalypse Now bar, the oldest bar in Saigon, and after we'd located it on a street map, Dougal and I left the hotel and went off to find it.

Walking along the city's streets for the very first time was exhilarating. At ground level you can feel the unadulterated rawness of it all. We reached the Apocalypse Now bar and went inside and ordered two cans of lager. The Vietnamese currency is the Dong, and we both had plenty of them on us. We also carried a fair amount of US dollars, in money belts strapped around our waists.

While we were drinking at the bar, I suggested to Dougal that we should go and visit the famous Cu Chi tunnels the next day. The Cu Chi tunnels are located about 50 kilometres from Saigon. During the Vietnam War, they were used by the Viet Cong guerillas, the VC, in their fight against the Americans and their allies, the South Vietnamese Army, or ARVN. The Cu Chi tunnel system was a vast jungle network of underground communication passageways, fighting positions, spider holes and trapdoors. At the height of the war in the late 60s the tunnels stretched for over 250 kilometres, from the outskirts of Saigon all the way to the Cambodian border.

The Viet Cong used the tunnels as hiding spots from American search and destroy operations and jungle patrols. They were riddled with all kinds of booby traps. The guerillas-built punji stake traps in the tunnels; camouflaged pits of sharpened bamboo sticks. They'd put hand grenades on the walls and ceilings, which would be set off when unwary US soldiers, known as tunnel rats, crawled through and touched the tripwires.

The VC even utilised Mother Nature in their war against the better armed American GI's. They'd tether venomous snakes, scorpions and centipedes to the ceilings, which added extra psychological fear on the part of the tunnel rats. The tunnels were dug out of laterite clay and were sometimes three levels deep, and the Viet Cong built kitchens, armament factories, sleeping quarters, makeshift hospitals and meeting rooms down there. They were ingenious in their construction. Dougal was adamant he wanted to see the Cu Chi tunnels as well.

After we'd drunk another few cans of beer, we paid the bill and left the bar and headed back to the hotel for some much-needed rest. While we were walking along the street, we were approached by two cyclo drivers. The Vietnamese cyclo is a three-wheeled bicycle with a front mounted seat, one wheel at the back and two at the front. It's a traditional form of transport and essentially a taxi on wheels.

One of the blokes asked us in broken English if we wanted to go anywhere in particular. We mentioned the Cu Chi tunnels, and they offered to take us there on mopeds the following morning. We agreed on a price of five dollars for each of them and asked them to take us back to the hotel in their cyclos, so they knew where to pick us up from the next day.

That night, I couldn't sleep at all again. There was too much adrenaline flowing through my body. At nine o'clock the following morning, we went and had breakfast upstairs in the hotel and at 10am, as arranged, the two guys pulled up outside on their mopeds. The weather was hot, and getting hotter by the minute, as we rode out of the city on our way to Cu Chi district.

The journey took over an hour, and I can remember waving to the locals who were relaxing in chairs alongside the road. Remarkably, every single one of them waved back to me. We arrived at the Cu Chi tunnels during the oppressive heat of the late morning, and after watching a short video about the history of the tunnels, we were taken on a guided tour of the area. It's even possible to go down and explore a section of the tunnels, which Dougal and I both did. Several of them had been widened to accommodate the bulkier frames of Western tourists, and it was an amazing, if claustrophobic experience, and an invaluable lesson in modern history.

After a few hours at the tunnels, we decided we'd seen enough for the day and indicated to the two moped drivers that it was time for us to leave.

On the way back to Saigon, we stopped off for refreshments at a drinks stall at the side of the road. This was when I first started feeling uncomfortable out there. I couldn't quite put my finger on it, but my gut instinct told me that something wasn't right. The woman serving the drinks appeared genuinely hostile towards us, for some reason. She was chattering away in Vietnamese to the two moped drivers and kept glancing over at Dougal and me with an almost hateful look in her eyes.

That's when it hit me, like a ton of bricks. I was becoming increasingly paranoid by now and felt more vulnerable than I had in a very long time. I hadn't slept for days, it was boiling hot, and here we were in a strange land, on the other side of the world, and to make matters worse, we couldn't understand the Vietnamese language in any shape or form. As the woman stared coldly into my eyes, with a look that sent shivers running down my spine, I paid her for the drinks, mumbled something sarcastically in English about how nice it was to feel welcome in her country, and we jumped back on board the mopeds.

Before we set off on the return journey to Saigon, one of the blokes offered to take us to his home, to meet the rest of his family. I remember politely declining and saying to him that maybe we'd go round there on another day. I explained to him that we were dog tired and needed to get back to our hotel to grab some sleep. When we arrived there, an hour or so later, Dougal handed one of the blokes a ten dollar note, the fee we'd agreed on the night before. One of them said no, it was supposed to be ten dollars for each of them; that was the deal. I thought they were trying to rip us off and had no intention whatsoever of letting them sting us for any more money. They started becoming visibly agitated and it was clear they weren't happy at all. Attempting to diffuse the situation, I recommended they come back to the hotel the next morning at ten o'clock, and I'd pay them the extra ten dollars. They talked briefly among themselves, and turning back towards us, reluctantly agreed to this arrangement, then rode off down the street on their mopeds.

Back in the hotel room Dougal said to me 'I can't quite work out why, but I'm sure there's something dodgy about those blokes. I don't trust them at all.' I totally agreed with him. I had a gut feeling that these two guys weren't who they were cracked up to be and spelt trouble. I thought about the situation we found ourselves in for a while. I conjured up a plan and told Dougal about it. I suggested to him that rather than hang about waiting for the blokes to turn up at 10am the following morning, we check out of the hotel an hour earlier at 9am and go and find another place to stay. Surely there was no way they'd track us down in a city of eight million inhabitants, I thought, and we'd be free to carry on enjoying our trip without hopefully encountering any more problems.

At bang on 9 o'clock the next morning, we checked out of the hotel and headed off on foot with our backpacks in the direction of Pham Ngu Lao Street. Pham Ngu Lao is a haven for foreign backpackers. It's chock full of budget hotels, nightclubs, bars, restaurants, travel agencies, souvenir shops and massage parlours. Eventually, we found a suitably priced guesthouse and booked a room for the night there.

Across the street from the guesthouse, was the Sinh Café. This was one of the first places in Saigon to offer budget tours to backpackers. It's a Vietnamese institution, and it's possible to travel the length and breadth of the country by coach or minibus, taking in all the major destinations. You can hop on or off at your leisure, and the prices are relatively cheap.

Dougal and I ambled over to the café to grab ourselves something to eat for breakfast and a drink of cold lager. One beer soon turned into another, and we were starting to feel a lot more relaxed by now. We eventually got chatting to other backpackers from various countries and were really getting into the whole vibe. Occasionally, a kid would come into the café, trying to tempt you into buying a postcard, a painting, a pair of sunglasses, a wristwatch, a fake Zippo lighter, or any other kind of souvenir from Vietnam.

The shoeshine boys were more tenacious and acted genuinely offended when you politely said no to them. They'd keep on and on at you, trying to get you to pay them a dollar or whatever for shining your shoes. They were a nuisance, to be honest, albeit a harmless one. People would walk up and down the street outside the café, offering massages, pedicures and suchlike.

At night on the street corners, things were a lot more sinister. Lurking in the shadows, down dark alleyways, shady characters plied their trade. There were drug pushers, hustlers and pimps, Vietnamese ne'er-do-wells and fly-by-nights. Undesirables. As you'd walk past them, they'd try and tempt you, whispering 'Marijuana? Opium? Heroin? Special massage?' Some of these people were police informants. If you bought drugs from them, they'd grass you up and identify you to the cops. You'd then be accused of committing a serious offence and ordered to pay a huge fine, sometimes as much as five hundred dollars. If you didn't have the money to pay it, you risked being arrested and sent to prison. On the other hand, if you could afford to pay the fine, the money would be divided equally between the corrupt police officer and the informant. That's how it worked out there.

There were other various scams occurring in Vietnam at the time, especially in the touristy areas of larger cities such as Hanoi and Ho Chi Minh. From fake and overcharging taxis to getting ripped off in bars and restaurants, you had to have your wits about you. Thieves and pickpockets blended in seamlessly with the crowds, and you had to be aware of opportunist drive-by snatch thieves, known by the Americans during the Vietnam War as cowboys. Riding on the back of mopeds, in an instant they'd grab your jewellery, bag, phone, or anything else you'd left unattended, before speeding off down the road.

There were unscrupulous men out on the streets, preying on the unwary and the vulnerable, trying to tempt them into investing in phantom properties or buying fake precious gemstones. Inscrutable people would grab your attention and invite you over to sit down and play rigged gambling games with them, the outcome of which invariably involved you losing every time and being quickly relieved of all your money.

While travelling around the country, I heard numerous stories of greedy cyclo drivers taking unsuspecting foreign tourists down seedy dead-end backstreets and alleyways and demanding they pay them extortionate amounts of cash for their ride. I was once told of an American guy who got into an argument with a cyclo driver over money. He was adamant he wasn't going to pay what the bloke was asking for, so eventually, the cyclo driver simply reached down into his bag, pulled out a pistol and shot him dead on the spot.

Getting involved with prostitutes was not a good idea and could spell disaster. One scam I heard about went like this: a Western male would be walking along a street at night, alone, when a prostitute, standing on the pavement, would solicit him by calling out things like 'Hey you, big boy, come here! You wanna have a good time with me right now? Me sucky sucky, boom boom all night! Me love you long time! Me good, me cheap. Only five dollar!' 'Me love you long time' is a line from the classic Stanley Kubrick Vietnam War movie, *Full Metal Jacket,* which incidentally, was filmed in the United Kingdom. The unwitting guy would invariably express his interest by walking over to the prostitute, her pimp more than likely hovering about somewhere in the shadows nearby. She'd then demand he pay her the money upfront. As the guy naively reached into his money belt, wallet, or whatever, for the five bucks, she'd grab him hard by the balls, momentarily incapacitating him, before doing a runner with all his cash. Of course, scams such as these can happen in any big city around the world; they aren't restricted to Vietnam.

One afternoon, in the city of Nha Trang, on the central coast of Vietnam, Dougal decided to wander off alone to do a bit of exploring. He was strolling along a road when a woman jumped out from behind a bush right in front of him. She beckoned Dougal to follow, and the two of them walked around the bush together and started kissing. One thing led to another, and without going into the gory details, Dougal was mortified when he felt a meat and two veg in the palm of his hand. Realising he'd been propositioned by a ladyboy, he made his excuses and beat a hasty retreat, leaving the ladyboy looking more than a little disappointed. Dougal returned to the hotel, his face a ghostly white and appearing more than a little perturbed. Shaking his head in disbelief, he told me what had just happened to him, and said 'I don't know if I can handle this country anymore. I really don't. It's mental.'

I'm not a monk, by any stretch of the imagination, and I won't disguise the fact I've had my own personal experiences with Southeast Asian ladies of the night on my travels over the years: some good, some not so good. Several of the stories I could tell you about are so crazy and outrageous they would blow your mind away, but what happens on tour stays on tour, I'm afraid.

At the time, I was a single Western male backpacker seeking fun, excitement and adventure in an exotic tropical foreign land thousands of miles away from home. It should come as no surprise to anybody that the temptations of the Orient are manifold. However, for obvious reasons, I'm sure you'll understand I'm not going to write about my experiences with prostitutes in this autobiography. Besides, it all happened a long time ago, so I'll say no more on the matter and leave it at that for now.

Sitting in the Sinh Café that morning, we witnessed a strange spectacle; an elderly Vietnamese man, with a Ho Chi Minh beard, jogging down Pham Ngu Lao Street, entirely naked, seemingly without a care in the world. As the day wore on, I started to feel quite pissed. Dougal and I had started drinking large bottles of Heineken and Tiger lager earlier in the morning, but they were relatively expensive, so we began buying bottles of the cheaper Vietnamese stuff. There was BGI, Bia Hanoi, 333 and Saigon Beer. Later, we discovered the delights of Bia Hoi. It was what the locals drank and was ultra cheap. On our trip in 1995, Bia Hoi was selling at just 12p a litre. It's 4 per cent in strength and tastes wonderful, I might add.

Other, more exotic, beverages on offer in Vietnam include snake wine. This might come in the form of a cobra, or a bamboo viper immersed in a bottle of extremely potent rice liquor, with the addition of a colourful variety of herbs. I remember one time in Saigon, a bloke sitting next to me on a table outside a bar was drinking a glass of bird Scotch whiskey, would you believe. There was a small dead bird immersed in the whiskey, and every now and then, the man poured a measure of the concoction into his glass. Gesturing towards me and smiling, he offered me a taste of the drink, but I politely refused. I'd like to think these creatures didn't suffer in any unnecessary way before they ended up in bottles of alcohol.

Back at the Sinh Café, I was having a rare old time. This all changed when Dougal suddenly walked over to me with a horrified expression on his face. He said 'You ain't gonna believe this. Those two blokes are sitting in their cyclos, right across the road from us!' I recall thinking, how the fuck did they find us? I stood up from the table and looked outside. Sure enough, there they were, with malevolent looks etched on their faces. Dougal went out to speak to them and came back inside the café and told me they said they weren't going away until we'd paid them the extra ten dollars they said we'd all agreed upon. I explained to him that they weren't going to get another cent out of me and carried on drinking.

The day was wearing on now, and evening was fast approaching. Those men were obviously going nowhere in a hurry, and I didn't want to take the risk of messing with them on their home turf in the darkness. They would have known every single alleyway and nook and cranny in Pham Ngu Lao Street, and as newly arrived travellers in Vietnam, we hadn't yet got our bearings and hardly knew where we were. It would have been suicide to try and escape from them in their own backyard. The whole scenario was developing into a waiting game, with neither side prepared to yield. The Sinh Café closed at 11pm so it was inevitable we'd have to bite the bullet and face them at some point.

Eventually, I'd had enough of all the bullshit and hatched a plan. I told Dougal to get his backpack ready, and when a vehicle stopped outside the café, obscuring the blokes' view of us, and at the word go, to run like his life depended on it. After we'd settled the tab, a van pulled up in front of the café. This was our moment; it was now or never. We dashed outside together, Dougal running in one direction, me in another.

Immediately, one of the blokes had me cornered. He grabbed a monkey wrench from a mechanic's toolbox which was on the pavement by the side of the road. Waving it menacingly in my face, he screamed 'Give me the money or I fucking kill you!' At that moment, in the unrelenting tropical heat, I remember thinking, I've barely been in the country thirty-six hours, and now I'm about to die in Vietnam. My heart was thumping, and it was like time had suddenly stood still, an out of this world experience is how I'd best describe it. Somehow, I managed to edge slowly away from my would-be Oriental assassin, back into the relative safety of the Sinh Café. I knew they couldn't touch us in there.

My body shaking, and in a complete daze, I sat down at a table and ordered myself a bottle of BGI lager, wondering if Dougal was okay. What had just happened to me was surreal. The manager came over to me, looking flustered, and said, in pretty good English, 'We never have problem in here like this before. It not good. I call police.' I couldn't even contemplate that scenario. The situation was rapidly developing into something that had the potential to end in complete disaster for us. The Vietnamese cops take no prisoners, especially foreign ones. The language barrier would have been our ultimate downfall. The two cyclo thugs could make up anything they wished. They might inform the police we'd defrauded or assaulted them, or worse, we were buying and taking drugs. We would've had to pay the cops a substantial bribe to persuade them to let us off the hook, but even that wasn't guaranteed to end this business. We could seriously find ourselves banged up abroad, in one of Ho Chi Minh City's notorious jails. We'd be incarcerated there with all manner of Vietnamese criminals – murderers, rapists, perverts; our futures uncertain. There was no doubt in my mind that this could turn into an absolute fucking nightmare.

Just as the manager was about to call the police, Dougal appeared in the café doorway, apparently unscathed. He told me the other bloke had threatened him with a broken bottle, but he'd managed to talk his way out of it. I breathed a huge sigh of relief, and then he said to me 'For fuck's sake Shaun, let's just pay them the money.' I finally saw sense and relented, and he walked across to our tormentors and gave them ten dollars.

Around ten minutes later, the guy who'd had a go at me with the monkey wrench strolled into the café as if nothing had happened and apologised for threatening to kill me. I looked him straight in the eye and politely told him to fuck off. He then sheepishly stared down at the tiled floor before turning away and skulking back to his cyclo outside. We checked to make sure the pair of them weren't hanging around there anymore and returned to the guesthouse.

I'm so glad I never took that bloke up on his offer of visiting his house to meet his family. He knew we were carrying comparatively large amounts of cash on us, and I'm sure he wouldn't have hesitated in killing us for it, if he had to. It wasn't beyond all reason that he'd have aggressive male relatives round there backing him up, if necessary, complicit in the whole carefully crafted scheme. At home, in his own domain, we'd be setting ourselves up like lambs to the slaughter.

As I lay there on my bed in the guesthouse, the paranoia really started kicking in. It reached the point it was nearly off the scale. The effects of the alcohol I'd drunk had all but dissipated, and I was convinced those guys were going to suss out where we were staying, break into our room with guns and blow us both to kingdom come. Every time I heard a sound outside our door, my heart would beat faster, and I prepared myself for the worst. As it turned out, the gruesome twosome never showed up, and we never saw either of them again.

Dougal and I learned a valuable lesson that day. We were naïve young men in a far-off land, in a country where the culture was completely different from ours. We were easy targets, and I guess we thought we were untouchable. We found out the hard way that we were not. In all my subsequent travels around Southeast Asia, and there have been many of them, I never let myself get into a situation like that again. That experience hardened me to the potential perils of travelling in a foreign country on the other side of the planet.

I knew we had to get out of Saigon, for our own sanity. I couldn't shake the feeling that we were going to bump into those blokes again. The next day Dougal and I walked over to the Sinh Café and booked a four-day tour to the Mekong Delta. The manager surprisingly seemed pleased to see us and told us the two cyclo drivers were opportunist gangsters, and although they were Vietnamese, they didn't have the necessary paperwork permitting them to reside in the country. The following morning, we checked out of the hotel, boarded a minibus and set off for the Delta.

As far as I can remember, there were around a dozen of us on this trip. Apart from Dougal and me, there was a young Israeli couple, a Dutch couple, three Germans, one Japanese and a guy from the USA called Marcel. We took to him instantly. He was a laid-back man of native American origin, from Santa Barbara, California, and had been travelling extensively throughout Southeast Asia at the time.

One of the Germans was an older, bearded man who we nicknamed Pagoda Pete. Incredibly, Pagoda Pete had been travelling around the world on his own, non-stop, for decades. The last time he had been in his own country was in 1952. Every time the minibus drove past a pagoda or temple, or even a simple Buddhist shrine, Pete would point at it, grow mad with excitement and ask the driver to stop the vehicle so he could take some photographs.

The Japanese guy was your classic solo traveller. He generally kept himself to himself, but eventually we got talking to him, and he told us he was a bachelor from Tokyo. He said he'd been backpacking around the globe for many years and had visited every single country on earth. In each of the countries he visited, he'd take thousands of photos with his camera. He then sent the reels back to his parents in Japan, and they stashed them in his bedroom, for him to look at when he finally came home. There must have been millions of them, when you think about it.

The funniest thing that happened on this trip into the Mekong Delta was when we visited Sam Mountain, a religious site near Chau Doc, on the Cambodian border. Dougal, Marcel and I were climbing up the steep steps of the mountain, when Marcel came across a Buddhist monk with his baby son. He bent down to gently pick up the baby, and as he did so, the infant pissed all over him, saturating his clothes.

When we got back down from the mountain, I was approached by a young lad. I couldn't understand what he was saying but gathered by the krama (traditional scarf) he was wearing around his neck that he was Cambodian. He was smoking a joint of weed and offered me a toke. I duly accepted, and it made the journey back to our hotel a lot more interesting.

On the fourth day, we left the delta and travelled back to Saigon. Over the course of the next few days, we hired the services of two friendly cyclo drivers, Mr Sam and his young sidekick, Hoang Vu. They took us to see some of the city's main attractions, such as the Independence Palace, the Reunification Palace and the Museum of American War Crimes, now called

the War Remnants Museum. Not long after, we went into the Sinh Café
and booked a ten-day tour. This trip consisted of travelling up on National
Route 1, by minibus, along the coast of Vietnam, where all the major cities
were located. Dougal and I had an awesome time, experiencing the wonders
of Vung Tau, Dalat, Nha Trang, Quy Nhon, Hoi An, Danang and Hue.

In the coastal city of Vung Tau, about sixty kilometres from Saigon,
we walked down to the city's picturesque beachfront and instantly became
the targets of a pair of opportunistic local cyclo drivers. The blokes were
persistent and wouldn't take no for an answer when we told them we weren't
interested at all in securing their services. One of them was particularly
persevering and kept trying to persuade us to let them take us to a place he
said served good food and cheap alcohol.

'You come with us now. We take you to great bar not far away. You eat
rice and peanuts and drink cold Vietnam beer. Have pretty girls and play
music. You like very much.' We politely declined his offer and walked off
up the street. The two cyclo drivers were not to be dissuaded though and
followed around a hundred metres behind. At long last, we managed to get
far enough away from them, and they gave up their attempt at persuading
us to hire them.

The tour guide on this ten-day trip was a short, rotund middle-aged
man called Mr Hai; Agent Hai, as Dougal and I christened him. During
the Vietnam War, Agent Hai worked for the Americans as an interpreter.
When North Vietnam won the war and reunified the country in 1975, he
was arrested by the communists and sent to a re-education centre in the
countryside. Because he was classed as an enemy and a traitor, he had one of
his thumbs cut off as punishment. Agent Hai spent many years imprisoned
at the re-education centre before being released.

Although he struggled with the English language and often appeared
worried he wasn't doing his job properly, I don't believe anyone on that tour
encountered any significant problems with Agent Hai. Understandably,
he was terrified something bad might happen to one of the travellers in
his charge, like getting lost, or worse, disappearing off the face of the earth
forever. All in all, I think Agent Hai was a genuinely good guy. He was

professional, informative, and tried his level best to make sure everyone enjoyed the tour as much as possible, and you can't ask for any more than that.

For me, the undoubted highlight of this tour was when we visited Dalat, a large city in Vietnam's Central Highlands. An incident occurred there which still makes me laugh to this day. It was one of the funniest things I've ever seen in my life, and I'll describe what happened in the next couple of paragraphs. Meanwhile, here's an interesting story. When the minibus pulled into Dalat, on our way to the hotel, the first thing we saw was the body of a man floating in a water fountain in the city centre. Apparently, he'd got drunk the night before, slumped over the edge of the fountain, fallen in and drowned, the poor bugger.

Anyway, part of the tour itinerary involved visiting this place, which stood beside a beautiful lake called Xuan Huong. Bizarrely, there were numerous Vietnamese cowboys there: guys riding around on horseback, wearing wide-brimmed Stetson hats, neckerchiefs, brightly coloured shirts, leather vests and trousers, and high-heel boots with spurs. It reminded me of an Indochinese Disneyland, and it was surreal. While we were wandering about, a boy came up to Dougal and me wearing a Mickey Mouse costume. He gestured to us that we should take a photo of him, with one of us stood next to him. After the picture was taken, he demanded we pay him one dollar. We told him he must be joking and walked off. Mickey Mouse was persistent, if nothing else. Wherever we went, he followed, and kept saying 'One dollar, one dollar. You give me one dollar!' He was becoming increasingly annoying and wouldn't leave us alone. In the end we gave him the money, just to make him go away.

A little while later, we came across the boy again. He was sitting down with several older Vietnamese men, gambling with the one dollar note we'd given him earlier. What really cracked me up was that the Mickey Mouse head part of the costume was placed on the ground right next to him. We finally got to see the boy's face. He glanced up at us with a startled expression, and we walked away, pissing ourselves. I guess you had to be there.

Although Danang, Vietnam's fifth-largest city, was on the tour itinerary, we didn't stop there for long because one of the people in the group, an Israeli guy, decided he didn't like the look of the place and didn't want to spend the night there. He thought Danang was a shithole. How he came to that conclusion so quickly I don't know. Up to then the group had only stopped off briefly at one café in the city for a cup of coffee. Maybe the guy was a clairvoyant and there was something about Danang that spooked him.

We did, however, get to visit the Marble Mountains, Ngu Hanh Son in Vietnamese, which are a cluster of five marble and limestone hills located inland, around a twenty-minute drive south from the city. The Marble Mountains complex is full of lush green trails, temples, caves and tunnels, and the views from the mountains of the surrounding countryside are spectacular.

As soon as we arrived at the Marble Mountains, Dougal and I began getting hassled by this young local woman. She was desperately trying to get us to buy a piece of marble from her as a souvenir and wouldn't leave us alone for a minute. She was persistent and went on and on about how she'd sell us the marble at a special price. Climbing up the stone steps of one of the mountains, she made sure she hung on to our coat tails, and try as we might, we couldn't shake her off. The woman kept repeating the words 'This marble beautiful. Look. See? You buy; you buy from me now. Please, only two dollar.'

She was becoming a blessed nuisance, to be honest, and even though we made it crystal clear we weren't interested in buying a chunk of marble from her, she wouldn't let it lie. Eventually, we reached the top of the mountain, and after totally ignoring her implorations for a good several minutes, she finally scowled at us and wandered off to find somebody else to pester.

Dougal and I spent a short time exploring the top of the mountain, before descending back down. When we reached the bottom of the steps, we were more than a little hacked off to see the woman standing there, waiting for us. 'You buy; you buy now from me! This, this! See? It beautiful!' she kept saying. Thrusting a small piece of marble in front of my face, she was rapidly becoming hysterical. 'I said you buy; you buy this now!' she screamed, in such a high-pitched voice that she sounded to me like a little twittering bird.

By now, the rest of the group had boarded the waiting minibus for the next leg of the journey, north up the coast on Highway 1 to the city of Hue, about one hundred kilometres from Danang. As the woman kept ranting at us unintelligibly, I turned towards her and told her she was 'dinky dau, dien caid au', which means crazy in Vietnamese. I'd had it up to here by now with her constant harassing, and she was seriously doing my head in.

She went ballistic when I called her dinky dau, and as the minibus slowly pulled away with all of us on board, she ran alongside it, pointing her finger at Dougal and me, incensed, with a demoniacal look in her eyes. She was shouting at the top of her voice, 'Fucky you! Me no dinky dau, you dinky dau! You dinky dau!' It was mental, or more in keeping with the situation, should I say crazy. Looking out of the rear window of the vehicle one last time, the woman was standing there freaking out, little chunks of marble in her hands. She was shrieking 'Me no dinky dau! You! You dinky dau! You dinky dau! Fucky you, fucky you!'

The distance between Ho Chi Minh City and Vietnam's capital, Hanoi, is around 1500 kilometres. Hanoi was the final destination on the tour, but Dougal and I only went up as far as the ancient imperial city of Hue, in central Vietnam. It was very near the end of our month-long trip, and we were fast running out of time. We took the Reunification Express train back to Saigon. With the train's spartan wooden seats and beds, it was an uncomfortable experience, to put it mildly, and the journey itself took twenty-seven hours.

The train moved at a snail's pace and seemed to stop at every single station along the way. To make matters worse, there were no real windows in the carriages, only small, shuttered, narrow slits built into the sides of the train. You couldn't look out and appreciate the striking views of the beautiful Vietnamese countryside, which was a bummer. No misty mountain ranges, no breathtaking azure waters of the South China Sea, no golden beaches, no shimmering rice fields, no tropical rainforest, no rural villages, no shady banana groves, no coconut trees, no farmers busy at work in their conical hats, no water buffalo wallowing in muddy wallows, no sunshine; only the dull interior of the train carriage to feast your eyes on.

The only time you got a proper glimpse of the outside world was when the train pulled into a station, and the doors opened to allow passengers on and off. It was hot and claustrophobic in those carriages, and there was no air conditioning. The journey seemed to go on forever. All you could do to occupy the time was try and stretch out somewhere and listen to music on a Walkman or read a book. Bear in mind that this was in February 1995, a long time ago, and I dare say travelling on the Reunification Express is very different nowadays; faster, and a far more comfortable experience.

Included in the price of a ticket for a ride on the Reunification Express is a basic Vietnamese meal, mainly a few pieces of beef, pork or chicken with rice or noodles. From time to time someone would walk down the aisles of the carriages selling snacks, cans of beer and soft drinks. Feeling tired, I'd crashed out on one of the hard wooden beds and unfortunately missed out on the food when it was time for it to be served. Upon waking up, I felt famished, and headed off looking for a member of staff to see if it wasn't too late to grab something to eat. Walking along the length of the train, I noticed how packed it was. There were people everywhere, crammed in like sardines, and in one of the carriages there appeared to be half of the entire Vietnamese Army. As I navigated my way past the young soldiers, they stopped whatever they were doing and stared at me in silence, looks of curiosity on their faces.

Eventually, I caught up with an official looking man in one of the front carriages, who agreed to let me have a meal. I don't recall what it consisted of exactly, but it wasn't the best meal I'd tasted by a long run. Anyway, it didn't matter, as at least I got to eat something in the end. The following morning, the train crawled into Saigon railway station, and Dougal and I took a cyclo ride to Pham Ngu Lao Street to find a hotel or guesthouse to stay in.

Our last night in Vietnam was one that will live in my memory forever. Mr Sam and Hoang Vu arrived at our hotel in the late afternoon and told us they were going to take us out for a free cyclo tour of Saigon. They said we'd both been loyal customers, and they wanted to repay us in some small way. Dougal and I were delighted and quickly got ourselves ready. As soon as we set off in the cyclos, I started wheezing. I realised I'd left my inhaler in the hotel room, but I didn't want to cause a fuss, and thought I'd be all right.

Mr Sam suggested we go and find something to eat, and recommended an authentic Vietnamese place he knew of, not that far away. We snaked through tiny alleyways until we arrived at a shabby looking eating house. I was feeling worse now and cursed myself for forgetting to bring my inhaler with me. We got off the cyclos and sat down at a table. I ordered four bottles of Tiger beer and looked at the menu. When it was time for us to order, I asked the woman serving us for water buffalo steak and chips. When she returned with the meal, a short while later, I was shocked to find that the steak was still frozen solid. I spoke to Mr Sam about it, and he called the woman over and asked her to get me another steak that was cooked properly.

Eventually, she came back with the steak and placed it on the table in front of me. This one was frozen also. I thought, what the heck, I might as well go ahead and eat the damned thing. I had a difficult job cutting the steak with my knife, it was that rigid. I only ate about a third of the meal before Dougal ordered a final round of Tiger beers, and we paid the bill and left the place.

I was sitting in the front of Mr Sam's cyclo and feeling worse by the minute. The wheezing wasn't abating, and on top of that, I was beginning to see all kinds of weird flashing lights and colours. It was as if I was hallucinating, and I felt terrible. Food poisoning. I asked Mr Sam to take me back to our hotel as I was unwell. He said he understood, but he had a surprise in store for us. He was adamant on taking us to one last place before he and Hoang Vu dropped us back at the hotel. He said the place in question was special, and we wouldn't regret going there.

I remember we went down this dark alley and pulled up outside a small, obscure-looking building. Donald and I got off the cyclos and followed Mr Sam and Hoang Vu inside. The place was dimly lit, with a few small tables and chairs scattered around. There was a pungent smell hanging in the air, and it was then that I realised we were in an opium den. I couldn't believe it. I recall thinking, I felt awful anyway, so I may as well smoke some opium. Who knows, it might even make me feel a bit better.

We sat down at a table, and Mr Sam went over to speak to a man on the other side of the room. He came back with a huge smile on his face, and two ready rolled joints of opium. The four of us smoked the joints between us, and the effects took hold immediately. We were virtually Comatose. Dougal later told me that after smoking the drug, he had felt extremely paranoid. He was convinced Mr Sam and Hoang Vu were trying to get us so stoned and intended to rob us of the last of our money before we flew home to the UK the next day.

As we left the opium den, before the cyclo ride back to the hotel, I was feeling worse than ever. We arrived at the hotel, and I wondered what the hell was happening to me. The flashing lights I'd been seeing earlier were becoming more intense by the second. We'd arranged beforehand for Mr Sam and Hoang Vue to pick us up from the hotel the following afternoon and take us to the airport on the back of their mopeds. My head was spinning, and Dougal had to help me off the cyclo and into the hotel lobby.

At the reception desk, he was holding me upright as he sorted out the keys to our room. With difficulty, he walked me over to the elevator and pressed the button. Seconds later the elevator door opened, and there standing directly in front of us was a Vietnamese family – a man and woman, and their two young children. At that exact moment, I slipped from Dougal's grasp, and collapsed on the concrete floor, banging my head and knocking myself unconscious in the process.

When I came round, I was lying on my back on my bed. There was a hell of a commotion going on in the room, and the exasperated hotel manager was standing at the end of the bed, screaming something in Vietnamese. Pointing his finger at me in accusatory fashion, he shouted 'Drugs! Drugs!' He was obviously extremely angry, and I thought, shit, I pray he doesn't call the police, or we could end up getting arrested on our last night in Vietnam. What an absolute bastard. I couldn't even imagine how bad the consequences would be, should that happen.

Fortunately, Dougal had the quickness of mind to diffuse the situation. Picking up my inhaler from the dressing table, he showed it to the hotel manager and mimicked the sound of a person wheezing to him. Mercifully, the man seemed to understand what Dougal was trying to explain to him. Shaking his head in frustration, he turned and walked out the door, then went downstairs to summon his wife. Minutes later, a plump middle-aged woman with large breasts appeared in the doorway. She walked over to my bed and straddled me. She then began repeatedly pressing down on my chest with both her hands and started rolling her eyes around, breathing heavily and chanting something in Vietnamese. It was a peculiar feeling, as if I was getting CPR and a massage, both at the same time. After she was satisfied I wasn't going to die on her, she left the room. I spent the rest of the night laughing uncontrollably and throwing up into a bucket at the side of the bed. I remember Dougal saying to me, 'You're fucking mental, you are.'

The following afternoon, Mr Sam and Hoang Vu showed up at the hotel on their mopeds. They walked into the lobby where Dougal and I were sitting, and upon seeing me, Mr Sam's eyes lit up. The man looked so happy, and I couldn't understand why. He told me he hadn't been able to sleep last night; he was so worried about me. He said he'd been crying, and he felt guilty about taking us to the opium den. He had genuinely thought I was dead, and that he'd be held personally responsible for the death of a falang (foreigner). He said if that happened, he'd be sent to jail for the rest of his life, where he'd be treated like an animal by the prison guards and forced to defend himself against abuse by violent inmates. It was something he couldn't bear even thinking about.

An hour later we picked up our backpacks and checked out of the hotel. We climbed on the back of Mr Sam's and Hoang Vu's mopeds, and they took us to Tan Son Nhut airport in time for our flight home.

I've been to Vietnam fifteen times so far. On the second and third trips, in 1997 and 2000, I travelled there with my then partner, who'd I'd been seeing on and off for the past couple of years. On the 2000 jaunt, she brought her five-year-old daughter along with us. I remember that when we went there in 1997, we booked a three-day minibus tour around the

Mekong Delta. We sat at a restaurant table down by the river in Chau Doc, with a dozen or so other backpackers.

I thought I'd order some rice wine and called a Vietnamese boy over and asked him to get me some. He walked off and returned with a see-through plastic bag full of the stuff. I paid him for it, and he poured it into a litre-sized bottle. I offered the wine to the other people sitting with us, and most of them accepted. I poured a small amount into their glasses, then took a large glug out of the bottle. I took a couple more swigs, then put the bottle down and opened a fresh can of beer.

In about half an hour, the rice wine started to kick in. I discovered later that it had concentrated in the bottom of the bottle. Because I was the last person to drink the wine, I ended up consuming the most potent part. Before long, I felt like I was losing my mind. I staggered back to our hotel with my partner and literally crawled up the stairs to our room. I sat down on the bed with my head in my hands. The effects of the alcohol were getting stronger, and I was rushing like an express train. I spent the whole night trying to fight against the tremendous potency of that rice wine. It was mental.

I didn't even realise I'd locked my partner out of the hotel room. She must have been banging on the door for ages before I finally let her in. She started screaming at me, 'Didn't you hear me knocking on the door? I've been stood outside on the landing for three hours!' I said I was in such a state I couldn't hear her. She then punched me in the face, breaking three fingers in the process. Two days later, back in Ho Chi Minh City, she went to the hospital and had her fingers snapped back into place. I spent the remainder of the holiday walking round with a black eye.

When we climbed aboard the minibus around 9 am the next morning, I was still buzzing my head off from the effects of the drink. I recall stopping for lunch at a restaurant in another part of the Mekong Delta. The waitress brought us over plates of purple and white stuffed calamari, and I was nearly sick at the sight of them. That evening, when we arrived at our hotel in Can Tho City, I was still reeling from the rice wine.

On that trip to Vietnam, while we were in Saigon, a boy we'd befriended invited my partner and me to his family's home on the outskirts of the city to celebrate Tet, the Vietnamese New Year, with them. 1997 was the Year of the Ox in the Chinese zodiac and Tet is the most important celebration in Vietnamese culture, and a national holiday in the country. A cyclo driver we'd been using called Mr Tam took us both to the house and I brought with me a case of BGI lager and packets of Marlborough cigarettes to give to the men in the family as presents.

We spent a good few hours with the boy's family, and although the language barrier proved to be a bit of a problem, we had a great time with them that day. Before we said our goodbyes in the late afternoon, one of the men, the boy's uncle, gave me a large plastic bottle full of dried venomous snakes as a token of his appreciation. I know it's hard to believe, and my brother was certainly having none of it when I told him, but one of the snakes had two heads. Thanking the boy for his family's hospitality, we left the house and walked over to Mr Tam, who was waiting to take us back to our hotel in his cyclo.

When we returned home from our Vietnamese adventure, I hooked up with my friend Sandy Henderson, known as Soz, and produced the bottle of snakes I'd been given in Saigon. I asked Soz if he fancied eating a piece of one of the snakes and he said why not, there was no harm in giving it a try. I'll never forget the sight of him and one of his mates casually strolling along Lymington High Street that evening, enthusiastically munching on these vipers as if they were lollipops on sticks. Unfortunately, Soz died not long after. He'd been to a dance music event at Elmer's Court Country Club in Lymington and decided to take a short cut home, along the railway track. He never made it. Stumbling into the live rail, he was electrocuted.

In early 2003 I travelled to India with my partner at the time, Naomi, for a two-week holiday. We arrived at New Delhi airport around 5 am. After clearing immigration, we walked out of the terminal, searching for a taxi to take us to our pre-booked hotel. As we headed towards the taxi rank, we began getting pelted with cockroaches. A group of local adolescent boys standing behind a wall were the culprits. What an introduction to India.

We managed to find ourselves a taxi, and the driver took us to our hotel. Upon arrival, we were shocked to find the receptionist had no record of our booking. He told us the hotel was full, and there were no rooms available. The travel agency we'd booked the hotel with had screwed up big time. Naomi and I ate breakfast in the hotel, then gathered our backpacks and walked out to hail a taxi to take us to another hotel. The taxi driver suggested that we should book one in the historic district of Parharganj, in the centre of New Delhi. He said the hotels there were a lot cheaper. We found a suitable place to stay in Parhaganj, and after checking in, we dropped off our stuff and strolled out to explore the neighbourhood.

New Delhi is a massive culture shock, as were all the places we visited on our two-week stay in India. Cows roamed freely in the streets, and there were stray dogs everywhere you looked. Multitudes of rats scurried about, and in the sky above us, vultures soared on currents of air. Parhaganj is a backpacker's paradise and absolutely teeming with people. The level of hustle and bustle was incredible. As far as the eye can see, there were shops, bars, restaurants, and vendors selling street food. There were colourful characters all over the place, and we saw many beggars wandering about the streets.

With the intention of seeing more of the city, we flagged down a tuk tuk. The driver, who was an elderly fellow wearing an old-fashioned tank top jumper, couldn't have been more discourteous if he tried. 'Where do you want to go? Where do you want to go?' he kept screaming at us. What a delightful person. Wandering around Parhaganj, men would suddenly appear as if from nowhere, beckoning for us to follow them down dimly lit alleys to who knows where. Seeing the menacing looks on their faces, there was no way on earth we'd even contemplate it.

One night, we decided to go for a walk along the main street in Parhagani. There were so many people about that we had a struggle to even move. Men would approach us, offering to sell us heroin, opium or marijuana and whispering in our ears, 'You wanna buy hashish? Best quality, very cheap. You want some?' In the doorways of travel agencies on the side of the street, dodgy looking people would try to entice you into going inside for a drink of chai, Indian tea. The chai would often be laced with drugs.

Out there, it's possible to buy Bhang Lassi, which is a traditional cannabis-infused Indian drink used in Hindu festivals and available for sale in government authorised bhang shops. I remember walking past one of these bhang shops one time. Peering through the window, I noticed a small group of Western backpackers in there, obviously suffering from the effects of bhang lassi. One of them was sitting at a table with his head slumped forward, and he appeared incapacitated; totally stoned out of his head. He looked terrible. In fact, he looked like Doctor Death.

The next day, Naomi and I went out for a late lunch at a pizza restaurant not far from our hotel. While were seated at a table inside, waiting to order, Naomi said to me she was feeling strange, and thought she might have been drugged. I couldn't work out how that could have happened. In the couple of bars we'd drunk in the previous evening, we'd kept a close eye on our drinks, and I didn't think we'd presented anyone with the opportunity to spike us. However, it wasn't beyond the realms of possibility. There had recently been several reported cases of travellers being drugged in New Delhi and waking up in such far-flung places as war-torn Kashmir – (stunningly beautiful but dangerous as hell), minus their passports and any money they'd been carrying.

After a few minutes, I began to feel somewhat strange myself. A short while later, the sensation thankfully abated, and we both started to relax at last. I suddenly realised that this was the power of the culture shock when travelling in India. Combined with the effects of jet lag, it can be an overwhelming experience.

That evening, Naomi and I went out for a meal at the iconic Gaylord restaurant on Connaught Place in the centre of the city. I recall ordering a bottle of Kingfisher lager, which tasted like gnat's piss. Apparently, some unscrupulous managers of restaurants and bars in India replace some of the beer in the bottle with water, to maximise their profits.

The next morning, we went out for a walk and picked up a local newspaper from a shop near to our hotel. Inside, there was a piece about the ceiling in the Gaylord collapsing the previous evening. Apparently, the incident had occurred only half an hour after we'd left the restaurant, and thankfully, no one in there at the time was seriously hurt.

That evening, we met an Indian Sikh guy who worked for a travel agency based in the city. He offered to take the both of us on a ten-day budget tour of Rajasthan in his classic white Ford Popular car. He explained to us that he'd struck deals with certain hotel owners and promised us we'd be saving a lot of money by signing up for one of his company's tours. Naomi and I thought it sounded like a great idea and decided to take him up on his offer.

The following morning, the man from the travel agency arrived at our hotel, and after checking out, he drove us to the world-famous Taj Mahal, in Agra, 200 kilometres from New Delhi. The Taj Mahal is a majestic ivory-white marble mausoleum, and it is beyond stunning when you see it for the first time. We spent several hours there, walking around the beautiful grounds, admiring the mind-blowing architecture, and wondering how anybody could possibly create something quite so beautiful. It turned into an unforgettable day.

That tour around Rajasthan was a fascinating experience. The itinerary included staying in cities such as Jaipur, Jodhpur, Pushkar, Udaipur and Jaisalmer. In Pushkar, the hotel we stayed in was a converted old Indian concrete fortress without glass windows. I recall sitting in the hotel's restaurant on the top floor one evening, looking down at masses of people celebrating at a local wedding. I asked our driver if we could join them, but he said there were a lot of drunken village guys down there who didn't have any common sense. He said they were ignorant of foreign travellers, and he couldn't guarantee our safety. He strongly advised against it.

There were many highlights on the tour. For instance, Naomi and I visited the world-renowned Ranthambore National Park, a large area of dense dry tropical forest, open bushland and rocky terrain, interspersed with lakes and streams. Ranthambore is known for its population of Bengal tigers and is one of India's major tourist attractions. We went on an early morning game drive there and were privileged to witness a family of tigers in their natural habitat. Two of the big cats, followed by their cubs, walked across the track directly in front of the Jeep we were riding in before disappearing into the brush.

When the ten days were up, we drove back to New Delhi. To say the roads in Rajasthan are dangerous is a gross understatement. Truck drivers over there present their own hazards, driving their vehicles much too fast and honking their horns constantly. A few times while we were driving on the roads, I was convinced we were going to have a head-on collision with one of these speeding juggernauts, sending us all to kingdom come. It wasn't uncommon to see dead animals on the side of the roads, dogs, cows and sheep, all mown down by the trucks.

Back in New Delhi, on our last day in India, our driver took us to a restaurant he knew for lunch before we were due to fly home later in the evening. I ordered a plate of fish in there, and when it arrived on the table, I couldn't but help notice how forlorn the poor thing looked, not that a dead fish is supposed to be jumping up and down with unbridled joy. It was probably a katla, a South Asian freshwater variety, and member of the carp family. It obviously hadn't been cooked properly. The fish tasted utterly raw and not very nice at all, but I wolfed it down anyway.

When we arrived in a taxi at the airport later, I began feeling as sick as a dog. It was obvious I was suffering from food poisoning after eating the fish earlier. I'd contracted the dreaded Delhi Belly. When Naomi and I boarded the plane and sat down in our seats, I realised I didn't have any sensation in my fingers. I felt like shit, and just before take-off, I started throwing up in one of the sick bags provided. An airline steward came over and wrongfully assumed I'd been drinking alcohol. He accused me of being drunk, but I'd only drunk two bottles of Kingfisher lager that day, and that was probably watered down, anyway. The flight home became the journey from hell for me, and I couldn't stop vomiting for hours. When we got back to the UK, I was so ill, I had to take a week off work.

In early 2004, I travelled to Cambodia for the first time, with Naomi. It's my favourite country, and I've been there seventeen times up to now. In the mid-1970s, the leader of the communist Khmer Rouge, Pol Pot, had taken control of the country, and for nearly four years he presided over one of the worse genocides in history. In the capital Phnom Penh, I hired a tuk tuk, and the driver took me to see the harrowing Khmer Rouge prison, Tuol Sleng. We then drove a few miles out of the city to visit the infamous killing fields at Choeung Ek.

Whilst in Phnom Penh, we stayed at a place called the King Guesthouse and became good friends with the family who owned it. The man who oversaw the whole enterprise was known to everyone as 'The King.' The only reason the man was still alive, having escaped Pol Pot's killing fields, was that during the Khmer Rouge regime, he'd bribed the regime's cadres with gold he'd hidden away, one piece at a time. He was the epitome of a true survivor, if ever there was one. On every occasion I stayed in that place, and there were many, The King treated me like a member of his own family. Once, before I flew back to the UK, he even gave me bottles of spirits from his private stock to take home with me.

The first time I stayed there, with Naomi in 2004, we met a guy who worked at the guesthouse called Thol. He's still my go-to man out there, and we always hook up whenever I'm in Cambodia. After a few days in the capital, we travelled north up to Siem Reap and visited the magnificent Angkor Wat temple complex nearby. Angkor Wat is one of the largest religious monuments in the world, and when you see it for the first time, it really blows you away, even more so than the magnificent Taj Mahal in India, in my opinion.

One morning two years later, in 2006, I bought a crate of Asahi Japanese lager from a shop in Phnom Penh. Apart from Thol and myself on the car journey up to Siem Reap, there were a couple of Australian guys that I'd met earlier travelling with us, and we necked all the cans of beer I'd brought with me for the journey and mixed them with a load of 10mg Valium tablets. At one point, we pulled over to the side of the road and started dancing around like idiots in an off-limits minefield. It was utter madness, but at the time, we simply didn't care at all.

Our little band of multi-national nutcases ended up bypassing Siem Reap and instead headed on up to the jungle town of Anlong Veng, in Oddar Meanchey province on the Thai border. Anlong Veng was one of the last strongholds of the communist Khmer Rouge movement, and it was there that Pol Pot met his ultimate demise. We visited his grave there; a pathetic pile of burnt-out old rubber tyres in the middle of nowhere, where the tyrant had been cremated without ceremony in 1998.

Two other countries I visited in the first half of the 2000s were The Gambia and Tanzania, in Africa, on both occasions with Naomi. The Gambia's a tiny country compared to the all the other nations on the continent and is known as 'Africa for beginners.' We stayed in a hotel in the bustling capital of Banjul for the duration of our five-night holiday and had a great time going out on various excursions, organised by a travel agency based at the hotel.

The only downer was the annoying, and sometimes intimidating, Gambia Bumsters – beach boys. Bumsters are basically young men who have no fear of approaching foreign tourists and attempting to engage in conversation with them. They tend to wear brightly coloured clothing and hang about in pairs or groups on beaches and outside tourist hotels, hoping to attract the attention of naïve Western holidaymakers. They're traders from the host community and they interact with foreigners with the idea of doing business with them. Bumsters are out for themselves and their extended families, and while Naomi and I were in the Gambia, we were repeatedly hassled by them. It's a well-known fact that Western women travel to the nation with the idea of meeting a young Bumster, falling in love, and eventually marrying him. Upon returning to their home country, it's not uncommon for many of these women to receive begging letters from them, asking for money and other gifts. The gullible and foolhardy fall into the trap of sending large sums of money to the Bumsters, hoping beyond hope that their relationships are genuine and meaningful. Unfortunately, this is rarely the case. According to these guys, it doesn't work like that; it's all about business with them and nothing else. I think that although these Gambia Bumsters can be a pain in the ass, ultimately, they're not a threat to your safety. Once you've sussed out their true intentions, you realise they're quite harmless, and relatively easy to deal with.

In Tanzania, we went on a couple of safaris in the Selous Game reserve, in the south of the country, now renamed in part Nyerere National Park. The Selous is a vast remote area of untamed wilderness and is bigger than Belgium. One of the excursions we'd booked beforehand involved trekking through the African bush on foot for two hours, a walking safari. Nature at its rawest. Our guide that day was a friendly older local guy who carried with him an antiquated rifle for protection. I remember thinking what a fat lot of good that gun would be if we happened to be attacked by some enraged wild animal after we'd unwittingly stumbled into its territory.

We were lucky enough to see many of Africa's most iconic species on that walking safari. There was a lone male lion half asleep under a bush; dangerously close to where we were walking. I saw impala, Cape buffalo, baboons, zebra and wildebeest in the Selous, and giraffes looking at us from above the treetops. I recall a nerve-racking moment when an enraged adolescent bull elephant mock-charged us several times on a dusty track. My heart was pulsating for hours after that experience.

Naomi and I were staying in lodges in a camp on the banks of the Rufiji River, the largest and longest in Tanzania, which snaked through the heart of the Selous game reserve. At night, hippos would leave the water to graze on the vegetation underneath the lodges. One afternoon, we went out on a boat on the river, where apart from the hippos, we saw numerous Nile crocodiles, either in the water, or lounging on the riverbank. In the evenings at the camp, I'd drink bottles of the Tanzanian Safari lager with my meal. I'd be so exhausted from the daytime trips out into the bush that I never drank more than three bottles of the stuff in one sitting.

I remember Naomi and me taking the hovercraft out from Tanzania's capital, Dar Es Salaam, to the island of Zanzibar in the Indian Ocean, which remains the hottest place I've ever been to in my life. At times, the baking, suffocating, dry heat was unbearable. While ambling along a beach on Zanzibar, I caught sight of the television presenter Judith Hann, sunbathing on the sand a few metres away with her head in a book. Judith Hann is most famous for co-presenting the BBC television series *Tomorrow's World* between 1974 and 1994. As I walked past her, I began jokingly humming the theme tune to *Tomorrow's World*, hoping to attract her attention. Engrossed in her book, she totally ignored me.

In 2005, I split up with Naomi. I was sad that our relationship had ended, but rather than moping around feeling sorry for myself, I arranged to fly out to Southeast Asia for the adventure of a lifetime. Travelling solo was an amazing experience, and one I'll never forget. I was in the region for approximately five months and visited eleven different countries while I was out there; Vietnam, Laos, Cambodia, Thailand, Myanmar, Malaysia, Singapore, Malaysian Borneo, Indonesia, Brunei and Hong Kong, in that order. Each country has its own special qualities, and suffice to say, I had a great time travelling around all of them. One of the highlights of this trip was Myanmar. Whilst in the country's capital, Yangon, I met an Irish guy at the hotel I was staying at called Rory Byrne, who was a journalist. We hit it off straight away. Rory and I were into similar types of music, and one Saturday night, we ventured out together to sample the delights of the city.

Rory had bought a bottle of Mandalay rum, and we'd sunk a few glasses of it before leaving our hotel. Mandalay rum is prime stuff, and we were in a boisterous mood as we walked around the streets of Yangon. Eventually, we came across a lively looking Burmese bar and decided to go inside for a drink. The place was packed with locals watching a football match on the TV. It was an Asian international World Cup qualifier between Myanmar and Bangladesh.

We ordered a beer and sat down among a group of men who were drinking some kind of spirit. To break the ice, I asked one of them what they were drinking, and ordered a few more spirits for him and his friends. Historically, people from Myanmar and Bangladesh don't like each other. The locals we were sat with didn't speak much English, but we somehow managed to engage in some good-humoured banter with them. While the football match was playing out on the TV, I jokingly asked one of the men which of the two countries he came from, Myanmar or Bangladesh. He replied, 'No Bangladesh. No Bangladesh!' As the drinks flowed, and the conversation grew more heated, the man kept repeating, 'No Bangladesh. No Bangladesh!' It was all good natured, and it was brilliant. 'No Bangladesh. No Bangladesh!'

A couple of days later, Rory and I booked a coach trip up to Pagan, in central Myanmar. Pagan is known as the Land of a Thousand Temples, and we had such a good time there. I recall sitting at an outside bar in the town one afternoon, drinking enormous glasses of gin and tonic. The G&Ts cost us the equivalent of 30p a throw and it tasted like there was a third of a litre of neat gin in each glass.

By nightfall, we'd both had our fill of gin, and headed off to grab a beer in another bar, just up the road. While we were in there, I needed to take a piss, so I walked out to the back of the place, looking for the WC. It was pitch black by now, and as I stumbled about in the darkness, the ground suddenly gave way beneath me, and I dropped straight down into a ten-foot-deep stinking latrine. The latrine had been loosely covered over with a flimsy piece of hessian cloth, and I'd unwittingly stepped right on top of it. I stood down there, helpless for a while, not knowing if I was going to be bitten by a pissed off venomous snake, that might well be slithering around inches away from me. Eventually, Rory came out of the bar looking for me and pulled me out of the hole. The next day, both hungover, we said our goodbyes. Rory was returning to Yangon, and I was continuing my journey on the road to Mandalay.

Other memorable highlights of that 2005 adventure included a day trip out to the famous World War Two Bridge on the River Kwai and a short train journey along the infamous Death Railway on the Thai/Myanmar border. I recall staying in a guesthouse for a week on an island in the middle of Lake Toba, in Sumatra, Indonesia. Lake Toba is the largest lake in Southeast Asia and one of the deepest in the world. While in Malaysian Borneo, I visited the Sepilok Orang Utang Rehabilitation Centre, in the state of Sarawak.

It was a wonderful feeling waking up in the morning in some hotel room and deciding where I fancied going to next. The Southeast Asia airline Air Asia made anything possible, and their flights were very cheap. One country I regrettably missed out on travelling to was the Philippines. I'd bought an airline ticket in Indonesia to fly to Manila but somehow managed to miss my flight. I guess it was a trip too far.

Sometime in 2006, I flew back to Phnom Penh, and as per usual, booked a room at the King Guesthouse. It just couldn't be anywhere else, really. A couple of my friends, Lamma and Ffi Maund, from the Bournemouth cowpunk band Pronghorn, were due to fly out to Vietnam and Cambodia for a two-week holiday for their honeymoon, and we'd arranged beforehand to meet up at the King towards the end of their trip.

One afternoon, I was taking a nap in my room when there was a knock at the door. I opened it to find Lamma and Ffi standing there with broad smiles on their faces. Happy to see each other, we immediately went downstairs into the lobby and ordered some bottles of Angkor beer. After a while, I suggested I go and pick up a bottle of Gordon's gin, which was relatively cheap in Cambodia, from the Lucky Supermarket, not far away on Sihanouk Boulevard. A guy working at the guesthouse said he'd take me there in his tuk tuk.

When I returned, the three of us wasted no time in getting stuck into the gin. We shared the bottle with some of the King's staff, who were on duty at the time and several tuk tuk drivers who were parked up outside in the street and even offered some to a group of fellow travellers arriving on a minibus from Vietnam, whom we'd never met before. After a few hours, things began to get slightly silly. We were sitting in the restaurant on the ground floor of the guesthouse when I grabbed hold of a tablespoon, poured some gin onto it and started snorting the stuff up my nose. Looking back, it was a ridiculous thing to do, but at the time, I couldn't give a damn.

Several days later, my Cambodian mate Thol and I accompanied Lamma and Ffi to the airport in Phnom Penh for their flight back to the UK. Their honeymoon was over, but we'd had a cracking time together out there. In a way, it felt strange waving goodbye to them, but life went on. Afterwards, Thol took me to a house on the outskirts of Phnom Penh to visit some Cambodian friends of his and introduce me to them. While we were there, we munched on some small shiny silver fish with pointed snouts and drank several cans of Angkor beer.

The following evening, I was sitting downstairs in the Guesthouse with the hangover from hell. Around 8 pm, a trio of middle-aged Western men walked into the lobby. They checked in at reception, sat down at the table next to me and ordered some beers. They were chatting among themselves, and by the sound of their accents, I discerned they were Australians.

There was something about them that made me think they might be Vietnam veterans. I plucked up the courage to go and ask one of them, and he said yes, they were indeed Nam vets. He invited me to join them at their table, and I ordered a round of Angkor beer for the four of us. One of the Aussies suddenly looked me in the eye and said 'Hey, you're not one of them nose drinkers, are you?' I remember thinking, how the fuck would these blokes, who'd obviously only just arrived in Phnom Penh, know about the gin snorting session? As it turned out, these guys had been drinking in a hotel bar in Bangkok the night before and had got talking with an English woman there. She'd asked them where they were headed to next, and they told her they were travelling to Phnom Penh, Cambodia, and were booked in to stay at the King Guesthouse. Utterly horrified, she'd exclaimed, 'I wouldn't go there if I was you. You don't wanna go there, they're all snorting gin up their noses in that place! They're completely mad, I'm telling you!'

As it materialised, the woman had been staying at the King the previous night and had witnessed the whole damned episode in the restaurant at the guesthouse. Unfuckingbelievable. Before the Aussie Nam vets turned in for the night, we arranged to hook up together in a couple of days and go out on a pub crawl around Phnom Penh.

Two nights later, the three Aussies and I met up in the guesthouse lobby and hammered a load of Angkor beer down our necks. We ordered a tuk tuk and travelled into the centre of Phnom Penh. We hit many bars that night, including Sharkey's, the Pickled Parrot, the Candy Bar, Foreign Correspondents Club, Blue Chilli, the Green Vespa, the Red Fox and the DV8. It was a proper pub crawl, and in all of them, we'd bought rounds of B-52's between us. B-52's were shots of coffee liquor, Irish cream liquor and orange-flavoured liquor, all mixed together, and if you drank enough of them, they'd knock your fucking head off.

In the tuk tuk on the way back to the guesthouse at the end of the night, my head was in a total spin. I recall being locked out of the King, and we had to bang on the door to awake the security guard, who was sound asleep in his hammock, so he could let us in. I was annihilated and had a hard time navigating the wooden steps up to my room on the top floor.

I remember suddenly feeling nauseous, and I didn't even make it to the bathroom. I threw up all over the stairs, and after fumbling around with the key, somehow managed to let myself into my room. I was lying on the bed, completely smashed, when I heard heavy footsteps plodding slowly up the steps. Then there was an almighty crashing sound, followed by man yelling 'Aaaahh! For fuck's sake, no!'

I went down for breakfast in a haze, about 7 am the next morning, and incredibly, the four Aussies were sat there at a table drinking bottles of lager. One of them had a bandage around his head, with a cartoon-style spot of blood seeping through it. He told me that after I'd staggered up the steps to my room after our pub crawl, he'd followed on behind me and slipped up in my puke on the landing. He'd smashed his head badly, and someone in the guesthouse had to call out an ambulance for him. He told me not to worry about it. He said it was no big deal, and he couldn't care less; he'd had a great night, and it was well worth all the pain. He then ordered me a bottle of Angkor beer.

These guys were proper hardcore, and I'm honoured I got to meet them. Breakfast in Cambodia would often consist of a bottle of beer first; usually Angkor, but sometimes Lao, Cambodian or Leo, followed by an omelette, toast and strong coffee, then yet more beer. In the pharmacies in Phnom Penh, you could buy a packet of forty 10 mg Valium tablets for five bucks a throw. It was like being in a sweetshop back home. I enjoyed taking the occasional Valium out there; they're great for hangovers. It's a benzodiazepine drug, and was known as mother's little helper, back in the 60s. Almost every time I had a tattoo done in Cambodia, I'd take a Valium tablet beforehand to relax. I'd also buy a few cans of lager and drink them in the tattoo parlour.

Peeping Toms played quite a few gigs throughout 2000 and 2001, the year Jon Webb joined the band as second guitarist. In 2002, Matt Walker replaced Martin Griffin on bass guitar. In 2004, the band performed at the very first 'Endorse It In Dorset' Festival, at Sixpenny Handley. Endorse It was a great, 10,000 capacity festival and took place over the course of the first weekend in August, in the beautiful surroundings of the Dorset countryside. Two years later, Matt left the band and Mikey Beardwood from The Fazers came in on bass.

My good friends, Lamma and Ffi Maund were the festival's main organisers, along with Graham Cullen. Over the next ten years, I performed there nine times, with either the reformed Cropdusters or the Peeping Toms. Endorse It in Dorset didn't happen for several years after 2011, but at the time of writing, it has been revamped and now takes place each September at the Cerne Abbas Brewery, near Dorchester.

Returning to the year 2000; The Cropdusters got back together for two big gigs in Holland. We played Rotown in Rotterdam and the Melkweg in Amsterdam. The band's line up for the dates was: Roger (guitar), me (vocals), Mike (bass), Cob (fiddle), Spike (drums) and Martin Griffin (acoustic guitar). It was a wonderful weekend, full of fun and debauchery, and reminded me of just how ace the country is.

When the band arrived in Rotterdam, it was great to discover Sully – not the frenzied biker I wrote about earlier but Spike's father, waiting to meet us at the venue. Coincidentally, both men shared the same name, Pewter O'Sullivan. Sully was a wonderful, generous guy; an Irishman from Cork, up to date with all the latest jokes and loved his Guinness with a passion. Sadly, Sully and his lovely wife Trish are no longer with us.

In March 2006, I got together with a woman called Kim, who I'd known for a long time. In truth, it was a whirlwind romance, and in October that year we got married. It didn't take long before we realised it probably wasn't the wisest of moves. Eventually, it became apparent to both of us that the marriage wasn't working and we made the decision to separate. We ended up getting divorced almost as quickly as we had got married. Kim and I have remained good friends, and my wife and I have been down to stay at her Air B& B in Cornwall.

It was in the summer of 2006 that we lost our great friend, Dusters fiddle player Cob Cook. He'd suffered a fatal heart attack and was only fifty-three years old. We were all distraught when we heard the news; everyone was in complete shock. Cob's funeral, at St Thomas's Church in Lymington, was so rammed solid with people it was incredible. It came as no surprise though. Cob was a much loved and well-respected man, and I believe his legacy lies most of all in the music he helped create with The Cropdusters. Make no mistake, he was such a vital component of the band that we could never have achieved what we did without him.

Following Cob's death, the remaining members of the Dusters got together and discussed how best to keep Cob's memory alive. We eventually agreed on organising a three-day charity music festival called Cobfest. The proceeds from the festival were earmarked to go to Wessex Heartbeat, the charity that supports the Wessex Cardiac Centre in Southampton. The band needed a new fiddle player on board to make this happen, and the obvious candidate was Ffi from Pronghorn. She was more than happy to join us, and so was her husband Lamma, who came in on the banjo.

CHAPTER 8

BACK IN THE ZONE

In February 1998, my daughter Nancy was born at the Queen Elizabeth Hospital in Portsmouth. She was born a few weeks early, and I remember those first few hours and days of holding this tiny little bundle of joy were quite scary, as she appeared so fragile. As Nancy has grown and developed into a beautiful, ambitious young lady, the world has become her oyster. I'm extremely proud to call her my daughter.

It was now 1999, and five years since The Cropdusters disbanded. I was desperate to get back in the groove and start making music again. My prayers were answered when Roger and a good mate called Michael O'Sullivan, nicknamed Spike, approached me, and asked if I was interested in reforming the Peeping Toms. I jumped at the chance. Spike was the Toms drummer, and another friend, Martin Griffin, played bass. With Roger on guitar and myself on vocals, we had the nucleus of a band together, and I couldn't wait to get started. We set to work rehearsing, in the barn up at Bampton's Farm.

We already had the original repertoire of Peeping Toms songs to fall back on, and over the course of the next several years, we wrote a host of new ones to add to our set. These included *Attention-Seeking Missile, Splinter, There's Always Room for One More Monkey, She's Not Like That, Inflatable Friend, We're All Casualties, Vulcan Hardware, Model Village, You Wanna Hope She Don't, Underachiever, Third World* and *Feel Like a Million Dong*, the lyrics of which were highly influenced by my experiences of travelling around Vietnam. The band also worked out a murderous cover version of the Enrigue Iglesias song *Hero*.

Meanwhile, a new pub had opened in Lymington, called the Thomas Tripp. The landlord of the Tripp was a great guy called Jon Burdge, and he supported local musicians. I think it was in '99 that we first approached Jon about the possibility of playing a gig in his pub. The live music scene in the town was non-existent at the time, and Lymington needed shaking up. Not since the heyday of the Old E in the early '80s had there been anything remotely happening on that front. It really was Deadsville.

Jon agreed to put the band on, and the show was an absolute stonker. It was the first of around twenty Peeping Toms gigs in the Tripp before the pub's closure in 2019. They were always special events, none more so than when the band played on the last ever night there. The pub was so rammed it was bursting at the seams, and towards the end of our set, we called Jon up onstage. He ended up throwing himself into the maelstrom of the mosh pit and crowd-surfed all the way to the back of the bar.

Jon Burdge took live music very seriously when it came to bands gigging in the pub. He built a solid wooden stage and installed sound-proofed windows. Playing at maximum volume was rarely ever a problem with nearby residents as they could hardly hear anything. Of course, there was always one who'd make it their business to complain about the slightest noise coming from the Tripp.

During the twenty-one years the Tripp was in operation, countless bands played there. It was the only venue in town that hosted regular live music events. Other pubs in Lymington would occasionally put on acoustic acts, but they were relatively tame affairs. The performers played their music at an extremely low volume so as not to upset the neighbours. Some places in Lymington and Pennington even brought in noise limiters, which would cut the music off if the volume reached a certain level. I hate noise limiters with a passion. They're the enemy. Looking back nostalgically at the Thomas Tripp, nothing in the area even remotely compared to it.

Jon was always good for a lock-in, and it wasn't unusual for my friends and me to be drinking in the pub until 6 am the following morning.

The Thomas Tripp was a unique establishment, full of larger-than-life characters. Every time the Toms played there, the atmosphere in the place was cutting edge. It was a throbbing island of intensity amidst a sea of apathy and indifference and is sorely missed by a lot of people. When the Tripp closed, Lymington reverted to its status as a ghost town.

Among other local venues Peeping Toms played at around this time was a pub in Ashley, New Milton called the Oak and Yaffle. At one gig there on a Saturday night, while we were midway through our set, this retard in the audience approached me and spat a gob load of phlegm in my face, sneering 'That's what punks do, innit?' I was a whisker away from smashing my SM58 microphone into his horrible ugly face. I'm glad I didn't because I would've been in a whole heap of trouble, and that's the truth. Other places Peeping Toms played at during the early 2000s included the Thomas Tripp's sister pub in Christchurch and another establishment in New Milton called the Rydal Arms.

The first Cobfest took place at Boldre Working Men's Club in deepest, darkest Pilley in 2007. I don't think that little village has seen anything like it before or since. There were vehicles parked along the main street for hundreds of yards, and there were hordes of punters gathered outside the club in the late afternoon, waiting for the doors to open. The Dusters headlined on the Saturday, and there were nearly 400 people in the club that night, most of them bouncing off the walls. It was a memorable, red-hot atmosphere in there.

Incredibly, over eighty kegs, containing eighty-eight pints of beer in each of them, were consumed at the event. I recall the sight of all these empty kegs piled up together in the club's garden at the end of the weekend. Some of the other acts who played at Cobfest were my mate Mark Baynes' death western band, Lady Winwood's Maggot, Pronghorn, Roshambo and The Fazers. Also appearing on the bill was an electronica/post-punk group called Continental Liaison. They were fronted by the unique and charismatic frontman Bam, real name Barry Elder. I'd known Bam for a long time, and was sad to hear of his passing, at fifty-three years old, in January 2024. The festival was enormously successful, and we managed to raise almost £5000 for the Wessex Heartbeat charity.

Buoyed by the success of Cobfest 2007, the following year we put on another event. Cobfest 2008 was held at Shorefield Country Park, in Milford-on-Sea, in April 2008. Around twenty-five bands played at the festival. Apart from The Cropdusters, other acts appearing on the bill included Some Dogs, Pronghorn, Lady Winwood's Maggot, The Highliners, The Mopes, Hip Fandango and The Curst Sons. It was great to have The Highliners perform at Cobfest 2008 because as I mentioned earlier, Mike and Bill used to play with them before leaving to help form the Dusters in '86. This event didn't raise quite as much money for charity as Cobfest 2007, but it was still a substantial amount.

This second incarnation of the band played several gigs between 2007 and 2011. The one that stands out the most for me was at the legendary 100 Club, in London's Oxford Street, supported by Some Dogs, Viva Las Vegas and Swill from The Men They Couldn't Hang, who performed a solo set. The 100 Club was a venue I'd wanted to play at for years. An old friend, and a regular at Dusters shows in the 80s, Tony Fraser, promoted the show that night, and it was a stormer. True to form, we organised a coach up from Lymington, and we sold out the venue, no problem. There were a lot of familiar faces at the gig, and I was delighted to meet up again with several members of the fabled Winchester Bovine Spongiform posse.

All the Endorse It in Dorset festivals The Cropdusters played were brilliant as well. Lamma always made sure we were either headlining on one of the stages, or coming on immediately before more well-established acts, such as Buzzcocks and New Model Army. Over the years, Endorse It in Dorset has hosted some great bands. The Damned, The Vibrators, The Beat, The Rezillos, Sham 69, Dreadzone, Peter and the Test Tube Babies, Vice Squad, UK Subs, Alabama 3, Goldblade, Dub Pistols, TV Smith, Attila the Stockbroker, Steranko, The Wurzels, and even the great Desmond Dekker, have all performed at the festival at one time or another.

CHAPTER 9

DELIVERANCE

In 2010 I volunteered to work in the Maranatha orphanage in Phnom Penh, Cambodia. At Heathrow Airport, a couple of hours before my flight out there, I was in the duty-free area sampling various free alcoholic beverages when I heard a familiar voice. Standing a few feet away, with his back to me, was Rampton, my old mate Sean Cranny, would you believe. What a coincidence. He was flying to Seoul, South Korea, where he was engineering the sound for a band at a music festival.

The assignment at the orphanage was a six-month placement, but I had to fly home after three months because I'd run out of money. While in Phnom Penh, I lived with a lovely Cambodian family, a man, his wife and their young son. Each morning, the wife prepared me a breakfast of coffee, toast and marmalade. Monday to Friday, I'd leave their house around 7.30 am and walk the short distance from there to the orphanage, to begin work at 8 am. At the orphanage, I'd teach the kids the English language to the best of my abilities until 11 am, then, because of the heat of the day, we'd all have a three-hour lunch break until 2 pm. After another couple of hours of teaching, it was time to go back to my hosts' house. I wasn't required to work weekends, and I'd spend them either travelling to other parts of the country, or sightseeing, and socialising and drinking in many of Phnom Penh's bars and nightclubs.

God only knows what that poor family I was staying with thought of me because there were several occasions where I returned to their house completely smashed in the evening, gliding stupidly across the wooden floorboards on their living room floor in front of them, before slowly climbing the stairs and collapsing in a heap on my bed. I must have done something right in their eyes, because I heard later that they were genuinely upset when I left my placement at the orphanage.

I was gutted when my time living with that ace Cambodian family came to such an abrupt end; not least because I convinced myself I had a serious crush on my hostess, who was roughly the same age as me. Seduced as I was by the exotic, overpowering allure of the Orient, she appeared to me as an insanely attractive Khmer woman. In my mind, she was beyond beautiful; obviously unavailable, but I still believed I was wholeheartedly in love with her. Looking back to those days staying under the same roof as that woman and her family in Phnom Penh in 2010, I must have been completely deluded.

I was flying into Phnom Penh so regularly by now, and becoming so familiar, that many of the local tuk tuk drivers and moped riders were openly calling my name out and waving at me as I was walking out of Pochentong Airport. 'Hey man, it's Shaun! He's back in Cambodia again! We're so happy to see you brother. Where do you wanna go? What hotel are you staying in? We must drink Ankor beer together, same as before brother!' It was a great, comforting feeling, being recognised like that by guys on the other side of the world, and I take it as a big compliment.

The first time Michaela and I went on holiday together was in April 2011. We flew out for a month of travelling around Cambodia and Vietnam. We arrived in Cambodia in time for the Khmer New Year. April is the hottest month of the year in that part of the world, and walking along the streets of Phnom Penh, the heat was palpable. The Cambodians are such friendly people and would welcome us into their homes and offer us food and drink. We even got invited to a wedding out there, and that was a wonderful experience. Khmer wedding ceremonies are a culturally rich affair. Steeped in centuries-old Buddhist tradition, they can last for up to three days and are awash with a myriad of bright colours, exotic food and dancing. The bride might wear up to seven different dresses over the course of the wedding and the father of the bride usually goes bankrupt after the event. He sees the marriage of his daughter as a status symbol and is prepared to sacrifice everything he has in ensuring the ceremony runs smoothly and is as memorable as possible.

One night in Siem Reap, Michaela and I bumped into some Australian youngsters who were out on the lash in Pub Street in the centre of town. We were in the bar of the hotel we were staying at, and I decided to match the Aussies drink for drink. I don't remember much about it, but the next morning, Michaela woke up and couldn't find me anywhere. Noticing the pile of clothes I'd been wearing the evening before strewn about the floor, she thought I'd got up to use the toilet during the night and must have wandered off downstairs to the hotel lobby bollock naked.

After jumping out of bed, Michaela heard groaning coming from beside it. She finally found me stuck fast between the bed and the wall. I'd obviously fallen down the side of the bed during the night, and managed to get myself hopelessly wedged in. I was shouting at Michaela to help free me from my predicament, but I was too heavy for her to move. She was wetting herself laughing, but with great difficulty she eventually pulled me out.

On another occasion in Cambodia, we were on the coach from Phnom Penh to Kampot. The coach stopped at Sihanoukville to let some passengers off, and I decided I was going for a pee, against my wife's better judgement. The coach drivers out there are renowned for not stopping to let passengers off to go to the toilet, and while I was pissing in a bush, the coach started to pull away without me. I remember it disappearing into the distance and wondered what I was going to do next. I flagged down a local moped rider and jumped on the back. He speedily caught up with the coach, which slowed down enough for me to hop on board.

In Vietnam, we made the obligatory journey to the Cu Chi tunnels, and when Michael descended into one of the tunnel shafts there, she had the misfortune to get bitten on the arm by a large and aggressive giant Asian centipede, which wasn't nice for her at all. She was in a lot of pain, but she's made of stern stuff and had no qualms in carrying on with our trip as if nothing had happened. Hospital was out of the question. It wasn't even an option. Hardcore would be an appropriate description, I'd say.

While in Chau Doc in the Mekong Delta, on the border with Cambodia, we were walking along a monkey bridge, which is a wobbly structure made from bamboo. We were trying to board a boat on the Mekong River, to take us back to Phnom Penh. Michaela had told me not to swing my backpack because the weight of it would act like a pendulum, and I'd fall off the bridge into the river. As you guessed it, I didn't listen to her advice. I was carrying the backpack in front of me when I picked it up and slung it straight over my shoulder. I was knocked off balance and crashed through the bridge's handrail into the reed bed below. Luckily, the tide was out. Michaela and some Vietnamese people who were present were bent up in absolute hysterics. They were laughing so much that they were unable to assist me back up. A young boy of about eight years of age, bless him, appeared from somewhere and did everything he possibly could to assist me. He eventually succeeded in helping me onto the boat, and I gave him a dollar for his troubles.

For my 50th birthday in January 2013, we arranged a party at the Freebird Bar & Grill in Phnom Penh. The Freebird is an American-style diner with superb décor and ultra friendly service. There's a great rock 'n' roll vibe in there, and they play some damned good music on their sound system. They also do a mean chilli con carne which is so hot, you sweat buckets the moment you taste it. Apart from Michaela and me there were some backpackers of various nationalities, and several local Cambodians, at my party.

After a brilliant night partying in the Freebird, Michaela and I took a tuk tuk back to our hotel. I was so hammered that when we arrived, I literally fell out of the tuk tuk and had to be helped into the hotel lobby by the young bellboy on duty. Michaela got the room key from reception, and I recall crawling on all fours through a conference room in the hotel. There were lots of Chinese businessmen in there, obviously at a late-night meeting. As I drunkenly crawled past them, they looked at me as if I was something from another planet. They just couldn't believe what they were seeing.

By far the largest number of travellers in Southeast Asia are other

Asians. You'd see hordes of Chinese people everywhere, and they tend to hang about together in large groups. They barely speak to one another and are constantly fiddling about with their mobile phones. There are always loads of Japanese tourists out there as well, relentlessly snapping photos of their friends and just about everything else, come to that matter.

Perhaps the craziest experience Michaela and I have shared while travelling in Southeast Asia was in Phnom Penh. While Michaela was relaxing by the poolside at the hotel we were staying in, I decided to go off for a wander. She advised me not to take our credit card with me because in those days, Cambodia didn't accept foreign cards in their machines; you had to go into the bank in person and show the officials your passport. Of course, me being me, I took the credit card with me and promptly lost it, resulting in Michaela having to spend around forty minutes on her mobile phone to get the card stopped. Now all our money was sitting in a bank account that we couldn't access, and we were only three days into a month-long holiday.

The new card was being sent to our home address in the UK. We knew we would be able to get hold of the money once the card arrived at home, as Michaela's daughter, Stephanie, could access the account and send the money to us via Western Union. In the meantime, my brother came to the rescue, as usual, and sent some money to us while we were waiting. We continued with our holiday and headed off to Phu Quoc Island, Vietnam, in the Gulf of Thailand.

When we turned up at the Cambodia/Vietnam border, my brother sent us some more money because the card had still not arrived. The nominated bank account was now in Vietnam. Unknown to us, because Vietnam is a communist country, any monies sent there must be withdrawn there. You cannot withdraw the money in any other country. This became apparent to us when we returned to Cambodia and tried to take some cash out from a bank in the southern city of Kampot. We were told that the only way we could access the money was to return to Vietnam and withdraw it there. I didn't go myself, because my brother, for whatever reason, and I can't understand why, didn't trust me with the money. The Western Union funds were linked to Michaela's passport, so I wouldn't have been able to access them anyway.

A Cambodian friend of ours in Kampot offered to take Michaela back across the border on his motorbike, even though she didn't have an entry visa. It was a risky situation because she was attempting to get back into Vietnam without one, and she could have been arrested on the spot. Anyway, the pair of them set off, and after an hour or so, arrived at the border crossing. One of the officials there recognised Michaela from a couple of days before. He and his colleagues found it highly amusing that she wanted to come back into the country, just to go to the bank. In a nutshell, they gave her an hour to visit the bank and return to the border, to ensure she then left Vietnam.

I was sitting drinking large glasses of red wine in the hotel garden in Kampot, feeling smug with myself, and half cut, when Michaela returned. She was a bright orange colour and looked like an Oompa-Loompa because she was covered head to toe in road dust. I made the fatal mistake of laughing at the state of her, and you guessed it, she ripped me a new one. She pointed at a minibus that was parked in the road outside the hotel, and said, 'We've got seats booked on that bus, and if you don't get up to our room three floors up, with no lift, and get the bags, I'm leaving on the bus without you. I don't care, as I have all the money, and I'll just buy new clothes with it in Phnom Penh.'

I don't think I've ever moved so fast in my life. I ran up the stairs to our hotel room, grabbed the luggage, and was at the bus ready to go with about a minute to spare. I recall it was a quiet journey back to Phnom Penh. Michaela refused to speak to me at all, although she finally chilled out when we got to the city, where she could relax by the hotel swimming pool. She said she could have killed me that day because of my behaviour. It's worth mentioning that my family believe wholeheartedly that I wouldn't be here today without the unwavering love and support of my wife.

Some of the people we encountered while travelling were strange, to put it mildly. At breakfast one morning, at a hotel in Phnom Penh, we were sitting on the opposite table to a family of South Koreans. There was a man, his wife, and their two sons whose table manners were atrocious. One of the boys, a podgy young chap, was cramming as much food into his mouth as quickly as possible with his chopsticks. There were noodles, pieces of egg and lumps of pumpkin porridge hanging out of his gob and dripping down onto his trousers. He was making a right mess of it all, and looked like he might explode at any given moment. He was turning a funny colour and sweating profusely, and his cheeks were puffed out and throbbing. He reminded me of a deranged giant hamster.

Michaela and I have enjoyed a lot of laughs on our travels around the world. For instance, while on holiday in Sri Lanka, in 2015, we booked a safari in Yala National Park, which borders the Indian Ocean in the south of the country. We were travelling through the park in the back of this Jeep, and I asked the driver to stop, as I needed to take a leak. I walked into a nearby thicket and surprised an adult Asian elephant, which was feeding on vegetation only a few metres away. My heart racing, I ran back to the Jeep as fast as my legs would carry me and clambered aboard. That was a close call and could have seriously ended in disaster.

On another occasion, also in 2015, we were in Luxor in Egypt, walking along the banks of the River Nile. This Egyptian bloke casually approached us and asked, in perfect English, if we wanted to go on a boat cruise on the Nile. We politely told him that we weren't interested, and quoting Shakespeare, he replied, 'Time waits for no man. I don't blame you.' That had us both in stitches for hours afterwards.

While relaxing by the side of a hotel swimming pool in Luxor one boiling hot afternoon, we heard gunshots coming from the other side of the river. The next morning, we were told a man had been murdered there the day before.

My old mate Richard Wallace had moved to Pai, near Chiang Mai in northern Thailand, several years previously. In February 2016, Michaela and I decided to fly out there and pay him a visit. We hadn't seen Wallace in ages and couldn't wait to catch up with him. After a few nights staying in a hotel in Bangkok, we travelled by coach up to Pai. We'd arranged beforehand to meet him in a place called The Pai Pub in the centre of town. The pub was run by a charismatic Australian guy, Rowan Brennan. Michaela and I were having a drink in there when Wallace showed up. We all had a great time reminiscing, and the music played, and the beer flowed.

The next morning, Wallace, Michaela and I hired some mopeds and headed off into the jungle to a place not far away called Thom's Pai Elephant Camp, which was run by a friend of Wallace's. The camp is a rehabilitation centre for abused Asian elephants. As soon as we arrived there, Michaela crossed over a shallow river in search of them. She found a group of the animals without any trouble and ended up feeding and washing one of them, an adult female. It was an amazing day overall. While Michaela was tending to the elephant, Wallace and I made the most of the cheap gin on offer at the camp. After a few hours, the three of us headed back to Pai on the mopeds. We stayed in the town for a few nights before saying goodbye to Wallace and returning to Bangkok to finish off our holiday.

Several years later, we were devastated to hear the news of Wallace's death out there in Thailand. There are many theories about what happened to him; one was that he'd suffered an allergic reaction after being bitten by some type of insect, which led to him having a fatal heart attack, but I'm not in a position to speculate in this book. I wasn't there at the time. All I know is it's another good man gone way too soon.

A month after visiting Richard Wallace out in Thailand, my beloved father died at the age of eighty-two at Southampton General Hospital. He'd been suffering from mixed dementia, Alzheimer's and vascular, for several years, and in a way, we lost him a long time before he passed away in March 2016. Dad had grown increasingly confused over time, although right up until the very end, he managed to remember who I was. Knowing this gives me a certain degree of comfort.

I've always been tremendously proud of what my father achieved during his lifetime. Coming from a poor background, he worked extremely hard throughout his life, first at his local grammar school in South Wales, then at university in Birmingham, where he obtained his BSc degree in Chemical Engineering. He then fulfilled his academic career by gaining his PhD, or Doctor of Philosophy, in Sociology, a research degree and an academic qualification of the highest level.

Dad worked for forty years at the Esso, later Exxon, oil refinery in Fawley, and I don't think he ever had a single day off, through illness or for any other reason. Because my father started out with nothing, he made sure my mother and we three children lived as good a life as possible and were well provided for. I sometimes think I must have been a bit of a disappointment to him, by not following in his footsteps by studying hard at school and going on to university. The word 'Underachiever,' as in the title of the Peeping Toms song, seems to ring true, somewhat.

In 2017, Michaela and I flew out to Australia to visit Kev Joyce and his wife Toz, who'd emigrated there decades before. They were living in a town on the Central Coast, and some other good friends of ours from Lymington, Will Devanney and his sister Kate, lived not far away. The first few nights we spent with Kate and her boys at her house. Kate is the epitome of the hostess with the mostest and welcomed us into her home with open arms. She insisted we made use of her bedroom because when we awoke in the morning, we'd have the best view from the house overlooking the stunning Avoca Beach.

After leaving Kate's, we then stayed at Will's place for a short while. Will and his wife Mary have a son, Callum. One evening, Will's brother Ronnie, who also lives in Australia, drove to the house for a get together in celebration of Callum's 18th birthday. He fired up a classic Aussie barbecue and the food tasted wonderful. Everyone had a great time catching up and reminiscing. Like Kev and Toz, the Devanneys had been living in Australia for an extremely long time, and we hadn't seen them in ages. While we were staying with them, the Devanney family treated Michaela and I like royalty and we can't thank them enough for their hospitality and generosity.

After a few days with the Devanneys, we said our goodbyes and went to stay with Kev and Toz at their house in Kariong. Michaela and I spent nearly a whole day at the Australian Reptile Park in Somersby, close to the city of Gosford. The park features reptiles such as saltwater crocodiles, Komodo dragons, various snakes, lizards and turtles. Other animals include kangaroos, wallabies, koalas and cassowaries. For arachnid enthusiasts, it's possible to observe Sydney funnel-web, redback and huntsman spiders there. While visiting the park that day, we were fortunate to get to hold baby Tasmanian Devils in our laps.

A massive highlight of our holiday in Australia was a trip into the stunning Blue Mountains National Park near Sydney. The Blue Mountains are an area of spectacular ever-changing landscapes and get their name from the blueish haze created by the mist emitted by the oil of the eucalyptus trees that cover vast swathes of the park. The day after we'd visited the reptile park, Kev drove the four of us there. It was a magical, unforgettable experience.

In 2019 and 2020, wild bushfires on an unprecedented scale devastated huge areas of the Blue Mountains. There's an iconic colour photograph of an exhausted firefighter standing next to a koala. They're both looking back towards the raging flames tearing through the tinder dry vegetation, and there's an element of heartbreaking tragedy captured in the picture.

Next on the agenda was New Zealand. An old friend of ours from Lymington, Duncan Gittins, had been living in Christchurch on the South Island for the past several years and invited us over to stay with him at his house there. Duncan's wife, Cat, their daughter and two young sons, who he jokingly referred to as the Kray Twins, were away in the city of Auckland on the North Island at the time we arrived. They returned home a few days later. After visiting various Christchurch attractions and sampling the atmosphere of some of the city's pubs, it was time for Michaela and me to say goodbye to Duncan and his family and fly on up to Auckland. After a short time spent in Auckland, we headed to Parua Bay, near Whangarei Heads on the west coast of the North Island to stay for a week with my old friend Cathy McColl, who'd relocated to New Zealand in 2001. We met up with Cathy at the Parua Bay Tavern before going back to her house. The place was rustic and remote, complete with stables for her horses and a building featuring a drinking bar and space for dancing and partying. While we were there, Cathy introduced us to a lot of her friends. Much of our stay in Parua Bay remains a blur to me, although I do remember we had a mental time of it.

Since we've been together, Michaela and I have certainly visited a wide array of destinations. One of the most memorable trips was back in December 2012, when we flew out for a Christmas and New Year's holiday in Cambodia and Vietnam, via Amsterdam and Guangzhou in China. On New Year's Eve in Phnom Penh, Michaela discovered that a band I was really into called the Cambodian Space Project were playing at a private organised function at the five-star Hyatt Regency hotel in the city. When we arrived at the hotel in the evening, we noticed all the guests, Cambodian and foreign alike, were dressed up to the nines. Everyone appeared so smart, and there we were in our T-shirts and jeans.

We hung around in the magnificent hotel lobby, complete with its interior waterfalls and lush tropical vegetation, for a short while, wondering how on earth we were going to gain access to this top-end function looking the way we did. I eventually came up with a clever idea. Approaching a member of the security staff, I explained to him that I was a journalist from the New Musical Express and Michaela was a freelance photographer. I told him we'd travelled all the way from the UK especially so we could write a review and take pictures of the Cambodian Space Project. The guy smiled at us and said no problem, and unbelievably, waved us both through to the outside area where the function was taking place. We were amazed to find all the food and drink was free that night and you could help yourself to as much as you wanted. We'd hit the New Year's Eve jackpot, that's for sure.

The Cambodian Space Project is a Cambodian psychedelic rock band, formed by lead singer and songwriter Kak Channthy and her Australian husband, guitarist Julien Poulson. Channthy has been described as 'the barefoot diva of the Cambodian rice fields' and 'the Khmer Amy Winehouse.' Tragically, she died in a tuk tuk accident after leaving a party at a hotel in Phnom Penh in 2018, at the age of thirty-eight.

The Cambodian Space Project revived the golden age of Cambodian rock music in the 1960s and early 1970s, before the terror of the Khmer Rouge, who took over the country in 1975, eradicated modern music and culture. Most of Cambodia's famous singers and performers at the time, such as Ros Serey Sothea, Sinn Sisamouth, Houy Meas and Pan Ron disappeared without trace under the brutal genocidal regime. They were almost certainly murdered in the killing fields. Indeed, it's estimated that up to 90 per cent of the country's artists and musicians were killed during the three years, eight months and twenty days the Khmer Rouge was in power.

The Cambodian Space Project were on fire that night. Channthy's beautiful voice, coupled with Julien Poulson's ace, twanging guitar sound, cut through the warm tropical air like a knife, with the rhythm section pounding away on their instruments alongside them. It was an exceptional performance by the band, and Michaela and I had a great time dancing to the music and drinking and socialising with them after the show. For me, New Year's Eve 2012 was undoubtedly the best one ever. As the clock struck midnight, heralding in 2013, we left the splendours of the Hyatt Regency and headed back to our more modest hotel, a short distance away.

Other notable holiday experiences Michaela and I have experienced, include a fabulous seven-day cruise around the stunning Norwegian Fjords and an awesome trip out to New York, where we stayed at a hotel in downtown Manhattan. Whilst in New York, we paid a sombre visit to the 9/11 Memorial at the World Trade Center site, the former location of the Twin Towers that were destroyed during the September 11th attacks. We also walked a few blocks from our hotel to the Dakota Apartments, scene of the murder of John Lennon by Mark David Chapman in December 1980.

CHAPTER 10

TASTE THE VENOM

In August 2013, with guitarist Jonathan Webb, I formed a brand-new band called Bamboo Vipers. I knew a guy from nearby Blackfield, Al Woodcock, who was a great guitar player. I asked him if he'd like to join the Vipers, and he nearly bit my hand off. I explained the project to him, and he told me he was gagging to get out there and play some gigs. His enthusiasm was infectious, and the three of us set about looking for a rhythm section. The original Bamboo Vipers drummer was a bloke from Southampton who ultimately didn't cut it, so we approached a young guy who lived locally called Jake Stillwell. Jake's dad, Gordy, was an old mate of mine, and he was well chuffed that we'd asked his son to join the band.

The Vipers still needed a bass player to complete the line-up, and we found one in the shape of Alex Rook. Alex was in a relationship with Jake's mother, so in that respect, it was ideal. I'd known Alex for years, since his time as bassist for local band Moosehead. The five of us began rehearsing in a unit at a place called The Granary, close by. The band were extremely prolific with songwriting, and within a short space of time, we'd written enough material for an album.

Some of our earliest songs were *Banged Up Abroad, Roger the Cabin Boy, God's Little Nimby, Crystal Methodist, Royal British Legion, Alien Friends Reunited, Biting Army, The Lord's My Shepherd's Pie* and *Wild Flowers*. All these tracks appeared on the Bamboo Vipers' debut album, *Dangling the*

Bait, which was recorded at Matt O'Donnell's Untapped Talent Studio in Southampton, and released on the band's own Santebal Records label in July 2014. Not long afterwards, I penned the lyrics to a brand-new batch of Vipers songs. These included *Silver Boots, Utopia, Transient, Haunted House, Payback, Malcontent* and *Collective Amnesia*; the latter featuring a line about the affable Lymington copper, PC Sawyer.

Our first gig was at the legendary 12 Bar Club in London's Soho, on a Friday night in February 2014. The 12 Bar was run by a lovely guy called Mark Webster, known to everyone as Barnet. He was the singer in his own rock 'n' roll band at the time, Viva Las Vegas, and was a well-respected face on the London alternative music scene. Over the course of the next year or so, the Vipers played around thirty gigs: the most notable shows being supporting the UK Subs twice at the Talking Heads music venue in Southampton.

We performed at several London venues, including The Borderline, The Hope and Anchor, The Dublin Castle, The Fiddler's Elbow and Nambucca. During this period, the Vipers played a few gigs at the Winchester Gate pub in Salisbury, which was, and still is, run by a friend of mine called Robb Blake. The Winchester Gate is a small, intimate venue, and the PA system in there at the time kicked some serious ass.

In April 2015, everything sadly came to a grinding halt with Bamboo Vipers when I contracted sepsis through a urinary infection caused by a benign lump on my kidney called an angiomyolipoma. On the funny side, not that there really is one, my right bollock had swollen to the size of a cricket ball, and I looked like the cartoon character Buster Gonad and his Unfeasibly Large Testicles in the Viz comic strip. It was damned uncomfortable; an absolute bastard, to tell the truth.

Initially, after feeling unwell, Michaela persuaded me to make an urgent appointment to see my GP. While waiting in the doctor's surgery I collapsed on the floor and the GP called an ambulance to take me to Lymington Hospital. At one point, as I lay there seriously ill in my hospital bed, I was given only twelve hours left to live. I survived this scare but wasn't in the right frame of mind to continue with Bamboo Vipers. It wasn't until a couple of years later that I felt the time was right to get the band up and running again.

In the months leading up to my illness, I'd been busy organising the County Fair music festival, which took place over the course of a weekend in May at the Three Tuns pub in Bransgore, Dorset. I'd booked over twenty bands to play at the event, but because I was so unwell, Bamboo Vipers had to pull out. It was heartbreaking because I'd put so much work into everything beforehand. I remember on the Sunday afternoon not feeling very well at all. I was pissing blood in the pub toilets, which was a bitch, but it wasn't all doom and gloom.

The Ukranians played a blinding set at the festival, as did The Morgellons and my friend Barnet's group Viva Las Vegas. My mate Mark Baynes' band Lady Winwood's Maggot, who I mentioned before, were damned good also, and so were the Wessex Pistols. The Morgellons' frontman, Vincent Mahon, is a good friend of Michaela and me, and we were all shocked to learn of the sudden death of their bass player, Mark Geraghty, recently. Mark was a face on the London music scene and played in some great bands during his lifetime, including Crisis and The Straps. He was also a well-respected gig promoter. He was a lovely guy, and although I only met him on a handful of occasions, he came across as warm and genuine.

Jonathan Webb and Al Woodcock were keen for the Vipers to carry on, but unfortunately, Jake and Alex had become disgruntled with the band and didn't really want to know anymore. It was obvious their hearts weren't in it. They both found travelling up to London to play gigs, or anywhere else for that matter, to be a chore. This left me scratching my head in bewilderment. One of them even complained he was too tired at the end of a working week, and was loathe to forfeit his Fridays and Saturdays in the name of rock 'n' roll. When I look back on it, it's unbelievable, really, but it was their choice and fair enough. They're both good guys and I wish them well with whatever they do in the future.

For me, the opportunity to play in a gigging band is a privilege. Music's either in your blood or it isn't, and you need to be bang on it 110 per cent if the whole thing's going to work. In fairness to Alex though, he held a responsible position in his father's timber business in Christchurch and was a busy man, but always put himself out, to drive the band and our equipment to the venues. In hindsight, I probably didn't appreciate his efforts enough.

All this ultimately meant we needed a new rhythm section. We got a drummer on board by the name of Ade Hood, who had his own rehearsal studio in nearby Hordle, but repeatedly struggled to find a suitable bass player. In fact, on subsequent Bamboo Vipers recordings at Untapped Talent, Jonathan played the bass on many of the tracks, as well as the guitar. Not an ideal situation by any means, although I'd say he proved to be a more than capable bassist and always got the job done.

I have a natural tendency to get myself lost, especially at international airports and European coach and train stations. My sense of direction is, and has always been, atrocious, to put it mildly. In fact, you could say 'Disorientated' is my middle name. I honestly don't know the reason why I manage to drift off the radar so frequently. Once, after a Vipers recording session at Untapped Talent one Saturday afternoon, I rushed out of the studio in a hurry with Jonathan Webb, so we could catch the next train back to Lymington. Realising I'd left my wallet and mobile phone behind, I raced back to the studio to retrieve them, leaving Jonathan waiting on the platform.

When I returned to the station, I boarded what I thought was the right train, expecting to see Jonathan on there. I couldn't find him, and because I'd got hammered that day, I sat down in one of the seats and fell asleep straight away. When I woke up, I found to my horror I was at the station in Woking, Surrey, almost seventy miles away from where I was supposed to be. I'd got on the wrong fucking train. Woking! The place is synonymous to me with having absolutely no sense of direction whatsoever, and pure unadulterated chaos. I still have nightmares about that train station. Woking. Ironically, my brother lives close by, in Weybridge. I'm sure he knows how disorientated I can be sometimes and wouldn't have been at all surprised to learn what had happened to me.

To make matters worse, I'd arranged beforehand to meet Michaela at

Brockenhurst station at a designated time. That time had long since passed, and when I didn't show up as planned, she was less than impressed, to put it mildly. It was a nightmare, but all in all, just another day in the complicated life of Shaun Morris. Maybe she was right all along in saying I should still be on reins, like when I was a headstrong toddler all those years ago, back in the early 60s.

Bamboo Vipers were doing just fine. Although we weren't gigging, due to not having a bassist, we were rehearsing regularly and writing new songs. We filmed quite a few videos to promote the music we'd recorded, and they proved to be a lot of fun in the making. The videos were posted on YouTube, and I personally think some of the better ones are *Inch High Private Eye, America, Don't Go Poking Around* and *Spacewaster.*

Don't Go Poking Around was an interesting one. As soon as a Vipers release becomes available for digital download, I plaster it all over the group pages I'm a member of on social media. Because the song's heavily influenced by Cajun music, I decided to whack it up, along with the accompanying video, on a specific group page. The group was initially set up, primarily, to showcase the traditional sounds of the swamps and bayous of Louisiana, in the deep south of the USA. I guess I was looking for a reaction to our music from the purists out there. In the event, I certainly got one. One of the comments written about *Don't Go Poking Around* was a stonewall classic: 'Goddammit! Who the hell is moderating this page these days?!' I take it that person objected to the band's take on Cajun music, which was laden heavy with powerful guitars and drums, and a miscellany of other appropriate sound effects. I think it's one of Bamboo Vipers' finest songs. Al Woodcock's slide guitar playing on it is an absolute peach. In my view, he captures the overall feel of the subject matter and nails it to perfection.

In 2018, we were devastated to hear of the death of Al, through sepsis. He was a wonderful guy, a fabulous musician and a great friend, and his passing left a huge void in our world. Al was a self-deprecating man, and it was only after his death that we learned one of his previous jobs had entailed tuning the pianos on the QE2 cruise liner.

Jonathan, Ade and I continued rehearsing with the Vipers for a while, but I craved much more than just band practices and making videos. I was desperate to get back out there and play live gigs. Was it too much to ask? Unfortunately, this was something Jonathan wasn't interested in doing, for whatever reason, and we eventually went our separate ways.

Although I was the only member of the band left, I was determined to reconstruct Bamboo Vipers. In 2022, I contacted a guy up in Kingston, Surrey, who played guitar in a band called Religion Equals Decay. His name was Iain Gibbins, and he was a fan of our music. Equally, I was into what RED were doing at the time. Bingo! After talking with each other on the phone a few times, we decided to get together and form another incantation of Bamboo Vipers.

Iain knew a great local drummer called Lee Duffel, who had a recording studio in his back garden. Lee played drums for the rock covers band Ransom, who mostly played gigs around the Home Counties. Initially, it was just the three of us, rehearsing together at Lee's studio in Kingston, but straight from the start, we realised we had something good going here. Even as a trio, the music sounded powerful as hell. Loud crunching guitar sounds and banging tribal drumbeats were the order of the day, and what the Vipers were all about now. There was no pussyfooting around and no prisoners taken, whatsoever.

Iain had a lorryload of tunes ready for the Vipers to use, and I began writing new lyrics. Our first digital release was the single *Champagne Socialist*, which came out in 2022. The same year, the band recorded and released two more singles; *Democratic Kampuchea*, which was the song about the Khmer Rouge's rule in Cambodia I'd been wanting to write for ages, and *Runt of the Litter*. In 2023, we put out another single, *Andrew Ridgeley Moment*. On these recordings, Iain played bass as well as lead and rhythm guitar.

Following this, we recruited two more members into the band; bass player Rich Bartram and a second guitarist, James Jenkins, both of whom were old mates of Lee's. The three of them had previously played together in the Kingston punk metal band Maniac. With the line up now complete, in September we performed our first gig together, a charity event at Boldre Working Men's Club. We had a run of T-shirts printed in time for the show, featuring the intimidating image of a Viper's head and emblazoned with the words 'Disgraced but Never Defeated,' which to me, felt perfectly apt at the time.

In early 2024, Bamboo Vipers recorded six songs for an EP titled *Songs Our Enemies Taught Us*. The track list for the EP is: *Boredom the Silent Killer, New Kinky Dimension, The Devil's Lettuce, Bandit Country, Jobs for the Boys* and *Punk in the Provinces*. My personal favourites from the EP are the glam inspired *New Kinky Dimension* and *Bandit Country*, the latter being more akin to a Cropdusters song, as opposed to the usual fast-paced Vipers material.

I wrote the lyrics to *Bandit Country* as a nod to the area where I live, down in the unspoilt wilderness of the New Forest. Ultimately, I wanted to capture the ominous feel and atmosphere of classic movies like *Deliverance* and *Southern Comfort* and drag the song kicking and screaming into the modern era. I think the words to the chorus pretty much sum up what I was trying to achieve by this: *The hills have eyes in bandit country/ Right bang in the heart of bandit country.*

In April, we played a double-header gig with the New Forest ska band New Tonic, at the Masonic Hall in Lymington. New Tonic's vocalist is a mate of ours called Steve Rutherford, nicknamed Tad. The show went under the banner Bandit Country Spring Smasher, and it was a cracking night; in fact, the sort of night the town hasn't seen in a long while. Spinning the tunes at the event was an old mate of mine, DJ PMT, aka Paul Briggs, who hails from nearby Holbury. Paul is frequently seen at gigs around town, especially the Southampton venues, The 1865 and the Engine Rooms. He's often accompanied by his good mates the two Daves, Dave Sharp and Dave Leggett. Like so many of us, the three of them possess an undying love of music.

The Masonic Hall is a great venue for live gigs, and as I mentioned before, in my opinion, vastly underused by promoters and bands. It has just the right balance of space and ambience. When the hall is properly illuminated, the whole thing looks superb. Add to that a decent PA system and stage, and you've got all the ingredients needed for a top, professional show. Events there are hosted by old friends of mine, Jan and Symon Wood.

In January the previous year, we hired the Masonic Hall for my 60th birthday party. Adamski DJ'd on the night and presented me with a birthday card signed by members of Killing Joke. He'd recently been playing on the same bill as the band at an outdoor festival abroad. My brother used his contacts, through his job in advertising, to get Bill Roache, of Coronation Street fame, to record a video link and personally wish me a happy 60th birthday. It was brilliant.

Soon after the Bandit Country Spring Smasher event, Iain Gibbins and the Vipers parted company, and he was replaced by guitarist Steve Hayward. For some reason, Iain had grown disillusioned with the direction the band was taking, and in hindsight, the decision to bring in Steve was a masterstroke. We immediately set to work writing new songs and rehearsed them at Lee's studio in Kingston and Untapped Talent in Southampton. Steve's first gig with Bamboo Vipers took place in late December, supporting Peter and the Test Tube Babies at the New Cross Inn in Southeast London. The show was a sell-out, and by all accounts, a riotous affair, and we did ourselves proud.

I married Michaela on the 4th of May 2013 at St John's Church in Boldre, Hampshire, and people still tell us it's the best wedding they've ever been to. We arranged it ourselves, with no input from anybody else. It was a fantastic day, and the sun shone for us. During the evening, at the wedding reception at Sway Village Hall, the Waterside hillbilly band the Trav Cats played a set, and I got up onstage with them and sang a couple of Cropdusters songs. Michaela and I lived in various local places before moving to a bungalow in Whitaker Crescent, Pennington in 2020, just as the Covid epidemic struck.

In May 2018, Michaela organised a charity event, which was held on a Friday night at Pennington Sports and Social Club. She wanted someone well-known to be the subject of a question-and-answer session, and we approached Rat Scabies, AKA Chris Millar, the original drummer for The

Damned. We were both thrilled when Rat agreed to come down from London and do it. As it was a charity event, he didn't want a fee; only his travelling expenses and a place to stay for the night, so we booked him a room at the Angel Hotel on Lymington High Street.

Rat travelled down from London on the train and Michaela picked him up from the hotel and drove him to the club. The evening went off splendidly. A good friend of ours, Simon Speechley, fielded the questions and it was immensely entertaining listening to some of Rat's stories of touring around the world with The Damned. He'd also brought some Damned records down with him, as raffle prizes, which was extremely good of him.

At the end of the night, Michaela, Rat and I went back to Jonathan Webb's house nearby for a bit of a session. Also present were Paul Briggs and his mates, the two Daves. At one point during the early hours of the following morning, Rat grabbed one of Jonathan's guitars off the living room wall and started playing Sex Pistols songs. At around 2 am, Michaela drove Rat back to the Angel Hotel. I think he enjoyed the short time he spent in Lymington. He was impressed by all the activity on the waterfront; the fishermen going about their business etc, and the town's bustling Saturday market.

The property we currently live at, in Whitaker Crescent, has a large back garden, half of which we didn't even realise was ours until a few weeks after moving in. One of the first things we did was erect a fence around the perimeter, to keep out the prying eyes of nosey neighbours. We bought a gorgeous Sprocker puppy and called him Tank, mainly because he resembled one by the way he moved about compared to his less rumbustious brothers and sisters, but also in honour of the Stranglers' keyboard player, Dave Greenfield, who'd recently died. Tank is one of my all-time favourite Stranglers songs.

Michaela's father, Gordy, has been an enormous help to us since we moved into our bungalow. He's a practical man, whereas I'm a DIY disaster. Gordy always comes round whenever we've needed assistance with a new project, often accompanied by his wife, Maz. Whether it's erecting garden fences or fitting a new bathroom or kitchen, there isn't a lot he can't turn his hands to. Michaela's very good at DIY herself, having learned the skills from her dad over the years.

Funnily enough, when the second incantation of my old band Peeping Toms started up in the late 90s, I wrote a song called *Vulcan Hardware*, named after a shop in New Milton, which isn't there anymore. The song is about someone who really hasn't got a clue about DIY, namely me. The opening lines to the chorus are 'You're a DIY disaster, and who you gonna blame? You cannot work any faster, it has always been the same.' I love the phrase 'Vulcan Hardware' and always thought it would make a great name for a band.

Because of my negative experiences with dogs in the past, I was initially unsure about getting a puppy on board, as Michaela had suggested we do. However, from the moment I set eyes on Tank, I was sold. I absolutely love him, and the two of us are damned near inseparable. Indeed, we call the patch of paradise behind our house Tank's Garden. Every day I look forward to taking him out for a walk around the countryside where we live. It's a liberating feeling for me,

and many of the recent Bamboo Vipers lyrics have been constructed when I'm out there with our dog.

I'd always wanted a garden large enough to accommodate my own pub. Not long after moving into our bungalow, the opportunity presented itself. My son-in-law Harley and I drove round to a house in Pennington Oval to collect an old garden shed which was being given away free by the owners. We didn't even bother to take the shed apart, but between us, we somehow succeeded in carrying it out into the road and tying it onto the roof of my car with some lorry ratchet straps that Harley had. We then proceeded to drive the short distance between Pennington Oval and Whitaker Crescent, and it must have made for quite a spectacle. It was the definition of health and safety gone haywire.

As we slowly passed through the village, trying to appear as anonymous as possible, an old mate of mine, coming out of Tesco with his bag of shopping, was forced to do a double take when he saw the shed sliding precariously around on the car roof. I think he was more surprised when he realised it was me at the wheel of the car, as not many people at the time knew I'd even passed my driving test. As we pulled up outside our bungalow, Michaela just stood there with a disbelieving look on her face, and said, 'What the fuck are you two doing? You're supposed to take the shed apart before you strap it onto the roof of the car, you pair of goons!'

A very good friend of ours, Lee McCullough, came round and laid down the basic foundations for my pub. Because of Covid restrictions, all the retail businesses were closed, so we tried our utmost to acquire as much stuff as possible, free of charge. We would trawl social media sites like Facebay on the lookout for a greenhouse, paving slabs, bricks, sand, fencing, garden furniture, decking, felt roofing, exotic plants, flowerpots, hanging baskets, bird tables, a fishpond and some decorative flamingos, you name it. The list goes on and on. We named my pub The Olde English Gentleman, after the infamous Lymington den of iniquity, and I immediately set to work transforming it into how I envisaged a shed bar should look. We put in two bright shiny orange Perspex windows, and I painted the outside of the shed midnight blue and the inside black and cedar red. Over the years, I'd amassed numerous souvenirs from my travels around the world, such as Vietnamese and Cambodian flags and scarves, and I made sure they were given pride of place in my new pub.

Michaela bought me a great wooden drinking bar and bar stools as presents, and we fitted a set of optics onto the wall behind it. I stacked the pub full of pint, wine and shot glasses, and covered the walls head to toe with tin signs, punk rock posters, flyers and stickers. I then bought a load of retro flashing Christmas fairy lights to illuminate the place. We laminated the floor and bought a bar fridge to go inside, and I thought the pub looked fucking ace. We'd achieved the desired vibe.

Not long afterwards, we obtained another garden shed from some local friends of ours, again for free. Result! This shed was significantly more robust than the original, and we put it right bang next to it. The discombobulated and invaluable Lee McCullough zealously cut an open doorway between the two sheds with his chainsaw, thereby doubling the floorspace. We called this grand addition The Snug, and we carpeted it out properly and bought a new sofa to put in there for extra comfort. This second, scaled down version of the Old E has been the centre point for the many parties Michaela and I have hosted, the icing on the cake. I'd like to think I put in a serious lot of time and effort into getting the bar exactly as I wanted it, and it's been a dream come true, to be honest. When the Bose Bluetooth speakers are turned up full and belting out the tunes in there, the whole place feels like it's literally shaking. Rock 'n' roll indeed.

When we first moved into our bungalow, we became acutely aware of this strange elderly bloke living in the house next door to us. We caught him spying on us through a hole in the garden fence on more than one occasion and realised straight away that he was a nosey so and so. He's the type of person who makes it their business to know everything that's going on in the immediate vicinity. There's not a lot that gets past his prying eyes. I guess there's always one.

Several months after moving in, we hosted an afternoon wedding party in our back garden. The nosey neighbour was caught red-handed standing on the roof of his house, peering through a pair of binoculars, trying to figure out what was going on. He was unable to see anything anyway, due to the large marquees and gazebos we'd erected in the garden, blocking his view.

A friend of ours happened to be walking along the road outside our bungalow that afternoon, and spotting him up on the roof, asked him what the hell he thought he was doing. Mr Nosey, caught off guard, started frantically waving his arms about in a panic, and stuttered, 'Oh, I don't know, these damned wasps. Honestly, no matter how hard I try, I just can't seem to be able to get rid of the damned things!' Why the man needed a pair of binoculars to sort out a wasp problem on his premises I have no idea.

Michaela and I travelled to Toronto, Canada in late November 2024 for a short holiday. We both had a brilliant time together in the city and were fortunate enough to journey out to see Niagara Falls, which was totally awesome. Everything was going swimmingly until, on the last day of our holiday, disaster struck. We were due to fly back to London on the Saturday evening, so in the afternoon Michaela ventured into downtown Toronto to do a bit of shopping, while I headed off to the English-styled Queen and Beaver pub to watch the West Ham v Arsenal game on live TV. While the football match was on in the pub, I drank four pints of German lager. When Michaela turned up to meet me there a couple of hours later, I was in a right sorry state. She tried three times to get me to leave, as we had a flight to catch in a few hours, but I could barely function properly. I couldn't speak, and my legs had turned to jelly. Eventually Michaela left me there on my own, saying she'd meet me at the airport.

All I can remember was the friendly Canadian manager of the pub coming up to me and saying 'Heh dude, are you okay? Thanks for popping into the Queen and Beaver. It's been lovely meeting you, and we've all really enjoyed your company here. We love your crazy stories and you've been great fun. However, I think you've had too much to drink and it's time for you to leave. Come on, I'll phone you a taxi to take you to the airport.' With that, I collapsed into his arms, babbling incoherently. I was completely battered, and didn't understand the reason why. There was no way drinking only four pints of beer would have put me in such a mess. Something didn't add up.

Not that I have any recollection, but the pub's manager ordered me a taxi to the airport. For some reason, en route, I must have asked the driver to drop me off at the Eton Shopping Centre in downtown Toronto, rather than taking me to the airport. Sitting there out of my mind, it was then that I realised I'd been spiked. Someone had slyly slipped drugs into my beer while I'd gone to use the toilet in the Queen and Beaver pub. I vaguely remember sitting in the shopping centre, on another planet, as a stranger walked by and helped himself to my pouch of tobacco, which was on the seat right next to me. I just smiled at him and wished him all the best. What the hell was going on?

Whatever drug I'd been spiked with, it was insanely strong, maybe spice or ketamine, or some other potent form of synthetic narcotic. I don't honestly know. What I do know, is I felt like I was losing my mind in that place and was convinced I'd never get out of there. I made it my mission to grab the attention of a couple of official-looking Canadian men in the shopping centre, and told them I thought I'd been spiked, and could they please help get me to the nearest hotel as quickly as possible.

Like a lot of people I know, or have known over the years, I haven't exactly lived the monastic lifestyle of a monk, by any means. I've been drinking alcohol since I was seventeen and experimented with various recreational drugs over the years, but this was on a completely different scale. At the end of the day, I was a helpless, fucked-up Englishman stranded on the other side of the world. The men I'd asked to help me ended up taking me to a hotel in the centre of town.

When I woke up the following morning, I had no idea where I was, and the effects of the drug were getting stronger, if anything. It was mental. I'd missed my return flight to the UK and didn't know if Michaela had flown back alone, without me, or was waiting for me at the airport. I left my hotel room around 6 am, took the elevator down to the lobby and asked the person on duty to phone a taxi to take me to the airport.

During the taxi journey, I explained to the driver what had happened. He was a friendly, understanding guy, and said to me, 'Wow man, that's not good. You know, it goes on all the time here in Toronto. I'm always hearing about it. You go to the washroom someplace, and while you're in there, somebody puts something in your drink. My advice to you is never leave your glass unattended. If you need to use the washroom, finish up your drink first, then if you want to, order another one from the bar in a fresh glass afterwards. Either that or change your habits.'

I asked the driver to stop outside a convenience store so I could buy a packet of cigarettes, and he pulled over to a place he knew would be open at that time of the morning. He let me smoke in his taxi and offered me a bottle of water. Half an hour or so later, the driver dropped me off at the airport. I paid him the agreed fare, thanked him for his advice, and walked into the terminal in a haze.

Michaela had taken my rucksack with her to the airport the previous evening, along with the rest of our luggage. The only things I had on me were my passport, credit card and mobile phone. Disorientated, I paced up and down the terminal not knowing what to do with myself. Staring at the departure screens, I couldn't make any sense of anything at all. I kept walking in and out of the terminal to smoke a cigarette. I was getting stressed now. I got it into my head that if I could find somewhere in the building that sold alcohol, then I'd drink a couple of pints of beer, hoping it would help me focus properly. There was no alcohol on sale anywhere in that part of the terminal building, so I bought some bottles of water and went and sat down.

I needed to keep my mobile phone switched off for long periods as I was rapidly running out of power, and the charger was in the rucksack Michaela had taken with her the previous evening. Turning on the phone, I looked to see how much money I had remaining in my online bank account. To my horror, I saw how much my short impromptu stay at the hotel I was taken to cost me; nearly £300. Without realising it, I'd spent the night in a five-star Hilton. Things were going from bad to worse.

Just then, my phone rang. It was Michaela, and she wasn't happy. She'd flown back to the UK alone, after I hadn't turned up at the airport and was already driving home from Heathrow. I explained what had happened and she advised me to book another flight as soon as possible, and said she'd call me back when she stopped at Fleet services on the motorway. I asked someone at the check-in desk if my original airline ticket was still valid. The person said it wasn't, and I'd have to buy another one. When I saw the price of the cheapest flight back to the UK from Toronto, I nearly died. I didn't have enough funds in my account to pay for it.

Agitated, I walked out the terminal to smoke another cigarette. Directly opposite the drop-off zone was a Radisson hotel. Hoping I might get a beer in there, I walked across the road and went inside. It was 8.30 am. I climbed a flight of stairs and located the hotel bar without too much trouble. The bartender said it wasn't open until 9 am, which was fine by me, and I wandered over to a computer nearby to access the internet.

Half an hour later, I ordered a pint of lager and sat down at the bar. I was soon joined by an Irishman from Dublin called Seamus, who'd also missed his flight home, would you believe. Convinced that if I drank a bit more alcohol, I'd finally shake off the effects of the drug I'd been spiked with, I necked down another two pints of lager before leaving the hotel and heading back across the road to the airport terminal.

Inside, I sat down and turned my phone back on, waiting for Michaela to call me. A short time later, she rang me, and I explained to her I'd checked my bank account and didn't have enough money in there to pay for a flight home. I also told her the drugs in my system weren't abating and they were still having a negative effect on me. Michaela said if she paid for another flight, it would clean her out, but she told me to hang on in there and she'd see if she could sort something out. After a couple more hours, she messaged me to let me know she'd booked another flight for that evening, through Aer Lingus via Dublin and Bristol. Thanking her profusely, and apologising for the sorry state I was in, I said I'd see her back at home the following night.

I don't really remember much about what happened over the next few hours, but I was dog tired and needed to get my head down somewhere. I stretched out over a row of seats and must have gone out like a light. Anyway, I awoke to find three police officers standing there in front of me. One of them asked me if my name was Shaun Morris. I replied to him that it was, and he told me they'd been trying to find me for the past three hours. Michaela had contacted the Toronto police, concerned that I hadn't boarded my flight to Dublin that evening as planned. Unbelievable. That was the second flight I'd missed in the last twenty-four hours. Apparently, staff had been calling my name out over the airport Tannoy, but I was too far gone to hear their announcements. What a waste of money.

The three Toronto cops were brilliant. Officers McLean, Thompson and Mortotsi, I can't thank you enough for all your help. They were aware of the current situation and told me the whole of the city's police force had been on full alert, looking for an English guy in his early 60s who was classed as vulnerable. Michaela had provided a description and they'd finally been able to locate me fast asleep in the airport terminal.

The upshot of all this was my brother Rich bailed me out in the end.

He paid for a flight back to the UK for me and I finally made it home two days later than expected. I honestly thought I'd be stranded in that airport, forever pacing up and down the terminal and nipping outside for a cigarette every five minutes, until I'd inevitably run out of money. The words 'downtown Toronto streets in the middle of winter, and cardboard box' had kept flashing in my mind. I'd convinced myself that this could be a distinct possibility. I offered my sincere thanks to my brother for what he did for me. I don't know what I would have done without him.

There were many lessons to be learned over that experience, but when you're someone like me, you never learn. That's the problem. You keep making the same mistakes time and time again, and I guess that will never change. Alcohol plays a big part, obviously, and I can truthfully say, that every time I've been in trouble with the law over the years, the demon drink has been involved. Whether being arrested and charged for crimes such as drunk and disorderly, or going missing at international airports, the outcome's invariably the same. A pattern develops, and when you drink too much alcohol, your inhibitions go flying right out of the window. An addictive personality and a natural performer like me stands no chance at all, not a hope in hell.

As we move into 2025, plans are afoot to go travelling again. It's Michaela's 60th birthday in November and we're going to have a holiday somewhere special. There are many countries on my wife's bucket list and it's down to me to make sure her dreams become reality, and she gets to visit at least one of them. At the time of writing, I've booked flights to a certain destination. I can't name the country in question in this book because Michaela will read it, and the holiday won't be a surprise to her.

CHAPTER 11

VENI, VIDI, VICI

As I sit here now in our bungalow in Pennington, looking out of the window into the back garden, I realise how fortunate I am. I have a lovely supporting wife and a dog that I adore, and I refer to the three of us as the Iron Triangle. There are several small-minded local people who disapproved of our relationship from the word go, and they set out to make Michaela's life uncomfortable. Whether they found her a threat or not, I don't know. They really haven't got a clue about what happens behind closed doors, not that it's any of their business anyway. These people haven't moved on from the 80s, for fuck's sake, and a couple of them are even wearing the same clothes they wore back then. I guess some folk will never change.

Most of the naysayers consist of a few jealous men and women who've done nothing constructive in their lives whatsoever; never been anywhere, never done anything. Nobodies. It's the village idiot mentality, and until you make a serious attempt at breaking out of the constrictive confines of where you're at, then your opinions count for nothing in my book. Leave it at that. I reckon Michaela's done an extremely good job in keeping me grounded. She's given me a happy home environment and saved me from myself. No other woman's managed to achieve that. We're soulmates, without a doubt.

I hardly go down the pub anymore because I have a happy home life. I think the Covid epidemic in 2020 changed things for a lot of people as regards going out and socialising. For me, the pub experience has never really been the same since the Covid outbreak. The general atmosphere's changed, without a doubt, and the days of stopping off for a few beers after work on a Friday afternoon, in a strange way, seem gone forever. Obviously, it's not that it doesn't still happen; of course it does. It just feels different nowadays. Before Covid, you'd walk into a pub and be greeted enthusiastically by someone shouting out at you from across the bar, 'All right mate, how's it going? What are you drinking? Come on, I'll get this!' These days, everybody seems a lot more serious and restrained in their behaviour.

At the end of the day, why would I want to go to a pub that's completely lacking in atmosphere and spend loads of money in there on alcohol when I've got my own bar right here in our back garden? I can buy beer from local supermarkets and shops at a fraction of the prices they charge in pubs. In any case, I don't have to put up with the bland, safe, horrible, formulated background music that gets played in many of them, catering to the majority of their customers. In the final analysis, I listen to the stuff I'm into whenever I want to, at whatever volume I choose; the louder the better, in my opinion.

Up until now, I've lived a life crammed full of adventure, and I wouldn't have it any other way. I suppose I'm luckier than a lot of people in that respect. I've always been wholly obsessed with music, like many of the folk I know, and essentially, it's a massive part of who I am. I've been involved in various bands for forty-five years now and played countless gigs in the UK and in countries across Europe. I've also written the words to literally hundreds of songs.

It's important for me to be in a band. It's such a creative outlet and a vehicle for artistic aspirations; coming up with lyrics to new songs, rehearsing and recording them and performing them onstage. I'm so pleased I managed to keep the whole Bamboo Vipers thing going when it looked for a while as if the band was finished for good. It's a real pleasure to play with my four bandmates from up in Kingston Upon Thames and we all put a lot of time and effort into what we do.

At the time of writing in early 2025 the Vipers have some serious gigs in the pipeline to look forward to, and I can't wait for us to get up on that stage again and perform our own music in front of an audience. The four-day annual Rebellion punk festival, which takes place every August at the Winter Gardens in Blackpool, Lancashire, is an event I'd love Bamboo Vipers to play at. It would be mental. Rebellion is the largest independently run punk festival in the UK, and Michaela and I have travelled up for it on several occasions in the past. It's massive, hosting over four hundred bands each summer, on seven separate stages at the venue. Thousands of like-minded people from all over the world descend upon Blackpool every year to take part in a long weekend of Punk, Oi! and Ska music, drinking and socialising, and getting generally messed up.

Most of the punters who attend Rebellion book rooms in bed and breakfast accommodation close to Blackpool Promenade over the course of the four days. I recall one B&B that Michaela and I were staying in which was located directly across from the beachfront. Downstairs at the breakfast table each morning, after ordering a full English, the friendly, chatty landlord would unfailingly ask us in his broad local accent, 'And would you like beans or tomatoes with that?'

It reached the point where we couldn't wait for him to ask us, 'And would you like beans or tomatoes with that?' It was comic relief, and in some ways, I regret that I didn't record his words on my phone for posterity, when I had the chance to. We could have sampled them for use on a future Bamboo Vipers recording, maybe. I remember the landlord also asking us, 'Have you had your fill of punk rock yet?' several times. 'No mate, never!' would be my reply.

The Rebellion Festival is the biggest annual event in Blackpool and brings a lot of much-needed money into the town. Apart from great hordes of punks and skinheads everywhere, there are many men and women out on stag dos and hen nights along the promenade. They can often be seen wearing outlandish fancy dress costumes of various sorts, contributing to the all-pervading, lively party atmosphere.

The noisy pubs, cafés, restaurants and amusement arcades are packed with legions of colourful people from across the globe having fun and enjoying themselves. Overall, it's a wonderfully unrelenting experience. With such a combination of sun, sea, alcohol and whatever, you'd think there'd be the potential for some serious trouble in Blackpool over the course of the weekend, but I can honestly say I personally haven't seen any; at least not in the Winter Gardens itself.

The toxic far-right movement in the UK have always had a presence when Rebellion's happening, albeit a relatively small one. However, at a recent festival, in the streets outside the venue, groups of these fascist morons were marauding about demonstrating, and they became embroiled in heated discussions and sometimes physical confrontations with punks and other Rebellion punters. Fortunately, as it transpired, these narrow-minded, intolerant far-right protesters were made to look like the idiots they are and were unceremoniously driven out of town.

Of all the countless bands I've seen play at the festival, I think Jello Biafra and the Guantanamo School of Medicine in 2018 have probably put on the best show. I was told a story about Jello at Rebellion one year. He was backstage in the large communal bands' dressing room, wearing a Spiderman costume, and was surfing across the tables helping himself to swigs of everyone's beer, wine and spirits.

I'm lucky enough to have been invited into that dressing room. In 2012, Steve Metcalfe, manager of one of my favourite bands of all time, The Boys, sorted Michaela and me out with backstage passes. Some of the other great performances I've witnessed at the festival include London veterans Cock Sparrer, 999, The Dickies, Idles, TV Smith, Chelsea, Hazel O'Connor and Irish band the Lee Harveys.

Bamboo Vipers all believe wholeheartedly in what we're doing and we're having a lot of fun at the same time. If people don't dig our music, then that's fair enough. At the end of the day, it's their choice. If everybody liked the same type of music, then the world would be a boring place, that's for sure. All I know, is it's a definite buzz being involved a band, and to be honest, I don't really know anything else. I love everything about it, and long may it continue. I think a line in the chorus to a Vipers song I wrote the lyrics to called *Runt of the Litter* is pretty much bang on: It's a hobby to you/ It's life and death to me.

I'm in my element when I'm writing the lyrics to new songs. I've just penned the words to two belting tunes a couple of my Vipers bandmates came up with: Rich Bartram's sinister *Heart of Darkness* and a James Jenkins composition titled *Microdot*. I wrote the lyrics to *Microdot*, which is about a tiny, frail elderly woman in Pennington who drinks a lot of spirits and chain smokes cigarettes. She rides around the pavements in the village on her mobility scooter, with scant regard for anyone else and she's a danger to people and to herself. The closing lines to *Microdot* are: 'Get out of her way, she's on a mission. Or she's gonna run you over.'

The beauty of Bamboo Vipers is that all five band members are more than capable of writing new songs on their own and providing the necessary creative input. If someone in the band doesn't like a particular idea, a tune for example, then that's fine, no problem. Put it on the backburner, or if need be, bin it completely. We all respect each other's opinions and it's completely how it should be – a democracy.

I feel privileged to have been afforded the opportunity to travel to so many remarkable countries around the world, and experience significantly different cultures from ours, and meet some truly wonderful people along the way. On a less positive note, I've found myself right at the centre of some dodgy and potentially very dangerous situations on my travels, and that's for sure. However, these were mostly down to my own irresponsibility at the time and only occurred in a small minority of the destinations I've visited over the years. The brave die sometime, but the cautious never live, as they say.

Like anyone else, I've made some bad choices in life, but ultimately, I followed the path I wanted to take. I could have been more determined to achieve something at school and college. Who knows, If I had, maybe I would have gone on to university, like my father and brother. I might have ended up in a high-powered job, earning lots of money, but all that doesn't really matter to me, and anyway, it's too late now. I've never really been one for material objects; as long as I've got my SM58 microphone, my

Bluetooth speaker and my ear buds, I'm happy.

You can't turn back the clock, and you shouldn't harbour regrets. I know it's a well-worn cliché, but life's too short. The lyrics to the chorus of a song I wrote for the Peeping Toms song *Underachiever* seem to sum it all up perfectly for me: '*Why didn't I concentrate? Why have I left it so damned late? Did I take the wrong path? Just wanted to have a laugh. Switch back to the 70s. Didn't know about the birds and bees. John Peel's on the radio. And I'm doing the pogo.*'

As I arrive at a new chapter in my life, it's time to sign off and say adios for now, amigos. I hope you've enjoyed the incredible journey I've been fortunate enough to have been on and documented to the best of my knowledge and ability, here in this autobiography. It's re-awoken a lot of long forgotten memories for me; most of them good, some not so good, I have to say.

Although it's been incredibly time-consuming and a real challenge, I've thoroughly enjoyed writing the book. I began working on it in September 2024, and it's taken me around six months to complete. It hasn't all been plain sailing, by any means. I've been getting up at stupid o'clock every morning to make the whole thing happen, and I've put my very heart and soul into the project. At the end of the day, I'd like to believe I've been as transparent as possible.

Attention-Seeking Missile is a no-holds-barred account of my life up and until now: punk in the provinces in its purest form. It's essentially a document of what I've personally experienced first-hand, for good or for worse. Some people might not like specific references I've made in the book, but if I left all of that out, then I wouldn't be telling the truth, would I? In that respect, I might as well have not bothered in the first place. Believe you me, it ain't been easy, and there's awful lot more I could have written, but I guess you must draw the line somewhere. Also, I'm not in the habit of incriminating anybody, other than myself.

Time inevitably moves on, and memories fade, of course, but it's been a thrillingly unconventional rollercoaster ride so far, that's for sure, and one I wouldn't swap for all the tea in China.

In writing this book, it's sad when I realise just how many of my friends, and people I knew of back then, aren't around anymore, especially the ones who died much too young. I guess in the end, they just ran out of time. That's life, I suppose, and there's not a lot you can do to change it. I hope to see you at the bar one day, who knows, on this planet, or maybe on another one somewhere in outer space. Onwards and upwards we go from here. As a wise old preacher once said: We came, we saw, we played a game of conkers. Over and out. Revo dna tuo.